ESL Grammar Quiz Book

for intermediate to advanced students of English as a Second Language

ALLAN KENT DART
The American Language Institute
New York University

Prentice-Hall, Inc., Englewood Cliffs, N.J. 07632

Library of Congress Cataloging in Publication Data
DART, ALLAN KENT (date)
    ESL grammar quiz book for intermediate to advanced
students of English as a second language.

    1. English language—Examinations, questions, etc.
2. English language—Grammar—1950–   3. English
language—Study and teaching—Foreign students.
I. Title.
PE1128.A2D35   420.7'6   81–15823
ISBN 0–13–283812–5   AACR2

Editorial production, supervision,
  and interior design by Frank Hubert
Manufacturing buyer: Harry P. Baisley
Cover design by 20/20 Services, Inc.,
  Mark Berghash

Printed in the United States of America
10   9   8   7   6   5   4

ISBN 0-13-283812-5

PRENTICE-HALL INTERNATIONAL, INC., *London*
PRENTICE-HALL OF AUSTRALIA PTY. LIMITED, *Sydney*
PRENTICE-HALL OF CANADA, LTD., *Toronto*
PRENTICE-HALL OF INDIA PRIVATE LIMITED, *New Delhi*
PRENTICE-HALL OF JAPAN, INC., *Tokyo*
PRENTICE-HALL OF SOUTHEAST ASIA PTE. LTD., *Singapore*
WHITEHALL BOOKS LIMITED, WELLINGTON, *New Zealand*

Contents

contents

contents

contents

contents

Introduction

ESL Grammar Quiz Book is a comprehensive survey of the English language for intermediate to advanced students of English as a second language. The book is appropriate for young adults at institutes, colleges, and universities, and for adults in continuing education programs. Young people (16 to 18 years) in senior high schools would also find the material interesting and meaningful.

As the text tends to favor no particular place or culture, *ESL Grammar Quiz Book* is appropriate for those who are not living in the United States, the United Kingdom, or other English-speaking countries.

Although the quizzes and their explanations in the *ESL Grammar Handbook* have been carefully graded and sequenced, for advanced students it is not essential that this order of presentation be followed exactly. However, for intermediate students (for whom much of the material may be new), I recommend that the order of the quizzes be adhered to since the book is semi-programmed, and the old material is constantly being reviewed within the context of the new.

Except for review quizzes, there is an explanation in the *ESL Grammar Handbook* for every quiz in this book. To make locating information easier, the number of a quiz corresponds to the number of its explanation in the *Handbook*. The page where an explanation can be found in the *Handbook* appears in the *Quiz Book* under the number of a quiz; for example:

QUIZ 1
handbook p. 1

The High-Intermediate Student

For less advanced students, it might be best for the teacher to select a topic (always stated at the beginning of each quiz), plan some oral exercises or other group activities,* and then introduce the topic to the class with the help of the explanation in the *ESL Grammar Handbook*. After this period of oral and perhaps writing practice, the students then take the quiz to see what they have remembered from the lesson. The duration of time between this explanation-*cum*-lesson and the time that the quiz is given can vary according to the needs of the students and the discretion of the teacher. Some teachers may prefer to postpone giving a quiz (perhaps a week) so that the quiz will act as a review rather than an introduction; still others may prefer to give a quiz as a homework assignment.

The Advanced Student

It is recommended that advanced students take the quiz first, then go to the explanation in the *Handbook*. In this way they will be testing themselves to see what they have learned from previous classes or self-study.

Giving, Taking, Correcting, and Scoring a Quiz

Taking a quiz need not be a pressure-ridden experience for students—they are testing themselves only in order to learn faster and improve their written and spoken English. Thus it is imperative that the teacher provide a friendly and relaxed classroom atmosphere.

For large classes, or classes that are not homogeneously grouped, it is often best to break the class up into smaller groups. The students may take and correct the quizzes among themselves under the teacher's supervision, or the whole group can take and correct a quiz together.

The amount of time to allow for a quiz should be determined by the proficiency level of the group. All the students must be encouraged to work rapidly, but it is important that everyone do each quiz completely. More important, taking a quiz ought not to be a race to see who is the fastest, the cleverest, or the most intelligent student in a class.

All the quizzes in this textbook can be easily scored. A quiz is always valued at 100 points. Each item is 10 points unless otherwise indicated at the beginning of the quiz.

The following samples show how a quiz can be properly corrected (note how a mistake is crossed out rather than erased):

score ___90___

REVIEW QUIZ H   information questions

Example: a. To ~~who~~ whom have you spoken (just) on the phone?

I've just spoken to _the president himself_ .

---

*A teacher's manual containing suggestions on how to use this book, supplementary exercises, and answers to all the quizzes is available to teachers upon request from the publishers.

introduction

score _80_

QUIZ 159   must and must have with have to

handbook p. 143

Example: a. A: Mr. and Mrs. Richhouse went on a trip around the world last year. B: My,
                ~~have~~ had   spend
          they *must* ~~had has~~ *to* ~~finish up~~ a lot of money.

score _70_

QUIZ 233   indirect speech

handbook p. 198

Example: a. "I don't ever eat anything fattening because I don't want to put on weight."
                          didn't   eat anything
        He told his doctor *that he* ~~doesn't~~ *ever* ~~ate nothing~~ *fattening because he*

        didn't want̸ to put on weight.

Formal and Informal Style

The terms *formal* and *informal* are frequently used in this text. Formal usage is
that style found in formal writing; for example, in a written report to be submit-
ted to the Security Council at the United Nations in New York, or cor-
respondence in the world of business, government, or education. An informal
style of writing would most likely be used in a letter to one's parents, a quick
note to a neighbor, or a short story depicting everyday life. Compare:

    formal: Why do you not sit down, Sir, and rest yourself?
    informal: Why don't you sit down and take it easy, Bill?

    formal: To whom do you wish to speak, Madam?
    informal: Who do you wish to speak to Ma'am?

People ordinarily use informal usage when they are speaking. Since the em-
phasis in the quizzes is on spoken English, most of the model sentences reflect
an informal style of writing. It is hoped that they also reflect that style of speaking used by a majority of people living in the United States today.

Acknowledgments

There are many people I wish to thank for the constructive criticism, en-
couragement, and interest they showed during the development of the manuscripts for *ESL Grammar Handbook* and *ESL Grammar Quiz Book*. I owe particular thanks to Fred Malkemes, a colleague and close friend of mine, and
Anna M. Halpin, my good friend and former neighbor.
    I must thank the administrations of the American Language Institute, New

York University, and the English Language Programs, King Faisal University, Dammam, Saudi Arabia, for giving me their support and allowing me to test the materials in my classes.

To the following at Prentice-Hall, I wish to express my appreciation: Marianne Russell, Pamela S. Kirshen, Gloria Pergament, Ilene McGrath, and Frank Hubert.

For her many suggestions and the strong motivating force that she provided, I wish to express by indebtedness to Linda Markstein, Professor, Borough of Manhattan Community College, City University of New York.

I feel an especially strong feeling of gratitude toward the students in my classes at New York University who participated in various stages of development of the manuscripts over a period of two years. I would like to thank them all: Alex Kuropatwa and Adrian Scappini (of Argentina), Victor Hugo Rojas (of Bolivia), Jarslav Nehybka (of Czechoslovakia), Gloria Mendieta (of Colombia), Jesus Perez (of Cuba), Carmen Mariano (of the Dominican Republic), Omkathaum Yehia (of Egypt), Miriam Herrera (of El Salvador), Kriton Giordamlis (of Greece), Yeuk Xam Cheng (of Hong Kong), Mehrdad Razavi (of Iran), Fabio Cordi (of Italy), Kosai Fujioka, Tohio Fujita, Noriko Imai, Sachiko Kanai, Sutsuki Swawshima, Atshushi Kono, Suzuki Kyoyasa, Masayoshi Kawasaki, Kaoyo Myata, Yasamasa Ogisu, Hideo Tanaka, and Mihoko Tanaka (of Japan), Mahmoud Elder, Mazen El-Mani, and Maher Mohammed (of Jordan), Hae Sook Chung, Eum Young Co, Byung Yun Jun, Hong Don Kim, Sook Hee Kim, Hyun Sik Ko, Jong Doo Lee, and Pyong S Yim (of Korea), Yan-Wen Chou, Li Ming Bian, Hong Jun Kao, Cynthia Shiah, Jian-S Wang, and David Yang (of the People's Republic of China), Sandro Testino (of Peru), Nan-Kuang Chang, Ai Hwa Wai, and Shen-Yuh Wu (of the Republic of China), Milagros Alvarez (of Spain), Jamal Thwayeb (of Syria), Suwanna Luckanakul and Suthasinee Sirikaya (of Thailand), Myriam Alarcón, Sally Bohorquez, and Franco Delnardo (of Venezuela), and Andrew Dang (of Vietnam).

Allan Kent Dart
New York City

QUIZ 1 spelling plural forms of countable nouns
handbook p. 1

Supply in the blanks the plural forms of the nouns in parentheses.

Examples: a. (mosquito) Darn it! There are a lot of *mosquitoes* in this room.

b. (parenthesis) Class, please check that all the *parentheses* in your compositions have been used correctly.

1. (wolf) There are a great many _____ in the forest surrounding us.

2. (watch) My grandfather always wears two _____ .

3. (dictionary) How many _____ are there on the second shelf?

4. (fish) What beautiful _____ there are in your aquarium!

5. (mouse) Keep your kitchen clean; you don't want to have _____ .

6. (goose) What long and beautiful necks _____ have!

7. (tax) We will always have death and _____ .

8. (attorney) How many _____ are there in your law firm?

9. (phenomenon) Natural _____ are fascinating to watch.

10. (piano) At the concert, there were one hundred _____ assembled on the stage.

score _____

QUIZ 2 distinguishing countable from uncountable nouns
handbook p. 3

In the parentheses indicate with a C or a U whether the underlined word in the sentence is countable or uncountable.

Examples: a. (U) Life is too short. (old saying)

b. (C) Some people say a cat has nine lives.

1. (   ) What beautiful deer !

2. (   ) You must carefully study the information in this confidential report.

3. (   ) Did you see some sheep on their farm?

4. (   ) We need a great deal of money to develop our country.

5. (   ) Oil plays an important role in international politics.

6. (   ) How does exercise help you?

7. (   ) My chemistry professor is involved mainly in research .

1

8. (   ) Our children have a lot of <u>fun</u> on their camping trips.

9. (   ) What do you think of the <u>news</u> in today's newspaper?

10. (   ) Don't forget to buy <u>meat</u> for dinner on your way home from work.

score _____

QUIZ 3   the possessive form of nouns
handbook p. 4

Fill in the blanks with an apostrophe (') or an apostrophe plus an s ('s). If no possessive marker is required, write an "X" in the blank.

Examples: a. Macy<u>'s</u> is supposed to be the largest department store in the world.

b. Where is the First Lady <u>X</u> and President's official residence?

c. Jesus<u>'</u> life lasted for only thirty-three years.

1. Doesn't Charles _____ father live somewhere in the middle of India?

2. None of my friends _____ friends are friends of mine.

3. John _____ and his brother's motorcycle is a Suzuki; they share it.

4. Mr. Jones _____ and Mr. Smith's drugstore is the best in town.

5. It is the media _____ responsibility to tell the truth.

6. Bob _____ and Dick's girlfriends are as different as day and night.

7. His pals _____ main interests are young women, sports, and cars.

8. Moses _____ life began as a poor foundling (discarded baby).

9. The Princess _____ life is quieter than the Prince's.

10. Barbara _____ and Ronald's house is just around the corner from ours.

score _____ (5 points each)

QUIZ 4   personal pronouns, demonstrative pronouns, and demonstrative adjectives
handbook p. 5

Circle the word in the parentheses that is correct.

Example: a. Are (these) / <u>those</u>) stamps here in my hand yours or mine?

1. I must speak to (<u>he</u> / <u>him</u>) about this matter at once (immediately).

2. John and (<u>me</u> / <u>I</u>) are going to take another grammar course after this one.

2

3. (*This* / *That*) book way up on the top shelf is a Webster's dictionary.

4. Are (*these* / *those*) papers over there on your desk his or yours?

5. Can you go with (*me* / *I*) to my friend's birthday party tonight?

6. Aren't those (*your* / *yours*) shoes under my bed?

7. I want you to keep this information a secret between you and (*me* / *I*).

8. Are (*these* / *those*) boys across the street students at our school?

9. Are (*these* / *those*) here on my desk yours or your secretary's?

10. My father gave presents to my sister, my brother, and (*me* / *I*).

11. (*These* / *Those*) figures in this report, Miss Brown, are not correct.

12. This is (*my* / *mine*) grammar book, isn't it?

13. These are (*our* / *ours*) children, all five of them.

14. Are these papers and letters (*their* / *theirs*) or yours and mine?

15. (*That* / *Those*) deer in the photograph look beautiful.

16. (*He* / *Him*) and I went to the game last Saturday afternoon.

17. At the movies my sister always sits between my brother and (*me* / *I*).

18. Are you going to meet (*he* / *him*) at the corner later?

19. Whose glass is this? It's not (*his* / *her*), is it?

20. Are these things (*their* / *theirs*), ours, his, or yours?

score _____ (5 points each)

QUIZ 5   prepositions of place
handbook p. 7

Fill in the blanks with appropriate prepositions.

around	between	in	to
at	from	on	

Examples: a. There are three rivers *around* the island of Manhattan.

b. Listen, Tommy, you have a head *on* your shoulders—use it.

1. Isn't that a lovely vase of flowers _____ the middle of the dining room table?

2. Please don't forget to write your name _____ the top of the page.

3. There is a large rose garden _____ my house and my neighbor's.

4. We're not very close _____ the next gas station, are we?

5. How far is New York _____ San Francisco?

6. There were about thirty people _____ the party last night, more or less.

7. The First Lady is always next _____ the President in time of crisis.

8. When I came into the classroom, you were sitting _____ the third row.

9. There are only a few people living _____ the South Pole.

10. I don't like to wear anything _____ my neck.

11. Mrs. Zimmerman's name is always _____ the bottom of a list.

12. Their chicken coop is _____ back of their house.

13. They live in Tahiti, a beautiful island _____ the South Pacific.

14. Shh, please try to quiet down, children; the baby is sleeping _____ her crib (a baby's bed).

15. Only wild animals and a few hermits live _____ those mountains.

16. Our son's school is _____ the corner of Main Street and Second Avenue.

17. A large water fountain is _____ the center of Washington Square Park.

18. There are a great many beautiful suburbs _____ the city of London.

19. August is _____ July and September.

20. We're now _____ the end of this quiz.

score _____

QUIZ 6   indefinite articles; *a* versus *an* before nouns and adjectives

handbook p. 9

Supply in each blank a or an.

Example: a. *An* inch is longer than *a* centimeter.

1. My neighbor has _____ husband who doesn't like to work.

2. His father belongs to _____ union which helps the workers get benefits.

3. There's _____ undercurrent of evil in that man's personality; he hates people.

4. Would you like to look at this? It's _____ article about your native country.

5. _____ hotel room in London isn't always so easy to find.

4

6. A good automobile mechanic can make fifty dollars _____ hour in some places.

7. Mr. President, Sir, it is _____ honor to meet you and the First Lady.

8. Would you like _____ orange or a banana with your breakfast this morning?

9. One of my best and oldest friends is attending _____ university in Sweden.

10. The gentleman sitting in the red chair is _____ heir to a great fortune.

score _____

QUIZ 7 "X article"

handbook p. 10

Supply in the blanks a or an plus an appropriate adjective chosen from the list below. If a or an is not required, write an "X" in the blank.

beautiful	historical	ugly	universal
dull	honest	unique	unnecessary
European	honorable	united	unusual
herbal			

Examples: a. Crime is *a universal* problem.

b. *An honest* fortune teller is not always easy to find.

c. Ladies and gentlemen, these are X *historical* moments in our lives.

1. What _____ children you have, Mr. and Mrs. Williams!

2. What _____ idea, Mr. Genius!

3. We'd like to take _____ trip this year; we want to go to Spain.

4. Sunday is _____ day in our small town; everyone sleeps late.

5. _____ nation is better than a divided one.

6. Those, Mr. Brown, are _____ questions to ask at this time.

7. What _____ expression you have on your face, young man! You look angry; your face is as red as a beet.

8. The judge in this case is _____ man. I hope.

9. They always have _____ people at their parties.

10. Excuse me, Miss, I'm looking for _____ shampoo.

QUIZ 8 noun modifiers
handbook p. 10

Supply in the blanks a *or* an *plus an appropriate noun modifier chosen from the list below.*

English	history	ink	quiz
gas	home	insurance	umbrella
herb	ice	opera	union

Examples:
a. His father is *a union* man; he strongly believes in workers' rights.
b. I dropped *an ink* bottle yesterday, but it didn't break, fortunately.

1. I can't play basketball tomorrow morning; I have _____ class.

2. Is there _____ station nearby? Our tank is almost empty.

3. Children, today we're going to have _____ lesson about King Arthur and the knights of the Round Table.

4. Laura Johnson is _____ fan; she goes all the time.

5. My neighbors have _____ garden right outside their kitchen door.

6. I'm looking for _____ stand to put in my hallway.

7. This is _____ book; the other one is a handbook.

8. Barbara Miller is _____ salesperson; she sells a lot.

9. Excuse me, I'm looking for _____ bucket.

10. What a fantastic baseball game this is! Johnny Jacobs has just hit _____ run. That's his fifth this game, isn't it?

score _____ (5 points each)

QUIZ 9 the simple present tense
handbook p. 11

Fill in each blank with the simple present tense of the base form stated in parentheses.

Examples:
a. (be) Time *is* money. (old saying)
b. (do) Our children *do* their homework at the school library.

1. (be) Deer _____ very peaceful animals.

2. (do) My roommate _____ his homework in the afternoons.

3. (be) Rice _____ a basic ingredient of Chinese food.

4. (have) An elephant _____ a relatively small brain.

6

5. (be) I _____ responsible for my own actions.

6. (be) People _____ difficult to understand, sometimes.

7. (carry) Her boss _____ a large briefcase to work every day.

8. (go) My neighbor _____ to work at 7:35 every morning; he's like a clock.

9. (play) Her little daughter _____ in the garden in the mornings.

10. (be) You _____ the best student in the class.

11. (spend) Our son _____ a lot of time at the library; he's a college student.

12. (be) Physics _____ a difficult but fascinating subject.

13. (play) Ted Jones _____ in a symphony orchestra; he's a violinist.

14. (quiz) Our grammar teacher _____ us every day.

15. (fly) My neighbors _____ out to California once or twice a year.

16. (correct) Mr. Sands _____ the class's homework every afternoon after lunch.

17. (do) Jane is a good student; she _____ her homework every night.

18. (be) You _____ all good friends of mine.

19. (see) Grandpa _____ better out of his right eye than his left.

20. (be) This _____ the end of the quiz.

score _____

QUIZ 10 negative verb phrases

handbook p. 12

Supply in the blanks appropriate negative verb phrases in the simple present tense.

Examples: a. (be) We *aren't* students of English as a first language.

b. (deliver) The mailman *doesn't deliver* mail on Sundays, does he?

1. (do) You _____ enough homework, Jackie; you should try harder.

2. (have) Los Angeles _____ a good public transportation system.

3. (be) I _____ a citizen of the United States.

4. (be) I wouldn't like to work in a store; people _____ easy to serve.

5. (cost) Fortunately, this _____ much.

6. (be) New York _____ far from Washington, D.C.

7. (mean) That word _____ anything.

8. (drive) His father _____ a car.

9. (go) Their son _____ to school yet; he's only three years old.

10. (have) Fish _____ very large brains.

score _____

QUIZ 11 yes-no questions; pronoun substitutes
handbook p. 13

Complete the following yes–no questions with appropriate verb phrases in the simple present tense. Use pronoun substitutes as subjects. Use only the verbs in the following list.

be   have   go   live   speak

Examples: a. A: What a beautiful woman my roommate is! B: *Does she have* a nice personality?

b. A: Her boyfriend is very cute; he's quite nice too. B: *Is he* a friend of yours?

1. A: Christopher and Janet Richards have a new apartment; it's beautiful.
B: _____ a good view of the Pacific Ocean?

2. A: Maria is a new student at this school. B: _____ English very well?

3. A: Jack and Janet are new students at this school, too. B: _____ in the same class with Maria?

4. A: My boyfriend and I have a car. B: _____ for drives in the country very often?

5. A: John is a student at the University of Delaware. B: _____ in a dormitory or an apartment in town?

6. A: My bike is from China. B: _____ a comfortable bike to ride?

7. A: Peter and Helen Davis live next door to me—they're both college teachers. B: _____ friends of yours or just neighbors?

8. A: Our house is on Fifth Street near the Cathedral. B: _____ the white house on the corner across the street from the post office?

9. A: George and Martha don't see each other very much. B: _____ to each other on the phone occasionally?

10. A: Robbie begins school tomorrow—I think he has everything he needs.
B: _____ a bag to carry his school materials in?

QUIZ 12 information questions
handbook p. 15

Using the following statements as cues, compose appropriate information questions. Use the information words *what, what color, what kind of,* or *where*. The *underlined* word in each sentence will be a clue to which information word(s) to use. Begin each question with a capital letter and end it with a question mark. Do *not* use pronoun substitutes.

Examples: a. *What kind of accent do you have?*   I have <u>a French</u> accent.

          b. *Where do you hide your money?*   We hide our money <u>in a teapot</u>.

1. _____ Robert has <u>blue</u> eyes.

2. _____ That word means <u>nothing</u>.

3. _____ Yellow and red make <u>orange</u>.

4. _____ Her eyes are <u>green</u>.

5. _____ Those shoes cost <u>fifty dollars</u>.

6. _____ This is <u>a Swiss</u> watch.

7. _____ I do my homework <u>at home</u>.

8. _____ We keep our car <u>in a garage</u>.

9. _____ I like <u>chocolate</u> ice cream.

10. _____ My sister lives <u>in Iceland</u>.

score _____ (5 points each)

QUIZ 13 expletive *there*; determiners
handbook p. 16

Circle the correct word(s) in the parentheses.

Example: a. There are ((*few*) / *little*) people living out in the middle of the desert.

1. There are (*a great deal of* / *quite a few*) mistakes in this recent report.

2. There is (*a little* / *a few*) rice on the second shelf in the cupboard.

3. We're having (*a lot of* / *much*) trouble with the machinery in the factory now.

4. My boss and I don't have (*no* / *any*) time to waste today; we're really rushed.

5. I've been reading (*a great deal of* / *quite a few*) exciting news recently.

6. There isn't (*any* / *no*) water running in the kitchen now, is there?

7. What (*few* / *little*) money there is in our savings account!

9

8. How (*much* / *many*) furniture do you need to buy for your new apartment?

9. Fortunately, my old car requires (*little* / *few*) repairs.

10. Unfortunately, the government wastes (*a great deal of* / *quite a few*) money.

11. Approximately how (*much* / *many*) coffee do you drink every day?

12. (*A great deal of* / *Quite a few*) research is being done at our university.

13. Mrs. Rogers always wears (*lots of* / *much*) heavy perfume.

14. We must finish this project as soon as possible; we have (*few* / *little*) time left.

15. Jack doesn't like (*much* / *many*) pepper on his food; it makes him sneeze.

16. My doctor says it's good for me to eat (*a lot of* / *much*) fruit every day.

17. We have (*some* / *any*) milk in the refrigerator, but we have very little cream.

18. There is (*some* / *any*) salt in this soup, but it still tastes bland.

19. They don't serve (*no* / *any*) alcohol in their house; they're very strict.

20. (*Much* / *Many*) time, effort, and thought went into our last project.

score _____

QUIZ 14   infinitives; *would like*
handbook p. 18

Supply in each blank the infinitive to do *or* to make.

Examples: a. Excuse me, Mr. Black, would you like *to do* a favor for me?

b. Listen, children, it's necessary for you *to make* your beds every day.

1. Like everyone, I don't like _____ mistakes, but I sometimes do.

2. I'd like _____ my exercises in the park this morning; it's a beautiful day.

3. It's not difficult _____ a quiz.

4. Is it absolutely necessary for me _____ a decision right away (immediately)?

5. Would you like _____ the dishes now or later?

6. I'd like _____ my homework at the library today. How about you?

7. Do you want _____ an appointment with the doctor for tomorrow or the day after?

8. Ladies and Gentlemen, our little daughter would like _____ a dance for you.

9. Mr. White, I'd like _____ a deal with you; I'll give you a thousand dollars for your old car. Is it a deal?

10. I don't like _____ the cleaning, the washing, and the cooking, but I have to.

score _____

QUIZ 15 impersonal *it*; duration with *take, last*

handbook p. 20

Using the following statements as cues, compose appropriate information questions. Use the information words _what_, _what color_, _what kind of_, _where_, _how many_, _how much_, or _how long_. Do _not_ use pronoun substitutes.

Example: a. _How much do those diamonds in the window cost?_

Those diamonds in the window cost _millions of dollars_.

1. _____

There are _90_ degrees in a right angle.

2. _____

We'd like to build our house _up in the mountains_.

3. _____

This word means _beautiful._

4. _____

It takes us _an hour_ to drive to work.

5. _____

I'd like to put my books _in your locker_.

6. _____

It takes _only three_ hours to fly from here to there.

7. _____

There is _no_ rice in that box.

8. _____

Robert Andrews drives _a green_ Cadillac convertible.

9. _____

The grammar class lasts _three_ hours.

10. _____

She takes _yoga and judo_ lessons every day.

QUIZ 16 adverbs
handbook p. 21

Supply in the blanks the adverbial form of the adjectives in parentheses.

Examples: a. (extreme) It's <u>extremely</u> cold today, so be sure to wear a heavy coat.

b. (late) How many times have you handed your homework in <u>late</u>?

1. (crazy) How _____ the dog is acting! Is he sick?

2. (fast) Just how _____ does blood flow through the veins of the human body, Doctor?

3. (heavy) How many times have I told you not to walk so _____ in the house? Please quiet down, children.

4. (graceful) When you're introduced to the Queen, bow _____.

5. (fast) That young man is always driving too _____; he's going to kill himself in that car someday.

6. (slow) The lion crept _____ toward its prey.

7. (possible) _____, you're doing the right thing in this matt r, but not one of your associates thinks so.

8. (hard) The students have been studying _____ and maki g a lot of progress.

9. (good) Just how _____ do you know the President, Sir?

10. (slow) Always drive _____ past a school, Miss.

QUIZ 17 linking verbs; adjectives versus adverbs
handbook p. 23

Circle the correct word in parentheses.

Example: a. The water of the great Mississippi River flows (<u>slow</u> / (<u>slowly</u>)) south to the river's mouth at New Orleans.

1. Only a few of the students in that class do (<u>bad</u> / <u>badly</u>) on the quizzes.

2. Did you get up early or (<u>late</u> / <u>lately</u>) last Sunday morning?

3. Your parents always dance together very (<u>smooth</u> / <u>smoothly</u>), don't they?

4. Yes, my neighbor across the street does behave (<u>strange</u> / <u>strangely</u>), doesn't he?

5. I must go to the doctor at once; I don't feel (<u>good</u> / <u>well</u>).

6. Yes, the average person in this country needs to work (*hard* / *hardly*) to make a living.

7. How often do you watch the (*late* / *lately*) movie on TV?

8. Mr. Warren, I certainly do feel (*good* / *well*) about the terms in the new contract; however, I'd like to make a few changes.

9. Yes, this sentence seems (*correct* / *correctly*), but it's hard to tell.

10. That man standing on the corner is looking at me (*strange* / *strangely*), isn't he?

score _____

QUIZ 18   exclamations

handbook p. 24

Fill in each blank with a, an, such, such a, such an, good, *or* well. *If a word is not required write an "X" in the blank.*

Examples: a. How *well* you cooked that goose!

b. What *X* sweet strawberries these are!

1. What _____ unique example of African sculpture that is!

2. What _____ interesting criteria you present in your argument, Madam!

3. The French Revolution was _____ historical event!

4. How _____ the boxer in white shorts fights tonight!

5. What _____ wonderful weather we've been having this spring!

6. You are _____ great friends! I love you all.

7. How _____ your children always are, Mrs. Jones! They're never naughty, nor do they ever misbehave.

8. My, what _____ ugly vase that is!

9. Oh, it's so cold out tonight; how _____ this warm bed feels!

10. How _____ this food tastes!

QUIZ 19 frequency adverbs
handbook p. 25

Supply appropriate verb phrases in the simple present tense containing the frequency adverb given in parentheses. Use only the verbs in the following list:

be   do   have   last   make

Examples: a. (often) He's an excellent student; he *doesn't often make* a mistake.

b. (always) My neighbor's wife *always has* on nice-looking clothes.

1. (hardly ever) Butch _____ his homework. What a poor student he is!

2. (ever) Mr. Dickens _____ nervous, nor does he ever get angry.

3. (occasionally) Bob _____ a mistake, but not often.

4. (never) Fortunately, our children _____ sick during the winter.

5. (usually) A good sweater, which is expensive, _____ a long time.

6. (seldom) A quiz _____ more than a few minutes.

7. (ever) My boss _____ a decision without thinking about it for a long time.

8. (always) They _____ a picnic on Sundays, only sometimes.

9. (rarely) A movie _____ more than two hours.

10. (ever) Her boyfriend _____ any money in his pocket.

QUIZ 20 yes-no questions with frequency adverbs
handbook p. 27

Supply appropriate words to complete the following yes–no questions with verb phrases in the simple present tense. Use the words at the left as subjects and the words at the right as verbs. Include <u>always,</u> <u>ever,</u> *or* <u>usually</u> *in the verb phrases, and begin each question with a capital letter.*

her husband	their son	your children	be	go
his sister	the workers	your husband	do	make
it	you	your mother and father	get	play
their daughter	your car	your neighbor		

name _____

Examples: a. *Do you ever do* your homework at the library?

            b. *Is it usually* cold, rainy, and windy in London during March?

1. _____ her appointments in the mornings?

2. _____ naughty, or do they ever get into trouble?

3. _____ with you to church on Sundays?

4. _____ a bonus at Christmas time?

5. _____ nice and warm in Florida in February?

6. _____ his chores in the mornings or the afternoons?

7. _____ a lot of noise when you start it?

8. _____ cards on Saturday nights?

9. _____ exercises when they get up in the mornings?

10. _____ satisfied with the progress you're making at school?

score _____ (20 points each)

QUIZ 21   information questions with frequency adverbs

handbook p. 28

Using the following statements as cues, compose appropriate information questions. Use the information words stated at the left. Use only subjects chosen from the list at the right.

how	when	foreign news	the patient
how long	where	the children	you
how often		a meeting	you and your wife
		meetings	

Examples: a. *How often do you and your wife go out on the town?* _____

              We go out on the town <u>once or twice a month</u>.

            b. *Where do meetings usually take place?* _____

              They usually take place <u>in this room.</u>

1. _____

    I most often keep my keys <u>in a small basket on that shelf</u>.

2. _____

    It <u>frequently</u> comes over the wire.

3. _____

They always do the dishes <u>in the evenings.</u>

4. _____

It usually lasts <u>more than two hours.</u>

5. _____

He usually feels <u>well</u> in the mornings.

score _____ (5 points each)

QUIZ 22 present participles
handbook p. 28

Make present participles out of the following base forms.

Examples: a. save *saving*

b. bring *bringing*

1. wait _____
2. lie _____
3. sing _____
4. hop _____
5. run _____
6. stay _____
7. benefit _____
8. swim _____
9. get _____
10. write _____

11. tie _____
12. begin _____
13. worry _____
14. bite _____
15. hope _____
16. die _____
17. prune _____
18. pop _____
19. hit _____
20. tighten _____

score _____

QUIZ 23 the present continuous tense
handbook p. 29

Place in the blanks appropriate affirmative or negative verb phrases in the present continuous tense. Use the verbs listed below. Include any adverbs in parentheses.

be	live	turn	wear
become	look	use	worry
begin	talk		

Examples: a. You *aren't wearing* any perfume today, are you, Millie?

b. (now) We'*re now beginning* this quiz.

1. My neighbors _____ foolish in this matter; they aren't using their heads.

2. (slow) Her hair _____ gray; she's almost sixty now.

3. We _____ this equipment only for the time being; ours isn't working right.

4. (always) A farmer _____ about the weather.

5. Listen, Ronnie, you _____ your brain; think before you speak.

6. Mr. Taylor, the man you wish to speak to, _____ on the phone at the moment; he can't speak to you right now.

7. (gradually) Our company _____ larger and more complex.

8. (always) An animal in the jungle _____ for food.

9. We _____ in a trailer for the time being; our house burned down in a fire several months ago.

10. Class, you _____ your dictionaries when you write your compositions, and you're making a lot of spelling mistakes.

score _____

QUIZ 24 contrasting verb tenses

handbook p. 30

Supply appropriate affirmative or negative verb phrases in the simple present tense or the present continuous tense.

come	go	rain	take	watch
do	hunt	sleep	try	wear

Examples: a. My roommate *doesn't go* to school every day, only three times a week.

b. I can't talk to you now because I *am doing* my homework.

1. Look! A man _____ to climb that big oak tree.

2. The Middle East is extremely dry; it _____ much there.

3. I can play my radio now; my roommate _____ .

4. (always) Christopher _____ a shower every morning; he sometimes forgets.

17

5. (often) Children, in general, _____ political programs on TV.

6. I _____ any perfume right now.

7. Grandpa _____ a walk in the park from time to time.

8. (seldom) A male lion _____ for food; the females in the pride do most of the hunting.

9. My lawyer _____ anything about my problem with the government for the time being; he wants the government to make the first move.

10. The international news _____ on (appears) at seven o'clock every evening.

score _____

QUIZ 25   yes-no questions

handbook p. 31

Supply appropriate words to complete the following yes–no questions with verb phrases in the simple present tense or present continuous tense. Use the verbs at the left, and use the words at the right as subjects. Use the adverbs in the parentheses when given.

cost	have	Flight 711	vegetarians
do	learn	his brother	your father
drive	leave	the patient	your grandfather
eat	live	rice	your roommate
enjoy	smoke	the students	your wife
get	worry		

Examples: a. *Does your father drive* to work every day?

b. (always) *Are your neighbors always worrying* about their children?

1. _____ in Casablanca only for the time being?

2. (ever) _____ meat? (How do they get protein?)

3. _____ a good horror movie once in a while?

4. (gradually) _____ better? Is he still in the hospital?

5. _____ a lot now? Is it cheaper than it was?

6. (sometimes) _____ a cigar after dinner?

7. _____ English little by little?

name _____

8. _____ for London every evening?

9. _____ any problems with your neighbor?

10. (ever) _____ his homework at the library?

score _____ (20 points each)

QUIZ 26   information questions

handbook p. 32

Using the following statements as cues, compose appropriate information questions. Use the information words stated at the left. Use only noun subjects chosen from the list at the right.

what	how long	a movie	your neighbors
what kind of	how often	your grandmother	the mailman
where		your husband	

Examples: a. *How often do your neighbors go on a vacation?* _____
           They go on a vacation <u>once or twice a year</u>.

      b. *Where is the gardener working today?* _____
         He's working <u>in the vegetable garden</u> today.

1. _____
   She usually eats <u>cereal</u> for breakfast.

2. _____
   He's now using a <u>Japanese</u> camera.

3. _____
   They mow their lawn <u>once in a while</u>.

4. _____
   It usually lasts <u>about an hour and a half</u>.

5. _____
   He's putting the package <u>on the front porch</u>.

QUIZ 27 adjective phrases; *the*

handbook p. 32

Circle the word in the parentheses that is correct.

Example: a. The TV set ((in,) on) the corner of the living room isn't working right.

1. The research in my company (*cost*, *costs*) a lot.
2. The sheep in our yard (*are*, *is*, *either*) old.
3. Excuse me, but the music (*in*, *on*) your radio is too loud; it's hurting my ears.
4. (*The*, *X*) oil costs a lot now, so we keep our house cool in the winter.
5. Mr. Jackson, the cost of these books (*are*, *is*) too high; it's unreasonable.
6. (*The*, *X*) eggs in this basket are fresher than those.
7. The man (*in*, *on*) the first row is the author of this play.
8. The deer in this park (*are*, *is*) very tame.
9. The people in my town (*gossip*, *gossips*) a great deal.
10. (*The*, *X*) life is wonderful. It's great to be alive. (old saying)
11. The food (*at*, *in*) the party is going to be Chinese, so bring your chopsticks.
12. (*The*, *X*) oil in this bottle is a little rancid.
13. The color of her eyes (*are*, *is*) blue, and they are always sparkling.
14. The large size of his feet (*make*, *makes*) it difficult for him to find shoes.
15. The police in our town (*know*, *knows*) what is happening.
16. The vase (*in*, *on*) the middle of the dining room table is an antique.
17. (*The*, *X*) money isn't easy to make these days.
18. The hair of a tiger (*are*, *is*) relatively short.
19. The data in this report (*is*, *are*, *either*) not accurate.
20. (*The*, *X*) water in the kettle is boiling.

score _____

QUIZ 28   neither, not one, both, *and* none

handbook p. 33

Circle the word in the parentheses that is correct. *Either* *means both words are correct.*

Example: a. None of my friends (*speak*, *speaks*, (*either*)) a second language well.

1. Neither of my children (*make*, *makes*, *either*) trouble at school.
2. Not one of the students ever (*forget*, *forgets*, *either*) to use an -*s* form when it's appropriate.

3. None of the people in my office ever (_play_, _plays_, _either_) around much.

4. Both of my parents (_work_, _works_, _either_) hard to make a living.

5. None of the equipment in my office (_are_, _is_, _either_) working right.

6. Neither of my English teachers (_are_, _is_, _either_) hard to understand.

7. Not one of my neighbors (_have_, _has_, _either_) a good lawnmower.

8. Both of my upstairs neighbors (_make_, _makes_, _either_) a lot of noise.

9. None of this laundry (_are_, _is_, _either_) clean.

10. None of my friends' friends (_are_, _is_, _either_) a friend of mine.

score _____ (5 points each)

QUIZ 29   compound pronouns and adverbs; _else_ and _besides_

handbook p. 34

Circle the word in the parentheses that is correct. _Either_ means both words are correct.

Example: a. She doesn't know (anyone, _no one_) in her husband's business life.

1. (_Nothing_, _Anything_) much happens in my little town on Sundays; it's dead.

2. Everyone in my class (_do_, _does_, _either_) the daily homework; it's easy.

3. Something else (_beside_, _besides_) your problems at work is bothering you.

4. No one in the class (_are_, _is_, _either_) as good a student as you are.

5. I don't want (_nothing_, _anything_) else from the store; the refrigerator is full.

6. (_Besides_, _Beside_) money, Mr. Smith, what else do you want in your life?

7. Does everyone in the class have (_his or her_, _their_) registration form?

8. Nothing in the stores (_are_, _is_, _either_) cheap now.

9. He's not a very good worker; he doesn't do (_anything_, _nothing_).

10. They have a lovely house (_besides_, _beside_) a large and isolated lake.

11. (_Anyone_, _Someone_) in my neighborhood doesn't have enough money to buy shoes for his children.

12. She and her husband usually go (_nowhere_, _anywhere_) on Monday nights.

13. Someone in my office (_is_, _are_) cheating the company.

14. No one else (_have_, _has_, _either_) a smile as beautiful as Mary Smith's.

15. (_Someone_, _Anyone_) else besides my neighbor is talking about me behind my back.

16. No one knows (_nothing_, _anything_) about the scandal in your family except me.

21

17. Everyone in the world (*want*, *wants*, *either*) peace for the next millennium.

18. I don't know (*someone*, *anyone*) in the Far East. Do you?

19. A convenient place for your new phone is (*beside*, *besides*) the bed.

20. We go (*everywhere*, *anywhere*) on our summer vacations.

score _____

QUIZ 30 prepositions of time

handbook p. 36

Circle the word in the parentheses that is correct. Either means both words are correct.

Example: a. The leaves usually fall from the trees (*at*, ⟨*in*⟩ *on*) early October.

1. (*At*, *In*, *either*) night is a good time to water the lawn in the garden.

2. They usually take their vacations (*at*, *in*, *on*) May, which is a nice time of the year.

3. My grandfather is like a clock; he wakes up every morning (*at*, *in*, *on*) dawn.

4. Lunch at my dormitory is usually served (*at*, *in*, *either*) 12:30.

5. What strange noises one hears (*at*, *in*, *on*) the night!

6. She often has about four cups of coffee (*in*, *during*, *either*) the morning.

7. His mother was born (*at*, *in*, *on*) July 24, 1933.

8. The international news always comes on (*at*, *in*, *on*) seven o'clock in the evening.

9. We're usually in our reading class from one (*at*, *in*, *to*) two o'clock.

10. They're serving champagne (*in*, *at*, *either*) the wedding today.

score _____

QUIZ 31 prepositions of direction

handbook p. 37

Supply an appropriate preposition from the following list.

at	from	out of	to	up
down	in	through	toward	

name _____

Example:　a. All roads lead *to* Rome. (old saying)

1. My boss never gets _____ work on time, and he seldom does any work.

2. There's no light in the stairwell, so be careful when you walk _____ the stairs.

3. Please get _____ this room, Robert, and never speak to me again.

4. Ladies and Gentlemen, we're soon going _____ the longest tunnel in the world.

5. Mommy, where does milk come _____?

6. Information goes _____ many channels before it reaches the President's desk.

7. What time do you usually arrive _____ London from your place in the country?

8. What a beautiful town and a lovely family you come _____!

9. It's Hadj (the holiest time in Islam), and hundreds of thousands of pilgrims are heading _____ Mecca.

10. We're arriving _____ the station now, children; get your bags.

score _____

QUIZ 32　expressing future time with the present continuous tense

handbook p. 38

Fill in the blanks with appropriate present participles made out of the following base forms.

arrive　　get　　go

Example:　a. Is the team *going* to the stadium soon?

1. We're _____ to the end of this quiz in a few minutes.

2. What time is the plane _____ to London tomorrow morning?

3. Are you _____ up to the top of the mountain on your next hike?

4. When are you _____ out of the office this afternoon, John?

5. Our bus from the airport to town is delayed, so we're _____ to our hotel late.

6. What time are you _____ to the reception this evening?

7. My family and I are _____ down to South America on our vacation next summer.

8. He's _____ to the class at exactly nine o'clock; he's always a very punctual student.

9. Excuse me, Conductor, is this train _____ in Singapore soon?

10. Our company salesman is _____ through your town on Friday morning; he'd like to pay you a visit at that time.

score _____ (20 points each)

QUIZ 33 expressing duration in the future; (for) *how long, probably, at least,* and *until*

handbook p. 38

Supply appropriate affirmative or negative verb phrases in the present continuous tense.

camp   live   stay   visit   work

Examples: a. We're *staying* in this town until next Monday morning.

b. (probably) My wife and I *are probably staying* in this hotel for at least three more weeks; we're just here for the time being.

1. I _____ in this department of the company until the end of the week; Friday is my last day.

2. (probably) What a nice resort this is! We _____ here until the end of the summer.

3. (probably) He _____ in our little town for long; he's like a nomad and never settles down in a place for more than a year or so.

4. (probably) The climbers _____ at the summit until tomorrow morning; weather conditions do not permit a descent.

5. My grandparents _____ with me for at least another week.

score _____

QUIZ 34 "X prepositions"

handbook p. 39

Circle the correct answer in parentheses.

Example: a. When are we reaching (*to*, Ⓧ) the summit?

1. The post office is near (*to*, *X*) the drugstore at the corner.

2. She's planning to enter (*to*, *into*, *X*) the University of California at Berkeley.

3. She's getting (_to_, _X_) home earlier than usual this evening.

4. I wouldn't like to enter (_into_, _to_, _X_) an argument with my neighbor; he's as strong as an ox.

5. I'm going to pay a visit (_to_, _at_, _X_) my lawyer to discuss this matter.

6. Yes, they're entering (_to_, _into_, _X_) the contest; they hope to win.

7. My roommate attends (_to_, _at_, _X_) school; she doesn't work.

8. We're very excited; we're visiting (_to_, _X_) the White House tomorrow morning.

9. I'm not driving my car (_to_, _X_) home; it's not working.

10. Our son is trying to get (_to_, _into_, _X_) Cornell University; he's already sent an application.

score _____

QUIZ 35   be going to + a base form

handbook p. 41

Fill in the blanks with appropriate affirmative or negative verb phrases with _be going to_ + a base form. Include in the sentence any adverbs in parentheses.

arrive	believe	graduate	stay
attend	enter	last	take
be	get	make	

Examples: a. (ever) Our son _isn't ever going to be_ the President, but he's going to be someone important and famous.

b. This beautiful weather _is going to last_ a long time; the radio says so.

1. We _____ at the reception on time; this delay is making us late.

2. Not one of my associates _____ the meeting tomorrow.

3. (never) We _____ to the station on time; this traffic is too heavy.

4. I have several house guests; they _____ with me until the end of the week.

5. (probably) I _____ the university this coming September.

6. (ever) He and his wife _____ a million dollars, but they're going to be happy.

7. My brother and I are only juniors; we _____ from the university until next year.

8. We _____ a break until 10 o'clock; we must finish this quiz.

9. Don't worry, Henry, we _____ there on time; I'm a fast driver.

10. (ever) No one _____ me when I tell this fantastic story.

score _____

QUIZ 36 be going to + be + a present participle

handbook p. 41

Supply appropriate present participles in the blanks.

do   make   run   wait
go   rain   sit   wear

Example: a. Jim, for how long are you going to be *running* today? Are you planning to do more than a couple of miles?

1. That lazy fellow is going to be _____ down for the rest of his life.

2. Jack isn't always going to be _____ to school; he's eventually graduating.

3. Ronnie, for how long are you going to be _____ your older brother's chores?

4. Mr. Newman, you're probably going to be _____ a great many errands for me today; I'm very busy.

5. I hear your daughter is going to be _____ to the university soon.

6. Just how soon are we going to be _____ more progress on this project, Ladies and Gentlemen?

7. How long is your baby boy going to be _____ diapers, Mrs. Taylor?

8. How long is the patient going to be _____ such a high fever, Dr. Madison?

9. For how long is it going to be _____? It certainly is wet outside.

10. Is there going to be anyone _____ for you at the station, Tiffany?

QUIZ 37   too, very, and enough
handbook p. 42

Fill in each blank with <u>too</u>, <u>very</u>, or <u>enough</u>.

Examples: a. What a *very* beautiful smile the woman in that painting has!

b. My grandfather says he will never be *too* old to enjoy a good cigar.

c. Is a thirteen-year-old girl old *enough* to wear lipstick?

1. Please relax, Mr. Smith, the doctor doesn't want you to get _____ excited; it's not good for your weak heart.

2. I am _____ glad to meet you, Sir; it is an honor.

3. This meat is certainly _____ tough, but I'm still going to eat it.

4. What a fantastic story! In fact, it's _____ fantastic for me to believe.

5. My grandmother is _____ old, but she goes to work every day.

6. He's not studying hard _____ at school; he's getting poor grades.

7. Is an eighteen-year-old boy or girl _____ young to vote in a presidential election?

8. Well, they're not _____ young to die for their country, are they?

9. Oh! That music is _____ loud; it's hurting my ears.

10. This food is certainly _____ rich and spicy. May I have some more, please?

score _____ (5 points each)

QUIZ 38   regular and irregular past forms; spelling and pronunciation
handbook p. 43

Make past forms out of the following regular and irregular base forms.

Examples: a. lay *laid*

b. work *worked*

1. permit _____   5. lie _____ or _____

2. swim _____   6. close _____

3. quit _____   7. connect _____

4. benefit _____   8. hang _____ or _____

9. teach _____   15. bet _____

10. spit _____ or _____   16. sweep _____

11. sing _____   17. copy _____

12. omit _____   18. shoot _____

13. slap _____   19. quiz _____

14. dive _____ or _____   20. play _____

score _____

QUIZ 39   the simple past tense
handbook p. 44

Place in the blanks appropriate affirmative or negative verb phrases in the simple past tense.

Examples: a. (do) We *didn't do* anything in particular last weekend; we slept a lot.

b. (drink) I *drank* two cups of coffee after dinner last night; I couldn't sleep well.

1. (serve) They _____ any champagne at the wedding last Saturday; it was too expensive.

2. (be) There _____ no people from my company at the meeting yesterday.

3. (lead) Adolph Hitler _____ the German people to destruction.

4. (hang) The world was shocked when the terrorists _____ the hostages.

5. (have) We _____ enough time to sit down for a minute all day yesterday; we were really busy.

6. (be) Life _____ easy for the poor people in my town during the last recession.

7. (eat) She _____ much dinner last night; she had no appetite.

8. (pay) He's in trouble with the IRS (Internal Revenue Service); he _____ his taxes last year and the year before.

9. (be) There _____ any sheep on my grandparents' farm; they raised only cattle.

10. (travel) We _____ nowhere last summer; we stayed home in our own backyard.

QUIZ 40   adverbs with the simple past tense

handbook p. 45

Supply in the blanks appropriate verb phrases in the simple past tense using the adverb indicated. Use only the verbs in the following list.

> be   drink   eat   get   have

Example: a. (always) The weather *wasn't always* nice on our summer vacation last summer; it rained on three or four days.

1. (ever) Not one of my friends _____ in the army during the war.

2. (usually) When I was a student at the university twenty-five years ago, I _____ much money in my pocket to spend, but I was very happy.

3. (always) When they were children, they _____ enough to eat; their family was very poor.

4. (seldom) During her pregnancy, she _____ sick in the mornings.

5. (ever) Not one of Mr. Green's business associates _____ at the hotel to pay him a visit during his stay there.

6. (never) My grandfather _____ alcohol.

7. (ever) Their last business enterprise wasn't much of a success; they _____ any credit at the bank.

8. (rarely) During the war, they _____ meat; there was none to be had.

9. (ever) During the last hurricane, neither of us _____ afraid at any time.

10. (hardly ever) During his vacation, he _____ out of his apartment; he was busy working on a manuscript.

score _____

REVIEW QUIZ A   contrasting verb tenses

Place in the blanks appropriate affirmative or negative verb phrases in the simple present tense, the present continuous tense, or the simple past tense.

Examples: a. (kill / slowly) Young man, with those cigarettes, you*'re slowly killing* yourself.

b. (leave) We missed the boat; it *left* almost an hour ago.

c. (begin) The class *begins* on time every day.

1. (get / usually) My neighbor _____ home from work at five o'clock every day.

2. (be) No one _____ perfect. (old saying)

3. (catch) What an amusing story this is! Several weeks ago, a policeman _____ a policewoman in the act of stealing.

4. (appear) That program _____ on TV now; let's watch it.

5. (do / ever) Neither of us _____ any exercises in the mornings; we're both very lazy.

6. (be / always) The police _____ honest.

7. (be) Life _____ easy for the poor people in my town.

8. (import) Saudi Arabia _____ oil.

9. (make) He _____ any money last year; his company went out of business, in fact.

10. (come / now) This quiz _____ to an end.

score _____

QUIZ 41 yes-no questions in the simple past tense
handbook p. 46

Complete the following yes–no questions with appropriate verb phrases in the simple present tense, the present continuous tense, or the simple past tense. Choose a subject from the group on the left and a verb from the right. Complete the short answers with appropriate words.

it	you	be	fight	live
Mary and Bob	your boss	come	get	make
Miss White	your roommate	enter	have	rain
the news				

Examples: a. (ever) *Does your roommate ever do* any homework for his class this semester? Yes, *he does*.

b. *Did you have* any trouble with your lawyer over that financial matter last year? No, *I didn't*.

c. *Is it raining* now? Yes, *it is*.

1. (ever) _____ much noise? Yes, _____.

2. _____ to yesterday's meeting on time?
No, _____.

3. _____ the university this coming fall?
No, _____.

4. (now) _____ over the wire good?
Yes, _____.

5. (ever) _____ during your vacation last summer?
No,_____ .

6. (usually)_____ in a good mood most of last
week? Yes,_____ .

7. _____ in a hotel for only the time being?
Yes,_____ .

8. _____ many problems at work these days?
Yes,_____ .

9. (always)_____ with each other when they were
married? No, _____ .

10. (usually)_____ to the office before you do every
day? Yes, _____ .

score _____

QUIZ 42 information questions in the simple past tense
handbook p. 47

Complete the following information questions with appropriate verb phrases in the simple present tense, the present continuous tense, or the simple past tense.

how long	what kind of dress	I	drive	make
how often	what kind of food	you	do	put
how much	what time	your husband	get	serve
what	when	your wife	go	spend
what kind of car	where	your vacation	keep	study
			last	wear

Examples: a. *How much did you spend* on your vacation last year?

b. *What kind of food are you serving* at your dinner party tomorrow night?

c. (usually) *Where do you usually spend* your summer vacations?

1. _____ my glasses? I can't find
them.

2. (usually) _____ out of school every
day, Roger?

3. _____ his bed? Once in a while?
Never?

4. _____ last summer? Did you have
a good time?

5. (most often) _____ her money at home? Is there a safe hiding place in the house.

6. (now)_____ ? Does it burn much gas?

7. _____ at the university this semester, Jennifer?

8. _____for your neighbor last week?

9. _____ on your vacation three years ago?

10. _____ to tomorrow night's dance, Laura?

score _____

QUIZ 43 *who, whom,* and *whose* in information questions

handbook p. 47

Fill in each blank with <u>who</u>, <u>whom</u>, *or* <u>whose</u>.

Examples: a. *Who* knows the answer to the riddle?

b. From *whom* is the Ambassador expecting to receive a reply?

c. *Whose* responsibility is it to see that our country's defenses are strong

1. Betsy, _____ do you love the best, your cat or your dog?

2. Of all the students in your class, _____ compositions are the best?

3. Sir, at _____ are you swearing?

4. Your Excellency, _____ did you visit at the White House yesterday morning?

5. _____ is the leader of this country?

6. _____ideas are you expressing, Mr. King, yours or your wife's?

7. For _____ did you vote in the last election?

8. _____usually corrects these quizzes?

9. _____ in your group do the members most often follow?

10. Excuse me, Ladies and Gentlemen, to _____do these car keys belong?

QUIZ 44   postponed prepositions

handbook p. 49

Place appropriate prepositions in the blanks.

        about   in   to
        at   of   with

Example: a. What kind of toothpaste do you usually brush your teeth *with*?

1. Who is your roommate always dreaming _____?

2. Excuse me, Mr. Whiteside, who are you speaking _____ on the phone?

3. What on earth is the professor talking _____? I don't understand a word.

4. Who does your favorite dancer usually dance _____ at recitals and concerts?

5. Who are you sitting _____ in class tomorrow?

6. What are you reading _____ in that book, John? It looks interesting.

7. Who are you staring _____ little boy? Don't you know it's rude to stare?

8. What pot are you boiling the lobsters _____? They're very big, you know.

9. What are you thinking _____, Mr. Dixon? Your past mistakes?

10. Whose bed are you going to sleep _____ tonight? Yours or your brother's?

score _____   (20 points each)

QUIZ 45   information questions; formal versus informal usage

handbook p. 49

Make information questions with who, whom, *or* whose *in response to the following statements.*

Example: a. (formal) *With whom does the Queen lunch tomorrow?*
             (informal) *Who does the Queen lunch with tomorrow?*
             The Queen lunches with *the King* tomorrow.

1. (formal) _____

   (informal) _____
   This gold watch belongs to *my grandfather*.

2. (formal) _____

(informal) _____

My mother met my father at *a neighbor's* house.

3. (formal) _____

(informal) _____

There are letters for *the Ambassador and his wife.*

4. (formal) _____

(informal) _____

Robert Maxwell knows *the President* in Washington, D. C.

5. (formal) _____

(informal) _____

We're voting for *nobody* in the next election.

score _____

QUIZ 46   information questions; information words as subjects
handbook p. 49

Make information questions with <u>what</u>, <u>who</u>, <u>whom</u>, *or* <u>whose</u>. *Observe the formal style.*

Example: a. *At whom did the convicted criminal swear?*
The convicted criminal swore at *the judge.*

1. _____

Thieves stole my wallet and your pen.

2. _____

The revolutionaries executed *the former dictator* at dawn.

3. _____

Those papers on the desk were *the director's*.

4. _____

Love makes the world go around. (old saying)

5. _____

There are messages for *Dr. Franklin and Mrs. Wilson.*

6. _____

Miss Crawford usually has confidence in *her lawyer.*

7. _____

Marie Curie discovered radium.

8. _____

Mine won the first prize.

name _____

9. _____

The Duke is sitting between <u>the Duchess and the Princess.</u>

10. _____

<u>A classmate</u> corrected my quiz.

score _____ (5 points each)

QUIZ 47   pronoun substitutes; *one, some; what* and *which*

handbook p. 50

Circle the correct word in the parentheses.

Example: a. (What,) Which) is your name?

1. (What, Which) time is best to make an appointment, one or two o'clock?

2. I have on a new bathing suit; do you like (it, one)?

3. (What, Which) is the formula for success?

4. This Jello is delicious; would you like (one, some)?

5. (What, Which, either) airlines fly across the Atlantic?

6. What beautiful eggs! I'd like a dozen large (one, ones), please.

7. Which (one, ones) of all these paintings appeal to you the most?

8. What a beautiful sculpture! Do you like (it, some)?

9. To (which, what) person in Cora Brown's family do you wish to speak?

10. Which one of the dogs (have, has) lice?

11. What beautiful shirts these are! Would you like to try (it, one) on?

12. (What, Which) woman in this room is wearing that seductive perfume?

13. What beautiful deer! Do you see (it, them)?

14. (What, Which) is your present address in Tegucigalpa?

15. That's an antique fan, and this is a new (one, ones).

16. Here are some nice stamps; which (one, ones) do you think is the most beautiful?

17. (What, Which) is the formula for carbon monoxide?

18. (What, Which) drawer are you putting the pillows in, the top or the bottom one?

19. To (what, which) address do you wish this package sent, this one or that one?

20. (What, Which) happens in your town on Saturday night?

35

REVIEW QUIZ B   reviewing plural forms of countable nouns

Give the plurals of the following nouns.

Examples: a. dream *dreams*

b. datum *data*

1. volcano _____
2. knife _____
3. ox _____
4. aquarium _____
5. fish _____
6. stomach _____
7. stimulus _____
8. surprise _____
9. roof _____
10. soprano _____

11. foot _____
12. tiger _____
13. play _____
14. couch _____
15. crisis _____
16. sheep _____
17. series _____
18. radio _____
19. phenomenon _____
20. berry _____

score _____ (5 points each)

REVIEW QUIZ C

Circle the correct word in the parentheses. <u>Either</u> *means both choices are correct.*

Example: a. She doesn't ever (<u>(do</u>, *does*) any favors for anybody; she's quite selfish.

1. Mr. Williams (', 's, *either*) job is less important than his wife's.
2. (*Do, Would,* *either*) you like to have some of this chocolate?
3. Half (*a, an, either*) hour of playing tennis is enough for me.
4. We're far (*to, from, at*) the end of this textbook.
5. What color (*of, X, either*) jacket would you like to try on, Sir?
6. How (*do, does*) research help us in our daily lives?
7. Would you please keep the answer to this question a secret between you and (*I, me*).
8. He has (*a, an*) unique personality; there's no one else like him.
9. Please put that bowl of fruit (*in, on*) the middle of the table.
10. We're staying at the student dormitory (*at, on, for*) the time being.
11. Jesus (', 's, *either*) life was very short; he lived for only thirty-three years.

12. Physics (*are*, *is*) a fascinating subject to study.

13. Would you please write your name on the dotted line (*at*, *on*) the bottom of the page.

14. He feels (*bad*, *badly*, *either*) about the poor financial situation in his family.

15. Well! How do you do? I am (*too*, *very*, *either*) glad to meet you.

16. Fortunately, none of the news (*is*, *are*, *either*) bad today.

17. He has (*enough money*, *money enough*, *either*) to go to the movies today.

18. It's (*too*, *very*, *either*) hot to work outside today, isn't it?

19. The local post office is near (*to*, *X*) the National Bank.

20. What (*do*, *X*) you usually do when you leave school in the afternoon?

score _____ (20 points each)

REVIEW QUIZ D

In each group of sentences, one sentence is correct; the other two contain one mistake each. Circle the letter corresponding to the correct answer, and then make appropriate corrections in the two remaining sentences.

Example: A. a. How often do you ~~make~~ *do* the cleaning in your house?

b. Does their young son ~~do~~ *make* much trouble at school?

ⓒ How often do you do the cleaning in your house?

1. a. Why are you always looking at yourself on the mirror?
   b. Who is that sitting on the third row of seats?
   c. What a beautiful red dress she's wearing to the party!

2. a. Our television set is on the corner of the living room.
   b. Their swimming pool is in the back of their house.
   c. The S.S. <u>Titanic</u> is at the bottom of the Atlantic Ocean.

3. a. There is people in the other room.
   b. The police catches a lot of criminals every day.
   c. A great many people in the world make a great deal of money.

4. a. You're mother is in the other room.
   b. What wonderful perfume! It's fragrance isn't familiar to me.
   c. Our house at the beach is yours for the summer.

5. a. That is a unusual painting.
   b. That, Ladies and Gentlemen, is an historical fact.
   c. I'd like a orange, please.

name _____ score _____ (5 points each)

REVIEW QUIZ E

Fill in each blank with only one appropriate word. If a word is not required (or it is optional), write an "X" in the blank.

Examples: a. There isn't <u>any</u> food in the refrigerator for the dog's dinner.

b. When are you going to be visiting <u>X</u> your aunt and uncle in Norway?

1. My mother writes a letter to my wife and _____ only once in a while.

2. Your sister _____ like to take another English course.

3. Mathematics _____ my daughter's favorite subject at school.

4. Approximately how many people _____ live in Shanghai?

5. There are only a _____ people in my conversation class.

6. Some of the students don't _____ their homework every day.

7. My roommate and I are lazy; neither of us _____ much housework.

8. Saudi Arabia _____ exports a great deal of oil.

9. They're subletting an apartment _____ the time being.

10. I'm going to school _____ the evenings and working during the day.

11. Are these mine? Yes, _____ are.

12. _____ how long are you going to be studying at the university?

13. Excuse me, when are you leaving _____ New Delhi?

14. Is your son planning to enter _____ the University of Texas this fall?

15. _____ of these three hats do you like the best?

16. _____ fish doesn't cost much.

17. We're going to be staying with our friends in Mississippi _____ two weeks.

18. He's _____ sick to go to school; he's in bed with a temperature of 102 degrees.

19. What a wonderful person I met _____ the Christmas party last Saturday night!

20. Yesterday, the Pope had _____ one-hour meeting with the President.

QUIZ 48   compound subjects and objects

handbook p. 51

Place in each blank the letter corresponding to the correct answer.

Example: a. This morning, I had a big breakfast of *a* with lots of hot coffee.
  a. ham and eggs   b. eggs and ham

1. Please give this package to _____.
   a. him and his sister   b. his sister and him

2. _____ are not going to attend their son's graduation ceremonies.
   a. He and his wife   b. His wife and he

3. My father likes _____ for dinner every night; he doesn't like fish or poultry.
   a. potatoes and meat   b. meat and potatoes

4. I need to buy some _____ at the stationery shop.
   a. pencils and pens   b. pens and pencils

5. _____ went on a trip to Nepal last fall; we went trekking for two weeks.
   a. My husband and I   b. I and my husband

6. While I was traveling in Latin America, I ate a lot of _____.
   a. chicken and rice   b. rice and chicken

7. _____, would you all please rise and sing the national anthem.
   a. Gentlemen and Ladies   b. Ladies and Gentlemen

8. I'm taking calculus, algebra _____ and advanced physics next semester.
   a. X   b. X or,

9. For our trip, first we need money; then we need _____.
   a. gas and a car   b. a car and gas

10. This is a secret between _____.
    a. you and I   b. you and me

score _____

QUIZ 49   compound verbs

handbook p. 53

Complete the compound verb phrases by filling in the blanks with appropriate forms of the base forms in parentheses. Include any adverbs.

Examples: a. (play) On New Year's Eve everyone dances, sings, and *plays* all night long.

   b. (ask) That young woman is always talking to the teacher and *asking* questions that can't be answered easily.

   c. (erupt) Mt. St. Helens exploded and *erupted* several times within a few weeks.

1. (write) No one in the class speaks and _____ as well as the professor.

2. (dig) My father is always working and _____ in the garden.

3. (get / rarely) She studies hard and _____ a low score.

4. (shoot) The woman, enraged with jealousy, _____ and killed her husband.

5. (do) He's always helping people and _____ nice things for them.

6. (lose / ever) She has a beautiful singing voice and _____ control of it.

7. (lie / almost never) She is a fairly honest woman and _____.

8. (do) Our little boy is always sitting in front of the fire and _____ puzzles.

9. (get) He lost his job and _____ any good offers for almost a year, but he finally found a fantastic position with a great salary.

10. (be / never) The elderly woman who is my neighbor has many friends and _____ lonely or depressed.

score _____

QUIZ 50 compound infinitives
handbook p. 54

Place in each blank a base form or an infinitive. Use only (to) make or (to) do.

Examples: a. Would you like *to do* me a favor?

b. I don't want to get nervous and *make* a lot of mistakes on the test.

1. Most scientists want to work at a laboratory and _____ important research.

2. Grandma would like _____ her hair in a different way for a change.

3. The government is trying to develop the industrial base of the country and _____ progress in social development.

4. Christy, I don't want you _____ faces at people on the street; it's rude.

5. I'm going to sit down right now and _____ my homework for tomorrow.

6. My friends and I want to go to the beach and _____ nothing but swim, rest, and play in the sand.

7. He needs to find a public phone and _____ a call to his roommate.

8. Now, Ladies and Gentlemen, Miss Raja is going to sing songs and _____ several dances native to Tamil Nadu, her birthplace in southern India.

9. The government is trying _____ work for the poor workers in my town.

10. Would you like to sit in a subway token booth and _____ change all day long?

score _____

QUIZ 51   compound adjectives and adverbs

handbook p. 54

Place in each blank a compound adjective or adverb. Make sure you change the adjectives in parentheses into adverbs when necessary.

Examples: a. (strange / foolish) How *strangely and foolishly* that little boy sometimes acts!

b. (nice / easy) Children, *please* is such a *nice and easy* word to use; please use it.

1. (fast / good) How _____ he does all his assigned work!

2. (slow / careful) He's a very fine craftsman and always works _____ _____.

3. (rich / happy) She's looking _____; she's always wearing beautiful clothes and has a big smile on her face.

4. (quiet / quick) Children, I'd like you to go to bed now, and I want you to go _____ . You have school tomorrow.

5. (good / sweet) How _____ this apple tastes!

6. (crazy / foolish) How _____ my neighbor downstairs sometimes acts!

7. (good / polite) What _____ children you have, Mr. and Mrs. Turner! They are a joy to have in my classroom.

8. (hard / good) How _____ that man works! The company should pay him more money.

9. (slow / methodical) Grandpa Smith always drives his car _____ _____.

10. (good / natural) How _____ this fresh salad tastes!

QUIZ 52   compound sentences with semicolons; *too* and *either*
handbook p. 54

Fill in the blanks with appropriate verb phrases in the simple present tense, the present continuous tense, or the simple past tense. Fill in the second blanks with <u>too</u> *or* <u>either</u>.

Examples: a. (get / ever) I never get into a bad mood; no one else in my family *ever gets* into one, *either*.

b. (forget) He often forgets to use -s forms; the others *forget* them, *too*.

c. (like) He didn't like the movie last night; his wife *didn't like* it, *either*.

1. (forget / ever) I never forget my friends; my friends _____ me, _____.

2. (think / always) I'm always thinking about my classes; my roommate in the dormitory _____ about his, _____.

3. (do / never) I didn't ever do much swimming last summer; my brother _____ much, _____.

4. (like / occasionally) I enjoy going on a hike once in a while; my roommate _____ to go on one, _____.

5. (cut / ever) She never cut herself on that machine; her co-worker _____ _____ himself on it, _____.

6. (want) I'm not going to the game; my sister _____ to go, _____.

7. (be / always) I'm never absent from school on Mondays; my teacher _____ there, _____.

8. (cheat / ever) I never cheat on tests; not one of my classmates _____ _____ on one, _____.

9. (be / ever) His father wasn't home much last winter; his mother _____ _____ there much _____.

10. (like) I don't like cowboy movies; no one else in my family _____ them, _____.

score _____

QUIZ 53   compound sentences with *and* and *but; miss*
handbook p. 55

Supply appropriate verb phrases in the simple present tense, the present continuous tense, or the simple past tense. Use only the verb <u>miss</u>.

name _____

Examples: a. Dear Mary, I love you, and I *miss* you very much; please write to me soon.

b. He got up late, but he *didn't miss* his train to the city.

c. Everything of value is in my luggage, but my camera *is missing*.

1. My grandmother isn't living now, and everyone in my family _____
    _____ her.

2. (always) Professor Jackson is a very forgetful person, and he _____
    _____ his appointments.

3. They called everyone else's name, but they _____ mine.

4. (ever) Mrs. Watson is a religious woman, and she _____
    church on Sundays, or holy days like Christmas and Easter.

5. I miss my friends on school vacations, but I _____
    homework.

6. (always) Her children are away at school, and she _____
    them.

7. All the checks I wrote to everyone last month are here on my desk, but a
    check to the phone company _____ .

8. (rarely) He's not a very sentimental person, and he _____
    his old friends back in his hometown.

9. My roommate _____ his family most during the holidays
    but I miss mine all the time. I'm really homesick.

10. He _____ the express bus, but he got to work on time.

score _____

QUIZ 54   compound sentences with *so*

handbook p. 57

Place in the blanks appropriate verb phrases in the simple present tense, the present continuous tense, or the simple past tense.

Examples: a. (eat / ever) They're Muslims, so they *don't ever eat* pork.

b. (have / never) They were always busy with their careers, so they *never had* any children.

c. (walk) The elevator isn't working, so I'*m walking* up the stairs.

1. (be / hardly ever) His apartment is small and very uncomfortable, so he
    _____ there.

2. (see) Bella Donna Rolanda is always very busy, so not one of her friends
    _____ her often.

43

3. (be / always) Gerald has a part-time job, so he _____ at school.

4. (worry / always) They have a sixteen-year-old daughter, so they _____ _____ about her.

5. (be / ever) George is always at his girlfriend's house, so he _____ _____ home with his parents.

6. (look) His wife is out of town today, so he _____ after the children.

7. (be / always) He grew up in a Chinese home, so there _____ rice on the table.

8. (put / never) He dislikes pepper, so he _____ it on his food.

9. (do / often) During last semester, Rosemary was always busy with her social life, so she _____ homework for school.

10. (eat / seldom) Mr. Reynolds is on a special diet, so he _____ out in restaurants.

score _____

QUIZ 55 abridged infinitives
handbook p. 57

Fill in the blanks with appropriate verb phrases containing abridged infinitives. Provide pronoun objects when necessary. Use only the verbs in the following list.

like   need   want   would like

Examples: a. My roommate hates to do the cleaning, but I *like to.*

b. They're coming to visit me tomorrow, but I *don't want them to.*

c. I gave the waiter a big tip, but I *didn't need to.*

1. Everyone in my family works hard, but no one _____.

2. I'm dropping out of school next semester, but I _____.

3. She quit school in the middle of last semester, but her father _____ _____.

4. My business partner and I aren't making much money now, but we _____.

5. My Dad is going to sell the family car, but my mother and I _____ _____.

6. Not everyone takes a trip around the world, but most everyone _____

_____.

7. I'm going to mow the lawn and water the flowers, but I _____.

8. Mr. Hudson, my writing teacher, is going to see this composition, but I

_____.

9. I'm not looking for a new job, but I _____.

10. Justin Johnson works from eight o'clock in the morning to eleven o'clock at

night, but his wife _____.

score _____ (5 points each)

QUIZ 56 *too, either, so, neither, and,* and *but*

handbook p. 58

Put appropriate words in the blanks.

Examples: a. *So* and *neither* are not easy to use, and *neither are* too and *either.*

b. (seldom) He often loses money at the horse races, but his wife *seldom does.*

1. The King never carries money, and the Queen _____.

2. Orlando never wears glasses, and _____ Rita, his twin sister.

3. Dickie Dunlap hit a home run in the game, and _____ three
other boys.

4. (rarely) Clara often loses money on a bet, but her clever husband

_____.

5. There weren't any keys on the desk, and _____ there any
money.

6. I don't ever come to class late, and not one of the other students

_____.

7. A baby boy needs a lot of attention, and _____ a baby girl.

8. (never) Wanda never studied much at school, and her twin sister

_____.

9. She'd like to go bowling, and _____ Bill, her roommate.

10. Goats are quite common in the Middle East, and sheep _____.

11. I was at that meeting, but not one of my co-workers _____.

12. (never) A sentence always has a subject, but a phrase _____.

13. You're learning a lot of new things in this course, and _____ I.

14. My classes aren't difficult, and yours _____ .

15. Red and green don't make purple, and _____ yellow and blue.

16. People on the street know about the scandal, and the communication media _____ .

17. The weather forecast isn't very good, and _____ the international news.

18. I don't want to change my schedule, and no one else in the class _____ .

19. He's very conservative in his political views, but not one of his friends _____ .

20. None of the newspaper reviewers liked that movie, and _____ _____ I.

score _____

QUIZ 57 complex sentences; *when, before,* and *after*
handbook p. 59

Place in the blanks appropriate verb phrases in the simple present tense.

Examples: a. (be) When the children *are* too quiet, something is wrong.

b. (take / always) You *always take* a shower after you play basketball.

1. (have / usually) Janet _____ anything to eat before she goes to her job.

2. (rise) I promise; when the curtain _____ , we're going to be in our seats. We're not going to miss a thing.

3. (come) No water _____ out when I turn on the faucet.

4. (cost) Food _____ much when you buy it at that store.

5. (have) When Alexander _____ a car, he takes a bus.

6. (lie) Uncle Ted always goes to sleep right away after he _____ down for a nap.

7. (rise) I'm going to be sleeping in my bed when the sun _____ tomorrow morning.

8. (be / usually) There _____ people in the house when I get home. I'm almost always the first one.

9. (happen) Andrew, before an accident _____ , please put that ladder away.

10. (get / always) After Richie eats ice cream, he _____ thirsty. I'm the same way.

QUIZ 58 *while*
handbook p. 60

Place in each blank an appropriate present participle; choose from the list below.

broil   do   get   work
defrost   figure   make   study

Example: a. While he's *studying* medicine at the University, his wife is *working* hard at a job; she's putting him through school.

1. I'm going to be _____ out these problems while you're _____ those calculations.

2. We're going to be _____ money on this project while we're _____ something for the community. I call that good business.

3. I'm going to be _____ the refrigerator while my sister is _____ the beds; that's teamwork.

4. While I'm _____ the salad, the steak is going to be _____.

5. While the days are _____ hotter now, the nights are _____ cooler.

score _____

QUIZ 59   complex sentences; *though, even though,* and *although*
handbook p. 61

Fill in the blanks with appropriate affirmative or negative verb phrases in the simple present tense, the present continuous tense, or the simple past tense.

Examples: a. (be) Although that money *wasn't* his, he spent all of it on useless luxuries.

b. (get / now) Though Grandpa *is now getting older,* he goes to work every day.

c. (have) I'm a happy person even though I *don't have* much money in the bank.

1. (play / hardly ever) Although he's a very fine pianist, he _____ _____.

2. (want) Dr. Scott, the patient in Room 37 _____ to get out of bed even though he's feeling much better now.

3. (be) Although there _____ no grammatical errors in the composition, the author had very little to say.

4. (do / always) Though some of the students _____ their homework, they usually do well in their class work.

5. (blow) I'm going for a walk even though the wind _____ hard.

6. (taste) This fish _____ very good even though I bought it fresh from the market this morning.

7. (lie / now) Although your grandmother _____ down, she isn't sleeping; she's only resting.

8. (take / never) My neighbor is always worrying about my problems even though he _____ care of his own.

9. (be) Although he _____ a careless child, he often hurts himself.

10. (eat) I'm not hungry at all even though I _____ breakfast.

score _____

QUIZ 60 complex sentences; *as soon as* and *until*

handbook p. 62

Place in each blank a base form or an -s form of one of the following verbs.

arrive	enter	go	reach
do	get	make	

Examples: a. Our company isn't going to grow until it <u>does</u> more research.

b. Your bedroom is going to look better as soon as you <u>make</u> your bed.

1. As soon as we _____ to Paris, we're going to have a wonderful dinner.

2. He's always a pleasant young man until he _____ into an argument with someone.

3. Until Mrs. Matson _____ her hair in a different way, she's going to look silly (ridiculous).

4. Billy Joe is going to change from a boy to a man as soon as he _____ the army.

5. Children, we're not going to be eating until we _____ our destination.

6. We're going to have trouble in our office until someone at the top _____ a decision about the company's future.

7. We're going to get off as soon as the bus _____ to the next stop.

8. As soon as you _____ at the station, please give me a call.

name _____

9. My dear, you're going to be happier as soon as you _____ some nice new friends in this town. Listen to your old grandmother.

10. We're going to start drinking tea as soon as the price of coffee _____ up again.

score _____

QUIZ 61   complex sentences; *because* and *since*

handbook p. 63

Place in each blank an appropriate verb phrase in the simple present tense, the present continuous tense, or the simple past tense.

be	do	play	take	wear
cost	love	run	water	work

Examples: a. Since the stove *isn't working* now, I'm going out to dinner this evening.

b. You feel tired and stiff now because you *didn't do* your exercises this morning.

c. (ever) The patient isn't getting better because he *doesn't ever take* his medicine.

1. Since the elevator _____ now, I'm walking up the stairs to my office.

2. Because it _____ automatic, there's no need to defrost your refrigerator.

3. (ever) Your lawn isn't green because the gardener _____ it.

4. (never) Since there _____ much food in the refrigerator (which didn't even work), the poor children often went to bed hungry.

5. Since the trains _____ now, I'm taking a taxi.

6. Because no one _____ him (he feels), he's a very lonely man.

7. Since she's only twelve years old, our daughter Elizabeth _____ _____ lipstick.

8. (always) Because my neighborhood in those days was a busy one, there _____ people on the street.

9. Marilyn Manners _____ the piano well because she seldom practices.

10. Because rice _____ much now, we eat a lot of it.

QUIZ 62   negative information questions; *why*

handbook p. 64

Make negative information questions with <u>why.</u>

Examples: a. (formal) <u>*Why does she not ever go out?*</u>
(informal) <u>*Why doesn't she ever go out?*</u>
<u>Since she's afraid of the streets at night,</u> she doesn't ever go out.

1. (formal) _____

(informal) _____
I'm not going to get the first prize <u>because I'm not good enough.</u>

2. (formal) (use <u>I</u>) _____

(informal) (use <u>I</u>) _____
I'm not a friend of yours <u>because you're not ever nice to me.</u>

3. (formal) _____

(informal) _____
My wife and I don't do exercises <u>because we're basically lazy.</u>

4. (formal) _____

(informal) _____
We didn't take our car with us <u>because it wasn't running right.</u>

5. (formal) _____

(informal) _____
I don't go to the movies <u>because I never have any free time.</u>

score _____

QUIZ 63   the emphatic form of the simple present tense;
conjunctive adverbs, *however*

handbook p. 65

Supply in each blank a verb phrase in the emphatic form of the simple present tense.

arrive   get   make
do   have   try

Examples: a. Although Roger tends to be lazy in the house, he *does do* the dishes once in
a great while even though he hates doing them.

b. Not all of the students get good grades; however, all of them *do try* hard.

1. Warren Williams, a very heavy guy,_____ exercises every
morning; however, he isn't very serious about it.

2. What a beautiful hotel this is! Yes, a nice hotel _____ a difference when you're on a business trip. Fortunately, our company is paying for it.

3. Yes, Miss Andrews _____ at the office on time every morning; however, she rarely does any work.

4. Our children seldom do the dishes, but they _____ a little housework.

5. (sometimes) He's one of the best students in the class; however, he _____ a mistake when he's speaking quickly.

6. No one in my office makes much money; however, everyone _____ _____ a great deal of work.

7. Hank Matthews never wins at a game of tennis; however, he _____ _____ hard.

8. Betty and Paul aren't very good secretaries, but they _____ to work on time every day.

9. They have a cleaning woman (maid) come in once a week; she never cooks, but she _____ all the heavy cleaning.

10. No, Mother, my stomach isn't upset; however, I _____ a headache.

score _____

QUIZ 64   the emphatic form of the simple past tense
handbook p. 67

Place in each blank a verb phrase in the emphatic form in the simple past tense.

do	enjoy	get	manage
eat	find	make	

Examples: a. No, we didn't enjoy the movie much, but we *did manage* to get into the theater for free (without charge).

b. The weather was terrible, ants and mosquitoes ruined our picnic, but we *did enjoy* ourselves.

1. No, Mother, I didn't touch my potatoes and vegetables, but I _____ _____ all my apple pie.

2. Yes, I really _____ an appointment, Miss, but you forgot to write it down.

3. Yes, it was hard for her to find a good job, but she _____ one, nevertheless.

4. He never did much for his wife when they were married; however, he _____ a lot for his children.

5. Yes, I _____ my bed, Dad, but it doesn't look like it, does it?

6. She never made many friends when she was at this company; however, she _____ to make a lot of enemies.

7. The actor in the play wasn't much, but we _____ the actress's performance.

8. Yes, the train was delayed in Milan for fifteen minutes, but it _____ to Venice on time.

9. Mr. Brown didn't want to do business with me; however, I _____ _____ a deal with his son.

10. I ran no errands yesterday, but I _____ a few chores around the house.

score _____

QUIZ 65   negative openings

handbook p. 67

Supply in the blanks appropriate verb phrases (emphatic form) in the simple present tense or the simple past tense. Use the words in the following list as subjects.

my grandmother	it	one
he	my birthday	she
I	my neighbors	they

Examples: a. (have / ever) Never, when he was a little boy, *did he ever have* other children to play with; he grew up on a farm and had no brothers or sisters.

b. (find) Rarely *does one find* inexpensive clothes that are nice in the stores these days.

1. (want) Not only _____ my money, but they asked for my help, too. And they live right next door to me.

2. (be / ever) No, my grandparents were never in Asia, nor _____ _____ in Europe.

3. (do / ever) Not once during the time that Jason lived here _____ _____ anything for his neighbors.

4. (come) Only once a year _____ , and I always give myself a present on the occasion.

5. (have) Young man, only once in a lifetime _____ one's youth, so enjoy yourself while you are young.

6. (see / ever) The patient seldom leaves her house, nor _____
_____ any of her friends.

7. (rain) Not once _____ when we were on our
vacation last year.

8. (have / ever) Seldom _____ nightmares, fortunately for me.

9. (do / ever) Never _____ her hair herself; she
always goes to a beauty salon. She cuts my grandfather's hair, however.

10. (lift) What an indolent (lazy) person! Never _____
a finger to help anyone. Do you know the man I'm talking about?

score _____ (5 points each)

QUIZ 66   tag questions

handbook p. 68

Place in each blank an appropriate tag ending. Observe the __informal__ style.

Examples: a. The police are taking bribes, *aren't they*?

b. The King loves and honors the Queen, *doesn't he*?

1. These are delicious, _____ ?

2. I'm not making a mistake, _____ ?

3. Time certainly goes fast, _____ ?

4. You'd like to buy a sports car, _____ ?

5. Everyone in the class wants to learn, _____ ?

6. I'm one of your best friends, _____ ?

7. This car cost a lot, _____ ?

8. Crime rarely pays, _____ ?

9. There's someone at the door, _____ ?

10. You're taking your coat with you, _____ ?

11. Her Majesty is going to sign the document, _____ ?

12. It's a marvelous day, _____ ?

13. There was no one in the room when you were there, _____ ?

14. Well, I am the president of this company, _____ ?

15. Most of your friends are going to be studying this summer, _____ ?

16. One seldom sees that kind of fruit in the market, _____ ?

17. I'm not ever going to be a millionaire, _____ ?

18. This is it, _____ ?

19. You were absent from yesterday's meeting, _____ ?

20. I was wrong when I did that, _____ ?

score _____

QUIZ 67   the imperative mood; titles
handbook p. 69

Circle the correct answer in parentheses. Either means both choices are correct.

Example: a. Never (*wastes,* (*waste*)) your time at school.

1. Please (*do, do do, either*) your homework regularly, class.

2. (*Lady, Madam, either*), please be seated in this chair while I'm serving you.

3. (*Do, X, either*) keep your desk neat and tidy, Miss Watson.

4. (*Sir, Mister, either*), give me a light, please.

5. Terry, please (*wash, do wash, either*) your face; it's really dirty.

6. (*Mrs., Miss, either*) Billington, please give me your husband's first name.

7. (*Teacher, Professor, either*), please explain the theory of relativity to us.

8. (*Do not, No, either*) spill any of that milk, Betsy.

9. (*Madam, Madame, either*) Ambassador, please call the State Department at once.

10. (*Sir, Gentleman, either*), please return to your seat.

score _____

QUIZ 68   *let's;* polite requests with *shall* and *would*
handbook p. 72

Circle the correct answer in parentheses.

Example: a. Let's ((*do,*) *does*) a quiz.

1. Mr. Evans, would you (*please stop, stop please, either*) at the ticket counter to book your flight.

2. Shall (*I, you, either*) fix some eggs and toast for your breakfast?

3. Let's do something exciting this weekend. (*Let's., Let's do., either*)

4. (*Do*, *X*, *either*) let's not have an argument over this silly problem.

5. Let's go shopping downtown today, (*or shall we*, *shall we*, *either*)?

6. Shall we have lunch early today? (*Let's.*, *Please do.*, *either*)

7. Would you please (*no*, *not either*) make so much noise, Billy and Betty.

8. (*Let's don't*, *Let's not*, *either*) take the subway to school today.

9. Would you (*please not*, *not please*, *either*) work at my desk, Ted.

10. Shall I tell you the story I heard about you? (*Let's don't.*, *Please don't.*, *either*)

score _____

QUIZ 69 reflexive pronouns

handbook p. 74

Fill in the blanks with appropriate reflexive pronouns.

Example: a. Do you believe you *yourself* are responsible for your actions?

1. We never let our little boy and girl be by _____ at night.

2. Let's give _____ a nice vacation this year.

3. When the washing machine is finished, it turns _____ off.

4. I don't like to listen to _____ on a tape recording.

5. It's best for the students to do their homework by _____.

6. Why is Mrs. Atwell always talking to _____? Is it because she's lived alone for so many years?

7. Our little girl fell out of the apple tree and hurt _____.

8. Bill, watch out! Don't cut _____ with that carving knife.

9. Why did Romeo kill _____?

10. Listen, children, you _____ are responsible for keeping your bedroom neat and tidy.

QUIZ 70   direct and indirect objects
handbook p. 75

Place in each blank <u>to</u>, <u>for</u>, *or* <u>X</u>.

Examples: a. Shah Jehan built the Taj Mahal in Agra as a tomb *for* his favorite wife.

        b. Tell <u>X</u> us the story of *Snow White and the Seven Dwarfs*, Mommy.

        c. The Russians sold Alaska <u>to</u> the United States for a relatively small sum of money.

1. They owe _____ my wife and me a great deal of money, so they never call us.

2. My neighbor is giving _____ himself a new car for Christmas.

3. My mother is always knitting something _____ someone in the family.

4. Dear, when you come home from work, please bring the evening paper _____ me.

5. Please send _____ me a post card when you're in the Far East.

6. How much money is the bank going to lend _____ you?

7. Please, you must promise; don't show these photographs _____ anyone.

8. Susie, would you please find _____ Daddy his slippers.

9. The company offered _____ him a very big salary, but he didn't take the job.

10. They cooked a big turkey _____ themselves on Thanksgiving Day.

QUIZ 71   separable and inseparable multiple-word verbs
handbook p. 76

Fill in each blank with the correct form of the multiple-word verb stated in the parentheses. Use the noun and pronoun objects in the following list.

    it   *my jacket*   *them*
    Jason   *the Queen of Nepal*

Examples: a. (cut down) The tree was almost dead, so we *cut it down.*

        b. (check out) This is a bargain, Ladies and Gentlemen, *check it out.*

        c. (count on) *Don't count on Jason*; he's never dependable.

1. (hang up) I _____ when I came into the room.

2. (deal with) Yes, all these problems are serious; I'm _____

_____ now.

3. (call on) The Queen of the Netherlands _____

yesterday afternoon for tea.

4. (lie down) Please be quiet children; your father is _____

_____ .

5. (take off) Isn't your coat warm? Why don't you _____

_____ ?

6. (tear down) There used to be a beautiful old church on that corner, but

someone _____ and built a parking lot.

7. (get rid of) I have cockroaches in my kitchen. What is a good way_____

_____ ?

8. (warm up) My coffee is a little cold, Miss. Would you please _____

_____ .

9. (wait for) What are you _____ , Dick? The

bus?

10. (put down) _____ ; he's a wonderful per-

son.

score _____

REVIEW QUIZ F   multiple-word verbs

Fill in each blank with the correct form of a multiple-word verb chosen from the list at the left. If a noun or pronoun object is needed, choose one from the list at the right.

blow up	figure out	try on	all the mistakes	me
cross out	go out with	turn down	him	the cards
deal out	go with	wake up	it	
do over	take care of	write down		

Examples: a. The dealer *dealt the cards out,* and I got the ace of spades.

b. My alarm isn't working, so please *wake me up* when you get up.

1. The person I met at the meeting gave me her phone number, but I _____

_____ .

2. What a beautiful pearl necklace! Shall I _____ ?

3. I don't want to wear this red scarf; it _____ this

yellow hat.

4. Yes, Dan knows Jane Wilson quite well; he _____ her all the time.

5. He proposed marriage to her, but she _____.

6. Yes, I _____ in the composition and put in the proper corrections.

7. It was a difficult puzzle, but I _____ with a little bit of help from some of my friends.

8. I'd like my lawyer _____ this problem for me; it's too complicated to do myself.

9. The letter was full of mistakes when I finished it; so I _____

_____.

10. The terrorists put a bomb in the Ambassador's car and _____

_____.

score _____

QUIZ 72   the past continuous tense
handbook p 77

Supply in the blanks appropriate verb phrases in the past continuous tense.

deal with	*hand out*	*stand up*	*tow away*
figure out	*lay off*	*take on*	*wake up*
get on	*show up*	*throw up*	*work out*

Examples: a. When I peeked into the baby's room, he *was waking up*.

b. The store wasn't making any money because management *wasn't dealing with* the customers properly.

1. While he_____ the problem, he was using a calculator.

2. (always) Even though he _____ in the gym, he wasn't getting any stronger; in fact, he was getting weaker.

3. The teacher _____ any new material when I got to class. She wasn't even there.

4. When I got to the patient's bedside, he _____.

5. Fortunately, Steve _____ when he suddenly passed out.

6. Just as I got to my parking place, the police _____ my car.

7. It was hard to find a job during the recession, and not many companies _____ new workers.

8. Since she and her husband _____ very well, she was miserable and unhappy.

9. While he was working for that company, he _____ at the office an hour or two late every morning; he was eventually fired.

10. When I last spoke to Robert Blake, he was worried because his company _____ a lot of people, and he didn't want to be one of them.

score _____

REVIEW QUIZ G   contrasting verb tenses

Fill in each blank with an appropriate verb phrase in the simple present tense, the simple past tense, the present continuous tense, or the past continuous tense.

Examples: a. (sniff) He *was sniffing* the fine old brandy as he was drinking it.

b. (mix) Water *doesn't mix* with oil.

c. (die) Historians tell us that Napoleon *didn't die* a happy man.

d. (arrest) Look! The police *are arresting* that woman.

1. (pay) He's in trouble because he _____ his taxes last year.

2. (study) Since Thelma _____ much, she gets low scores.

3. (sleep) When the teacher looked up from his notes during the lecture, a few of the students _____ .

4. (run) The water _____ in the kitchen. Can't you hear it?

5. (make) Blue and yellow _____ orange.

6. (work) Someone new _____ at my desk when I walked into the office today. A few minutes later I found out that I had been fired.

7. (faint) Margaret _____ when she received the bad news in a telegram.

8. (meet) His mother and father _____ at a school picnic in 1954.

9. (take off) The professor _____ his coat when he came into the room.

10. (take on) When I went to that company for a job interview, they _____ new people; business was poor.

name _____ score _____ (20 points each)

Fill in each blank with an appropriate form of <u>be going to</u> + *a base form, choosing from the list below.*

call off	give out	stay up	take up
give away	pass up	take on	

Examples: a. She *wasn't going to stay up* late and wait for her daughter to come home, but she finally decided to when she became worried.

b. My office *was going to take on* ten new workers, but they fired five instead.

1. They_____the meeting, but they put it off until the next day instead.

2. She_____engineering at the university, but she found out that she liked the subject very much.

3. We_____that opportunity, but we decided to take advantage of it instead.

4. He_____all those old clothes, but at the last moment he decided to get rid of them.

5. The teacher_____some grammar exercises for the students to do, but he decided to assign a composition instead.

score _____

QUIZ 74   the simple future tense
handbook p. 80

In each blank, place an appropriate verb phrase in the simple future tense, choosing from the following list.

be	find	remember	surrender
commit	get	speak	tell
end	love	study	

Examples: a. (never) Mommy, *I'll never tell* a lie again; I promise.

b. We will fight for our freedom; we *will not surrender* to the enemy.

1. (always) There _____hope for a better world.

2. It_____a long time before this century comes to an end. Time goes by so fast.

3. (soon) This news program _____, children, so please be patient. *Your program is coming on in only a few minutes.*

4. (ever) "I_____to you again," she said to her boyfriend in a moment of anger.

5. (always) I_____your birthday; it's on the same day as mine.

6. You_____hard, class, and do better on the final examinations than all the other students in the school.

7. (ever again) "I_____a mortal sin," he promised his priest in the confessional.

8. (eventually) The world_____peace.

9. "My darling, I_____you until the moment I draw my last breath," she said.

10. (never) "I_____to school late again," the little boy promised his mother as he was crossing his fingers behind his back.

score _____

QUIZ 75 probably

handbook p. 82

Supply in each blank an appropriate verb phrase in the simple future tense. Use the verbs below. When needed, use the pronoun object it.

be	get along with	knock out	split up
come	grow up	pass out	steal
fix up	keep	show off	

Examples: a. (ever) None of my friends *will ever steal,* lie, or cheat; they're all honest people.

b. (probably) It'*ll probably be* a nice day tomorrow, so we're going to the country.

1. (probably) My boss _____ to the meeting tomorrow; she's too busy.

2. (soon) Class, I have new material for you; I _____.

3. (eventually) "The people of the world _____ each other in peace and harmony," the minister said during his sermon.

4. (probably) My neighbor has a new car. He likes to brag a lot, so he _____ _____ to everyone in town.

5. (probably / never) She's a childish young woman of twenty-two; she _____; she'll always be girlish. It's part of her charm.

6. (never) Oh! This boring moving _____ to an end.

61

7. (probably / ever) What careless neighbors I have! Their house doesn't look very nice; they _____ .

8. I predict the Californian _____ the New Yorker in the third round at Madison Square Garden tonight.

9. (never) They're very happy together, and they _____ .

10. (always) I _____ my word. I promise.

score _____

QUIZ 76 the future continuous tense

handbook p. 83

Fill in each blank with an appropriate verb phrase in the future continuous tense. When an object is needed, use the pronoun it.

bring out	do over	rain	think about
clear up	give away	take off	wait on
come out	happen	tear down	

Examples: a. (always) He closed his letter with, "I'*ll always be thinking about* you, dear."

b. (probably) My company is developing a new product; we'*ll probably be bringing it out* early next summer.

1. (surely) It _____ a lot when you are in London, so take a good raincoat and umbrella.

2. (probably) When you go to Washington, D.C. in early April, the cherry blossoms _____ .

3. (soon) "A great many new and exciting things _____ in your life," the fortune teller told me as she was gazing into her crystal ball and telling me my fortune.

4. She _____ her children for the rest of her life; she's devoted to them. She's their slave.

5. (soon) Summer is coming, so we _____ on our vacation.

6. (probably) This old furniture isn't worth much; I _____ .

7. (probably) This composition still isn't very good; I _____ .

8. (soon) That post office is getting old and dilapidated; the city _____ _____ .

9. (probably) It _____ today or tomorrow; the radio says we're not going to have much more rain.

10. (soon) We _____ , so fasten your seat belts.

QUIZ 77 yes-no questions in future tenses

handbook p. 85

Complete the following yes–no questions with appropriate verb phrases in the simple future tense or the future continuous tense. Provide subjects, and supply objects when needed.

it	arrive	put up	it
you	begin	rain	him
your flight	come on	see off	you
the class	discuss	sleep	
the news	have	take up with	
they	point out	wake up	

Examples: a. *Will your flight be arriving* at Orly Airport the same time as ours? . . . I hope so.

b. This is a really serious problem. When you go to church tomorrow, *will you talk it over with* your minister? . . . I've been thinking about it.

1. _____ these ideas with anyone during the meeting tomorrow? . . . No, I won't. I'd like to wait a while.

2. (probably) Bob is a good friend of yours, isn't he? _____
_____ at the airport tomorrow when he leaves for Australia? . . . Of course I will.

3. _____ as soon as the teacher arrives? . . . . It always does.

4. (probably) Your aunt and uncle live in Acapulco, don't they? _____
_____ when you go there on your next vacation? . . . They usually do.

5. _____ when I get home? I wouldn't like to disturb you. . . . . I'll still be up.

6. You know where the bank is, don't you? _____
to me while we're driving through town this morning? . . . Sure, just remind me so I won't forget.

7. I'm going to take a little nap. _____ at seven o'clock? I'd like to hear the news and weather forecast. . . . But I won't be here.

8. (probably) _____ when the sun rises tomorrow morning? . . . No, I always watch it rise.

9. This is a serious situation; _____ your lawyer? . . . It's not that serious.

10. (probably) When we go out tonight, _____ ? . . . Probably, it's that time of year.

QUIZ 78 information questions in future tenses
handbook p. 85

Make appropriate information questions. Use <u>who</u>, <u>whom</u>, <u>whose</u>, or <u>why</u>.

Example: a. (formal) <u>With whom will you be sharing a room?</u>
(informal) <u>Who will you be sharing a room with?</u>
I'll be sharing a room with <u>an old school friend</u>.

1. (formal) _____

(informal) _____
We won't be giving ourselves a vacation this year <u>because we are fixing up
our house</u>.

2. (formal) _____

(informal) _____
I'll be riding to the game in <u>my roommate's</u> car.

3. (formal) _____

(informal) _____
My husband won't play golf with me <u>because he always loses when he
does</u>.

4. (formal) _____

(informal) _____
I'll probably send the reply to <u>the most important person on the committee</u>.

5. (formal) _____

(informal) _____
My mother won't go shopping with me <u>because I can never make up my
mind</u>.

score _____ (5 points each)

QUIZ 79 regular and irregular past participles
handbook p. 86

Make past participles out of the following regular and irregular base forms.

Examples: a. behave *behaved*

b. stink *stunk*

1. cut _____   5. hang _____ or _____
2. pray _____   6. itch _____
3. lie _____ or _____   7. kneel _____ or _____
4. prune _____   8. shrink _____

9. speed _____ or _____   15. lay _____

10. clap _____   16. benefit _____

11. forget _____ or _____   17. get _____ or _____

12. ferry _____   18. cast _____

13. read _____   19. knit _____ or _____

14. scratch _____   20. bear _____ or _____

score _____

QUIZ 80   the present perfect tense; the duration of an event, *since* and *for*

handbook p. 86

Place in each blank <u>since</u> *or* <u>for</u>.

Examples: a. My grandpa has had his car <u>for</u> more than thirty years.

b. Germany has been a divided country <u>since</u> the end of the Second World War in 1945.

1. _____ billions of years, our galaxy has been in existence.

2. Korea has been a divided nation _____ April 15, 1953.

3. _____ thousands of years, people have wanted to explore the outer reaches of our solar system.

4. My best friend and I have known each other _____ our childhood.

5. _____ 53 years, my grandparents have been man and wife.

6. This class has been in session _____ the latter part of September.

7. Frank and his sister Cora have lived in the same house _____ at least seventy years. They're always sitting on the front porch and watching the traffic go by.

8. _____ June 1, 1980, Jack and Jill, my brother and sister-in-law, have been married.

9. It's been a relatively long time _____ World War II.

10. _____ at least 2300 years or so, Buddhism has been the major religion of eastern and central Asia.

QUIZ 81   *since* in time clauses; *ago; ever*

handbook p. 88

Put in each blank an appropriate verb phrase in the simple past tense.

accept	fall down	show up	tell
buy	fall out	take off	throw up
cut down	hang up on	take up	

Examples: a. He's been on a diet ever since his wife *bought* him a scale more than a
month ago.

b. Our garden has looked better ever since we *cut down* that ugly old banana
tree.

1. Christopher has been very happy with his girlfriend ever since she
_____ him that she loved him.

2. My sister hasn't gone skiing ever since she _____ and broke
her left leg.

3. Warren has been a much happier man ever since he _____
yoga and meditation when he went to India five years ago.

4. My neighbor's wife has looked like a movie star ever since he
_____ a lot of weight—at least fifty pounds.

5. Mark Masters has been a happy man ever since Gloria B illings
_____ his proposal of marriage a few weeks ago.

6. Yes, the patient has felt a great deal better ever since he _____
and got rid of all those poisons in his system.

7. Darling, this party has been a success ever since you _____.

8. He's been rather worried about his appearance ever since his hair
_____ about ten years ago.

9. The woman sitting next to me has been asleep ever since this plane
_____ seven hours ago.

10. She's been angry and quite upset ever since her boss _____
her an hour ago.

QUIZ 82   contrasting verb tenses
handbook p. 89

Supply appropriate affirmative or negative verb phrases in the simple present tense, the simple past tense, or the present perfect tense.

Examples: a. (be) A house *is* not a home. (old saying)

b. (be / ever) Grandpa *hasn't ever been* in a doctor's office; he's really healthy.

c. (occur) The American Revolution *occurred* more than two hundred years ago.

1. (have) Since he has no job, he _____ money now.

2. (teach) Gregory Stone _____ English at an elementary school in a small town on the island of Sumatra in Indonesia from 1978 to 1980.

3. (be) Alex and Anna _____ married for at least ten years; they seem to be a very happy couple.

4. (be / never) You _____ home when I called, which was at least five times.

5. (whistle) This is a wonderful tea kettle; it _____ when the water comes to a boil.

6. (have) Hugh Brown _____ his gold watch ever since his father gave it to him on his sixteenth birthday almost fifty years ago.

7. (die) Adolph Hitler _____ a happy man, I believe.

8. (be) I _____ here for only a few years; I like it a great deal.

9. (meet) Gwen Davidson _____ her husband, Ted, when she was a student at the University of Colorado at Boulder, where he was teaching.

10. (be) According to many people, Christopher Columbus _____ the first European to come to the New World. They say the Vikings were.

QUIZ 83   yes-no questions; *as long as*
handbook p. 90

Fill in each blank with <u>have</u> (<u>has</u>) + subject + past participle. Use the subjects at the left and the verbs at the right below.

I	be	know	work
Tom	have	study	

Examples: a. <u>*Have you had*</u> your watch as long as I've had mine?

b. <u>*Has Tom been*</u> in love with Alice as long as she's been in love with him?

1. _____ a friend of yours as long as I have?

2. _____ English as long as you have?

3. _____ his car as long as you've had yours?

4. _____ for this company as long as you have?

5. _____ you as long as my husband has?

score _____

QUIZ 84   information questions
handbook p. 90

Make information questions. Use (<u>for</u>)<u>how long</u> or (<u>for</u>)<u>how many</u> + seconds, minutes, etc.

Examples: a. <u>*How long has the United States been independent from Great Britain?*</u>
The United States has been independent from Great Britain <u>since July 4, 1776</u>.

b. <u>*For how many years have you been out of high school?*</u>
I've been out of high school for <u>twenty-five</u> years.

1. _____

We've had our washing machine for <u>seventeen</u> years.

2. _____

I've lived by myself <u>ever since I left my parents' home ten years ago.</u>

3. _____

My father has known your mother <u>longer than your father has known mine.</u>

4. _____

My wife and I have had our house <u>ever since the day we got married thirty years ago.</u>

5. _____

My patient has been in a coma for <u>more than twenty-four</u> hours.

6. _____

My husband and I have lived by ourselves <u>ever since all our children got married.</u>

7. _____

I've known you and your wife since <u>New Year's Eve, 1940.</u>

8. _____

I've had mine <u>as long as anybody else in the class has.</u>

9. _____

My brother has known my wife <u>longer than I have.</u>

10. _____

I've lived with you and your brother in your parents' house for <u>five</u> years.

score _____

QUIZ 85 events at an indefinite time in the past; *recently, finally, already,* and *just*

handbook p. 91

Supply appropriate verb phrases in the present perfect tense. Use the following adverbs of indefinite time:

recently finally just

Examples: a. (get) John Doe is much happier now; he's <u>*recently gotten*</u> a raise in salary and more retirement benefits.

     b. (fix) At last! My landlord *has finally fixed* the leak in the kitchen; the tap isn't always dripping now.

1. (begin) Please be quiet, David; the news _____.

2. (meet) How happy my husband and I are! Our son _____ a wonderful young woman whom he wants to be his wife.

3. (come) My, it certainly is cold out; I _____ into the house, and my hands are as cold as ice.

4. (decide) The president of the company _____ to resign and retire to Florida; I move into his position when he leaves.

5. (inherit) How fortunate for him! He _____ a million dollars from a distant second cousin whom he didn't even know.

6. (see) "Why, you're as pale as a ghost." "Yes, I _____ one."

7. (lie down) It's about time! Baby Bobby _____ for his afternoon nap.

name _____

8. (have) We _____ a great deal of rain, and all the parks and gardens in our town look green and lovely.

9. (finish) I _____ my homework; now I can go to bed.

10. (have) David Dawson _____ an operation; he's at home now and convalescing (getting better).

score _____ (20 points each)

QUIZ 86 adverbs of indefinite time in yes-no questions; cause and effect

handbook p. 93

Complete the following yes–no questions, using the subjects and verbs listed below. Use only the present perfect tense.

Bella Donna	you	catch up with	inherit	see
Daddy	you and your wife	go	make up	turn down

Examples: a. (recently) A: <u>Has Bella Donna recently inherited</u> a lot of money? B: Yes, she has, Jennifer. She's going around town in fancy clothes and driving a brand new Rolls-Royce.

b. (finally) <u>Have you finally made up</u> you face, Miss Superstar? Are you ready to go out in front of the camera and act your heart out?

1. (already) A: Mommy, _____ to work? He doesn't seem to be anywhere in the house or out in the yard. B: Yes, he has, Timmy, and so has your older brother.

2. (just) A: Grace, _____ a ghost? Your face is as white as a sheet. B: No, I haven't; I just feel a little dizzy.

3. (finally) A: Jack, _____ ? B: Yes, we have, Ronald. We love each other too much to split up.

4. (finally) A: Andrew, _____ the rest of the class? You really missed a great deal of work while you were away, didn't you? B: Yes, I did, Sir, and I've fallen behind a lot; however, I'm managing to keep up, I think.

5. (finally) _____ John for good? It was his fifth proposal of marriage to her last night, wasn't it?

70

QUIZ 87   adverbs of indefinite time with the simple past tense
handbook p. 93

Place in each blank the appropriate past form of a multiple-word verb. Each verb phrase will require an object; choose one from the list on the right.

call up	clean off	clean up	it	them
chop up	clean out	clear up	me	this table

Examples: a. A: Have you heard about the big scandal in the Palace? B: Yes, a friend of mine just *called me up* a few minutes ago and told me all about it.

   b. The vegetables are ready for the stew; I already *chopped them up* fifteen minutes ago.

1. Jason, please don't put your toys in that closet; I just _____ this morning, and I don't want it to get messy again so soon.

2. Yes, Doctor, I had a very bad rash on my arm (I don't know what it was), but some ointment (I don't know what that was, either) finally _____

   _____ .

3. Our waiter finally _____ about a half hour ago, but he hasn't come back to take our orders.

4. My desk is a mess; I just _____ yesterday morning, and today it looks like a bomb has hit it.

5. No, that's not a problem of mine anymore; I went to my lawyer last week, and she finally _____ .

QUIZ 88 negative yes-no questions with adverbs of indefinite time

handbook p. 94

Make appropriate negative yes–no questions using only the present perfect tense. Use a direct object if necessary.

a construction company	break out	move away	a house
a revolution	buy	pass away (die)	it
her husband	lay off	put away	some workers
it	make up	tear down	them
they			

Examples: a. The children's toys are all over the living room floor.
(already) *Haven't they already put them away?*

b. What's happened to the big yellow house down the street on the corner?
(finally) *Hasn't a construction company finally torn it down?*

1. Are Bob and his brother still living in this town?

(recently) _____

2. Doesn't the woman in apartment 2E look unhappy?

(recently) _____

3. Are Laura and David Browning still living in an apartment?

(finally) _____

4. That company isn't doing so well now; business has been slow.

(just) _____

5. What's been happening in that country? It's so small and far away, no one ever hears or reads much about it.

(recently) _____

QUIZ 89 *any longer, anymore,* and *no longer*

handbook p. 95

Fill in each blank with an appropriate verb phrase in the present perfect tense.

break off	grow out of	pick up	take advantage of
clear up	grow up	put down	take on
get over	pick out	run out of	wear out

Examples: a. (finally) There's no longer rioting and shooting in the streets; the government *has finally put down* the terrorists.

               b. The patient doesn't have a rash on his chest anymore; it*'s cleared up* with treatment.

1. We no longer need a baby-sitter for our children; they _____ _____ a lot.

2. He's not waiting for the bus anymore; he _____ patience.

3. (finally) Richie no longer wears these clothes; he _____ them.

4. I'm not using my typewriter any longer; it's old and it _____ _____.

5. (recently) Those two countries _____ diplomatic relations; they no longer trade with each other, either.

6. (already) That company isn't hiring anymore; they _____ _____ enough workers.

7. (already) We no longer speak to each other; he _____ me far too many times.

8. (finally) The patient isn't coughing and sneezing any longer; she _____ _____ her cold.

9. Our son no longer keeps his room neat and tidy; he _____ _____ some bad habits from his roommate at the university dormitory.

10. (already) Thanks, but I'm not looking for a Father's Day present anymore; I _____ a beautiful tie for my Dad that he will love.

QUIZ 90   *yet* in negative statements

handbook p. 95

Complete the following sentences with appropriate verb phrases in the present perfect tense. Provide objects when needed.

call out	grow up	tow away	it
chew up	pick up	try out	my hamburger
fix up	show up	wait on	them
grind up	take advantage of	work out	us

Examples:
  a. Ellen and her husband are bored here because they *haven't taken advantage of* the many wonderful things this city has to offer yet.

  b. I've been waiting a long time for someone to call my name, but no one *has called it out* yet.

1. I'm waiting for the butcher; he _____ yet.

2. Our neighbors have been in their house for more than ten years, but they _____ yet.

3. Please don't try to swallow all of that meat in one gulp, Billy; you _____ yet.

4. John is a very childish young man; he _____ yet.

5. Yes, we really do have a problem with our new production schedule; we _____ yet.

6. Dickie, why are your toys all over the house? You _____ _____ yet.

7. Sir, we've been at this table for more than an hour, but no one _____ _____ yet.

8. I've been here for two hours, waiting for a friend; but he _____ _____ yet.

9. My brand new car is parked outside on the street; they just delivered it a few minutes ago. I _____ yet.

10. That car has been parked illegally in front of our garage for at least a week, but the police _____ yet.

QUIZ 91   *still* in the simple present tense
handbook p. 96

Place in each blank an appropriate verb phrase in the simple present tense with <u>still</u>.

be	live	smoke
do	make	speak
have	owe	wear

Examples: a. Susan Anderson <u>*still lives*</u> with her parents; she hasn't gone out into the world on her own yet.

b. (ever) I <u>*still don't ever make*</u> my bed in the mornings. I didn't like to do it when I was a child, and I still don't like to do it.

1. My roommate _____ me money; she hasn't paid me back yet.

2. (ever) Timmy _____ chores around the house; he's always been a lazy boy.

3. My grandmother _____ hats; she hasn't changed with the times—she's very old-fashioned.

4. I _____ a doctor; I haven't finished medical school yet.

5. Jeff Stone has lived in France for more than twenty years, but he _____ _____ French well.

6. Yes, Christine Crawford is still going to school; she _____ her degree.

7. My roommate _____ ; he hasn't given up the dirty habit yet.

8. (never) Dick Davis is coming to school more regularly, but he _____ _____ any homework, nor does he ever pay attention in class.

9. Our neighbors _____ home from their vacation; they haven't come back yet.

10. I _____ English as well as I'd like to; I need more practice.

QUIZ 92   *still* in the present continuous tense
handbook p. 97

Supply in each blank an appropriate verb phrase in the present continuous tense with *still*.

bark	eat	live	spray	wear
complain	feel	overcharge	think	work

Examples: a. My boyfriend and I *still aren't working*; we haven't found jobs yet.

b. Their baby boy *is still wearing* diapers; he's not toilet trained yet.

1. My grandfather is very old-fashioned; he _____ suspenders.

2. (always) Sandra Williams, one of the most romantic persons I know,

_____ about Roberto, a man she met in Mexico almost five years ago.

3. My mother has gotten rid of the ants in her kitchen, but she _____

_____ all the time; she doesn't want them to come back.

4. Yes, Chris, your baby sister _____ with a spoon; she hasn't grown up enough yet to use a fork.

5. (always) Mrs. Drake, my next door neighbor for many years, hasn't changed much; she _____ .

6. Yes, Martha and Jack _____ together, and they're very happy.

7. (always) I've taken my dog to a good dog trainer, but he _____

_____.

8. The patient has taken his medicine religiously; however, she _____

_____ well.

9. I _____ , and I've had at least fifty job interviews.

10. (always) Everyone says Bill Maxwell is honest, but he _____

_____ his customers.

QUIZ 93   yes-no questions with *still*

handbook p. 97

Complete the following yes–no questions with appropriate verb phrases in the simple present tense or the present continuous tense with still.

Bill	Alice	be	keep up with	put up with	take off
Bob	Jane	go out with	live	smoke	wait for
Jim	you	hang around with	put by	speak	work out

Examples:　a. (usually) *Do you still usually take off* every weekend, or do you just stay in town?

　　　　　b. Gloria, *are you still waiting for* your boyfriend, or has he finally shown up?

1. _____ with an accent? Yes, she does, but only a little bit; she'll eventually get rid of it completely.

2. _____ with his parents? No, he isn't; he's finally found a nice and cheap apartment for himself.

3. (always) _____ ? No, he's not; he's finally given it up.

4. _____ those young boys down at the pool hall on Broadway? No, he doesn't; he's finally smartened up.

5. _____ your roommate's sister? No, he doesn't. He's recently found a new girlfriend.

6. (always) _____ a little bit of money every month? Yes, I am; it's important to have some money set aside for an emergency.

7. _____ single? Yes, he hasn't yet found the right woman.

8. (usually) _____ at the gym every day? Yes, I do.

9. _____ her difficult boss? No, she doesn't.

10. _____ his class, or is he falling behind? Of course he is; he's a very smart student.

QUIZ 94   yes-no questions with *yet*
handbook p. 97

In response to the following statements, make appropriate negative yes–no questions containing verb phrases in the present perfect tense. Use yet.

it	*the surgeon*	*bring out*	*put on*	*any weight*
he	*you*	*clean up*	*rise*	*his mind*
the sun		*cut out*	*take off*	*it*
		make up		

Examples: a. Dick Downes, my roommate, can't make a decision; he's in a terrible dilemma. He doesn't know what to do.
Hasn't he made up his mind yet?

b. It's still quite dark out, and there's a heavy dew on the lawn.
Hasn't the sun risen yet?

1. Alex is still too heavy; he watches his diet, however.

    _____

2. The kitchen is still a mess; the sink is full of dirty dishes, and there are puddles of water on the floor.

    _____

3. John eats a lot, but he's still a little thin.

    _____

4. The patient has a tumor on his right leg, and it's rather serious.

    _____

5. Our company started developing this product almost ten years ago.

    _____

score _____ (20 points each)

QUIZ 95   information questions with *yet*
handbook p. 98

Make appropriate negative information questions with why *containing verb phrases in the present perfect tense. Use* yet.

our plane	*call on*	*look up*	*him*
she	*clean out*	*quiet down*	*it*
they	*give up*	*take off*	*your closet*
you	*look over*		

Examples: a. I'm a little surprised, Danny; you're being a lazy boy today.
<u>Why haven't you cleaned your closet out yet?</u>

b. The new French ambassador has already been here for six months, and he still hasn't seen or met the Queen.
<u>Why has he not yet called on her?</u>

1. Smoking is one of the worst things for your health; you really shouldn't smoke.

   _____

2. Listen, Angela, why are you asking me for a definition of that word?

   _____

3. The children are acting restless and being noisy this evening, and it's almost ten o'clock.

   _____

4. Why are we delayed? We've been sitting here for two hours. What's wrong?

   _____

5. I need your opinion on this report as soon as possible, Mr. Jackson.

   _____

score _____

QUIZ 96 *yet* with abridged clauses and infinitives

handbook p. 98

Put in each blank an appropriate verb phrase in the present perfect tense.

ask out	grow out of	put up	run into
blow out	knock out	ring up	run out of
give up	put down	run away	speed up

Examples: a. (ever) I <u>haven't ever put down</u> my roommate for any of his shortcomings, and he's been just as considerate of me as I have of him.

b. Rickie <u>hasn't grown out of</u> these trousers yet, but I expect him to any time now.

1. I _____ my lawyer yet, but I'm going to any day now.

2. (ever) No inmate in that prison _____ yet, but everyone in the town surrounding the institution is afraid one will.

3. My roommate _____ my sister yet, but he wants to.

4. Our production _____ yet, but we expect it to any time now.

5. (ever) I _____ any of my old friends in this town yet (it's a new place for me), but I probably will.

6. That light bulb _____ yet, but it will in a few more days.

7. (ever) No one _____ the champion yet, but someone will someday.

8. Our enemy _____ yet, but we expect them to within a few more days of heavy fighting.

9. My mother _____ any strawberries yet this year, but she will when they're ready to pick from our garden, which will be in a few more days.

10. Our company _____ money yet, but we expect it to within a few more months.

score _____

QUIZ 97   *have yet* + **an infinitive**

handbook p. 100

Fill in each blank with <u>have</u> *or* <u>has</u> *plus* <u>yet</u> *plus an appropriate infinitive. Provide objects when needed.*

call on	knock out	ring back	turn on	anyone
help out	lay off	speed up	work out	it
hold up	pass up	try out		me

Examples:

a. What a beautiful typewriter! Yes, I just bought it yesterday, and I *have yet to try it out.*

b. (still) The new Russian ambassador has paid a formal visit to everyone important in the capital, but he *still has yet to call on* the President and the First Lady.

1. I've called him up at least fifteen times (he's always out, his secretary says), and he _____ .

2. (still) Winnie, I've asked you many times to do some work around the house, but you _____ your mother and me.

3. Business hasn't been so good, but the company _____.

4. (still) The newspapers say he's one of the biggest bank robbers in the city, but he _____ a major bank.

5. I've slept everywhere and on everything, but I _____ a water bed.

6. They're very good businesspeople; they _____ a good opportunity.

7. My! This is really a difficult puzzle; I _____ .

8. I know many people like that kind of music, but it _____ .

9. The teacher has told Betsy that she must work faster, but she _____ .

10. (still) Yes, he's a good boxer, but he _____ the champion.

score _____ (20 points each)

QUIZ 98 *still* with the present perfect tense

handbook p. 100

Complete each sentence with a negative verb phrase in the present perfect tense with *still*. Provide the object *it* when needed.

| break down | catch on | cross out | take care of |
| bring out | clear up | make up | |

Examples: a. The company said they were going to publish the book in January (it's almost April now), but they *still haven't brought it out*.

b. It stopped raining a couple of hours ago, but it *still hasn't cleared up*.

1. You must perform tonight, Bella Donna; the show begins at eight o'clock (it's now 7:45), and you _____ .

2. I've had my old car for more than twenty years, and it _____ .

3. (ever) My lawyer seems to be worried about my situation; however, she _____ .

4. I asked my boss to take my name off that list, but he _____ .

5. I'm sorry, I know your joke must be funny, but I _____ .

name _____   score _____   (20 points each)

QUIZ 99 *still* in negative questions
handbook p. 101

Make appropriate negative information questions with <u>why</u> containing verb phrases in the present perfect tense. Use <u>still</u>. Provide objects when needed.

he	get rid of	slow down	him
she	knock out	split up	it
they	pass out	throw out	them
you	show up		

Examples: a. Miss Jackson, why are all these old magazines lying around in the office?
<u>Why have you still not thrown them out?</u>

b. I've been waiting for my friend for almost two days.
<u>Why has she still not shown up?</u>

1. Dear, I've asked you several times not to drive so fast.

_____

2. Our class has become very large. There are almost sixty students now.

_____

3. The boxer in white shorts has been hitting the other guy with a lot of heavy punches.

_____

4. I don't know why I keep all these old dishes; many of them are cracked.

_____

5. That man has had at least ten or fifteen cocktails, but he's managing to stand up, more or less.

_____

score _____

QUIZ 100   repeated events in the past
handbook p. 102

Fill in each blank with an appropriate verb phrase in the present perfect tense.

break out	fall in	hand out	turn down
catch up with	get rid of	run out of	work on
call down	go out with	take on	write down

Examples: a. My roommate *has fallen in* love four times since he started at the university only three months ago.

b. Three serious epidemics *have broken out* in the past six months, and the government has done almost nothing about it.

82

1. The boss _____ Dick Jefferies more than twice, so he doesn't fool around in the office so much anymore.

2. Anna Thompson _____ Roger Reeves at least a dozen times; he's going to ask her again, however, to marry him. I think she's going to say yes this time.

3. Paul Peters _____ his roommate's sister only twice, yet he wants her to become his wife; he's really fallen in love.

4. What a trip! We _____ gas three times since we set off less than a week ago, but we're having a great time.

5. My company _____ fifty new workers this week, yet business hasn't gotten better.

6. His father, an architect, _____ five major projects this year.

7. Excuse me, I _____ your name twice, but I've lost it both times.

8. Yes, I _____ the gophers in the garden twice, but they've come back both times.

9. Charles Wells _____ the class quite a few times, but he usually manages to fall behind again.

10. The teacher _____ new material three times this week. We're loaded with homework.

score _____

QUIZ 101   questions about repeated events in the past

handbook p. 103

Complete the following yes–no and information questions with appropriate verb phrases in the present perfect tense.

he	you	drop out of	listen in on	try out
she	your roommate	give away	stand up for	turn down
the champion	your secretary	give out	take advantage of	wear out
		go out with	try on	work out

Examples: a. Janet, *has your roommate taken advantage of* you more times than you have of her? . . . I've never taken advantage of her.

b. Just how many typewriters *have you worn out?* You're very hard on one, aren't you? . . . I've gone through at least ten.

1. How many proposals of marriage _____ ? . . . That's none of your business.

2. _____ Alice many times since he first met her at your Christmas party last year? . . . Every weekend.

3. Bill, _____ fifteen or sixteen registration forms to the class? . . . I've passed out only eleven.

4. How many times _____ at that gym? . . . Never.

5. I hear you're looking for a new car, Mr. Williams. How many different models _____ since you decided to get rid of your old car and buy a new one? . . . Only three.

6. Mrs. Johnson, how many times _____ that gown? Haven't you made up your mind yet? . . . I just can't decide.

7. Professor Anderson, how many books _____ or sold since you decided to dispose of your personal library? . . . More than a thousand.

8. Dick, how many times _____ school and decided to go back and try again? You have a great deal of determination. . . . Five or six, I guess.

9. Mr. Rogers, _____ Henry Forbes more than once in a court of law, or is this the first time? . . . Sir, this is my fifth time.

10. How many phone calls with your wife _____ ? . . . I don't think Miss Clark has ever done anything like that.

score _____

QUIZ 102 negative verb phrases with *ever*

handbook p. 104

Supply appropriate verb phrases in the present perfect tense with <u>ever.</u>

blow out	catch on to	pass up	take up
break out	fall in	show off	turn away
call on	go over	take care of	turn down

Examples: a. I *haven't ever caught on to* one of my neighbor's jokes; they're always very complicated.

b. The new ambassador *hasn't ever called on* the King because he has never been asked.

1. To my knowledge, a major revolution _____ in that part of the world.

2. Not one of our children _____ love; they're all still too young.

3. He's a very clever guy; he _____ a good opportunity.

4. No one _____ that house; so it's run down quite a bit.

84

5. Yes, he's a very smart young man, yet he _____ anything seriously at school or in the business world. He's still looking for the right direction to take.

6. I've had my car for three years, yet not one of my tires_____
_____.

7. They're very rich people, and they've always been generous with their good fortune. They _____ a beggar or poor person who appears at their door.

8. We've been in this hotel for a week (it's costing us a fortune), yet no one _____ our beds.

9. She's a very talented woman with a good brain and beautiful looks, yet she _____ any of her achievements to her friends. She doesn't like to brag.

10. No one _____ these reports carefully; they're full of grammatical errors and illogical reasoning.

score _____ (20 points each)

QUIZ 103   questions with *ever*

handbook p. 104

Complete the following yes–no questions with appropriate verb phrases in the present perfect tense with <u>ever</u>.

| Alex | they | call up | look after | put by | talk over |
| Lisa | you | hand in | make out | show up | |

Examples: a. <u>*Have you ever called up*</u> a friend just as he was getting into the shower? . . . Yes, that just happened to me the other day.

b. <u>*Have they ever talked over*</u> this problem? . . . Yes, they have, once or twice.

1. _____ at one of your boss's meetings late? . . . Never, I'm always on time.

2. _____ any money for the day when she may need it? . . . Yes, she has.

3. _____ any of your neighbor's children? . . . Yes, I have, and they're wonderful.

4. _____ well when he goes to the horse races? Or has he always been as unlucky as I have with the horses? . . . He's won only peanuts.

5. _____ any of the homework for your class, Miss Brooks? He seldom ever did any in mine. . . . He's the best student in the class.

REVIEW QUIZ H   information questions

Make information questions. Use (for) how long, how often (how frequently), how many times, what, whom, or why. Observe the formal style.

Example: a. *To whom have you just spoken on the phone?*
I've just spoken to the President himself.

1. _____
Since there is a transportation strike, I'm not going to go to school today.

2. _____
My wife and I have lived in this town since 1978.

3. _____
I've been in love three and a half times.

4. _____
We'd like to give ourselves a new car for Christmas.

5. _____
There has been a message for you.

6. _____
My brother gives me a ride to my job once in a while.

7. _____
I haven't sent out any Christmas cards because I've lost my address book.

8. _____
It usually takes us three hours to drive to our cabin in the mountains.

9. _____
I want to talk with you about my boss and yours because the two of them are always talking about us.

10. _____
I'd like to talk to you about your brother because he owes me some money.

score _____

QUIZ 104   the present perfect continuous tense; *lately*

handbook p. 104

Put in each blank an appropriate verb phrase in the present perfect continuous tense.

do	make out	save	use
go out of business	revolve	speak	work
grow out of	run	stand	

Examples: a. The pyramids *have been standing* for more than five thousand years.

b. Because of a major difference of opinion, my neighbor and I *haven't been speaking* to each other for years, but we're beginning to write to each other.

1. The earth _____ around the sun for billions of years.

2. Lately, Billy _____ his clothes faster than his twin brother, Bobby, has.

3. Dr. Johnson _____ a great deal of important research in microbiology lately.

4. My car _____ right lately; I'm taking it to the garage for some repairs.

5. Since it's not been so hot lately, we _____ our air conditioner much—we're saving a lot of expensive energy.

6. You _____ your chores lately, Eddie; everyone in the family has to do his or her share of the work.

7. I _____ on the railroad for fifteen years; I've seen a lot.

8. He _____ well in his business lately; the competition hasn't been so clever as he has.

9. Because the inflation isn't so bad now, we _____ more money.

10. Because of the recession, a lot of companies _____ lately.

score _____

QUIZ 105 *so far, until now,* and *now*

handbook p. 107

Fill in each blank with an appropriate verb phrase in the present perfect tense or the present perfect continuous tense.

blow out	go with	pass up	show up
break out	have	sell	work on

Examples: a. We *haven't had* any problems with our car on this trip until now.

b. Yes, Ray and Kathy *have been going with* each other for a long time now.

1. Two flu epidemics _____ in the country so far this year.

2. We _____ a wonderful time on this vacation until now; we've run out of money.

3. Ronald Banks _____ at work late for a long time now; he's going to get called down for it.

4. I _____ a nice and quiet apartment until now; some noisy neighbors moved into the place above mine a few days ago.

5. We _____ much rain until now; we've been lucky on this vacation.

6. This book is going to be a best seller; it came out only four months ago, and it _____ 150,000 copies so far.

7. (ever) I _____ a good business opportunity until now; I just don't want to have anything to do with that company; they're not dependable.

8. Oh, I _____ this project for more than three years now. It's finally coming to an end. At last!

9. Bill Baldwin _____ a good job until now; he quit it yesterday afternoon.

10. Since the beginning of this trip, three tires on our car _____ _____ so far. What's going to happen next?

score _____

QUIZ 106 questions

handbook p. 108

Complete the following yes–no and information questions with appropriate verb phrases in either the present perfect tense or the present perfect continuous tense.

the army	check out	lock up	put down
the guide	cross out	look after	run away from
the police	grind up	point out	sell
you	have	put by	show up

Examples: a. Sir, just how many animals *have run away from* this zoo in the past six months? . . . Where have you heard such a rumor?

b. *Have you been having* many parties lately, Mrs. Bailey? . . . Yes, I have been.

1. For how many days _____ your neighbor's five children? . . . Three, and that's three too many.

2. How many bank robbers _____ so far this month? . . . Not one, which is unusual.

3. How many copies of this book _____ so far? . . . Millions.

4. Chef, how many pounds of beef _____ for the meat loaf? . . . 300; we've got a big crowd.

5. _____ all of the important architectural features of the cathedral during our tour today? She hasn't missed anything, has she? . . . I don't think she has, dear.

6. Who _____ this story, Mr. Black? I don't think it's true. . . . My wife has, and she doesn't lie, Mr. Grant.

7. _____ many mistakes in your recent compositions? . . . No, I haven't been, Professor.

8. Mr. and Mrs. Peabody, how much money _____ for your retirement? . . . More than a million.

9. (finally) _____ the revolutionary forces, or are they still occupying the capital and the Presidential Palace? . . . Sir, the army has run away.

10. How many people _____ for this meeting so far? It looks like a lot. . . . I'd say more than a hundred.

score _____

QUIZ 107   the present perfect tense in subordinate clauses
handbook p. 108

Supply in each blank an appropriate affirmative or negative verb phrase in the present perfect tense.

catch up with	deal with	get away with	make up
chew up	figure out	give out	move away
clear up	fool around	look over	size up

Examples: a. Even though the police *have sized up* the situation accurately, they still don't know what to do about it.

b. Since you *have moved away,* I have missed you very much.

1. Miss Saunders, you should do some extra homework every night until you _____ the rest of the class. You've fallen behind.

2. Since the teacher _____ the final grades yet, the students are all very nice to him.

3. Jason and Helen aren't going to be happy until they _____. They don't like it here.

4. Because you _____ your food, Cindy, it's hard for you to swallow.

5. You won't be such a worried person as soon as you _____ this situation with your lawyer. Why don't you deal with it today? Stop putting it off.

6. Because you _____ this matter quickly, you might be heading for a lot of trouble with your neighbors. Take care of it as soon as you can.

7. (ever) Though I _____ in the office, my boss often calls me lazy.

8. Mr. Grimes, please let me know as soon as you _____ this puzzle.

9. Although I _____ this report very closely, it looks like a well-written one.

10. Because Slippery Joe _____ so many crimes, the police are always watching him.

score _____

QUIZ 108   the present perfect tense with *when, before,* and *after*

handbook p. 108

Put in each blank an appropriate verb phrase in the present perfect tense.

clear away	*move into*	*sell out*	*take off*
clear out of	*make up*	*stand up*	*talk over*
get over	*ring*	*take advantage of*	*warm up*

Examples: a. (finally) When you and your husband *have finally moved into* your new house, you'll be a much happier woman.

b. Mr. Greene, after you *have sold out* all this merchandise, you'll be a rich man.

1. When my neighbors _____ all that junk in front of their house, their yard will look much better, and so will mine.

2. I can sleep anywhere; I'll be fast asleep before this plane _____ _____ .

3. Dear, after I _____ this soup, it'll taste like a million dollars.

4. (finally) When I _____ my mind, I shall let you know my decision; meanwhile, please don't call me, I'll call you.

5. When the King _____ , it means that this meeting is over.

6. Mr. Livingston, before you _____ this matter with your landlord, please consult with your attorney; he knows how to deal with it.

7. When the bell _____ , it means all of the students should be in their seats.

8. After you _____ this unhappy affair, you'll have a much better understanding of yourself.

9. My boss never gets upset when someone _____ his good nature.

10. After the students _____ the classroom, I'm going to correct their final examinations.

QUIZ 109   *have got*
handbook p. 109

Put in each blank have, has, haven't, *or* hasn't.

Examples: a. Why *haven't* you got any money in your bank account? I haven't got a job.

b. He hasn't got a large apartment; nor *have* I.

1. Bob Butterworth hasn't got a car, and neither _____ any of his friends.

2. How much time _____ your boss got to talk to me about my project?

3. _____ anyone in this room got a car?

4. Excuse me, Ma'am, _____ you got a quarter to spare?

5. I've got a secret, and so _____ you. If you tell me yours, I'll tell you mine.

6. Sir, no one in this city _____ got a name as important as yours.

7. I've not got any school today, and my sister _____ either.

8. You _____ got a match, have you?

9. Excuse me, _____ you got a dime?

10. We _____ got a lot to learn, and we haven't got much time.

QUIZ 110   *have got to* + **a base form**
handbook p. 110

Place in each blank an appropriate verb phrase with have got to + *a base form.*

clear up	put off	slow down	take advantage of
get along	see off	sort out	take up with
pass up	sharpen up	squeeze in	wrap up

Examples: a. I'*ve got to clear up* this situation with the phone company right away.

b. Richie, you'*ve got to wrap up* that present before you take it to Nancy's birthday party.

1. (just) Listen, Peter, your boss _____ this deal; he'll make a million.

2. This room is crowded, I know, but we _____ five more students.

3. We _____ the meeting until tomorrow; there are no available rooms.

91

4. (just) You _____ , Sam; you're driving like a maniac.

5. Mr. Blank, your secretary _____ all the mail; there may be some important letters in that pile.

6. (just) I'd love to stay with you longer, but I _____ .

7. I _____ some friends at the airport, so I'm taking off from work this afternoon.

8. (just) I don't want to, but I _____ this golden opportunity because I've already got too many irons in the fire. (old saying)

9. My wife has a great many legal problems that she _____ her attorney.

10. Listen, men and women, this is the army; you _____ . You're marching like a bunch of scouts.

score _____

QUIZ 111   questions with *how come*

handbook p. 111

Supply appropriate verb phrases in the blanks. Use only <u>do</u> or <u>make</u>.

Examples: a. Children, how come you *haven't made* your beds yet? It's almost time to go to school.

b. You're a carpenter, Mr. Robinson, how come you *didn't do* the alterations on your house yourself?

1. Betsy, how come you _____ your chores before you left the house for school this morning?

2. (ever) Her husband isn't always at work, is he? How come he _____ any of the housework? His wife never has a moment to sit down.

3. Listen, little boy, how come you _____ faces at me while I was speaking to you? Don't you know that's rude?

4. You're a fine architect, Mr. Walters; how come you _____ any projects in San Francisco since your arrival here almost two years ago?

5. Weren't you being a little rash? How come you _____ such an important decision so quickly?

6. Mr. Treadwell, I'm curious; how come your company _____ any business with mine? Don't you like our service?

7. Excuse me, Professor, how come we _____ any quizzes since the beginning of the week? Isn't the class ready to go on?

8. (ever) Her hair seldom looks nice; how come she _____ it in a better way? Why doesn't she go to a beauty salon?

9. I'm curious, Frank; how come you _____ more money than your boss is? You do more work than he does.

10. Mr. Cameron, how come you _____ any homework since the beginning of the course?

score _____

QUIZ 112 *even* in negative verb phrases

handbook p. 111

Fill in each blank with an appropriate negative verb phrase with even.

Examples: a. (be) I'm not tired, Mother; I'*m not even* sleepy—I don't want to go to bed yet.

b. (do) He hasn't cleaned the house up at all; he *hasn't even done* the dishes yet, and he's expecting guests for dinner.

1. (be) This food isn't very good; it _____ good enough for a dog to eat.

2. (say) That customer won't give you a tip; he _____ thank you.

3. (spell) Her spelling is poor; she _____ her name correctly.

4. (know) His knowledge of grammar is limited; he _____ what a past participle is, but he does speak well.

5. (open) You haven't been doing any studying, Bobby; you _____ _____ a book since you sat down almost two hours ago.

6. (sit) My secretary isn't working much today; he _____ at his desk now.

7. (accept) That policeman won't ever take a bribe (he's very honest); he _____ a cup of coffee offered by someone.

8. (know) They're poorly educated people; they _____ the alphabet.

9. (get out of) His weekend was a very lazy one; he _____ the house.

10. (be) No, you didn't see me at the game; I _____ there.

QUIZ 113   another versus other(s)

handbook p. 112

Place in each blank <u>another</u>, <u>other</u>, *or* <u>others.</u>

Examples: a. He's leaving his wife for <u>another</u> woman.

b. Are there <u>other</u> highways in the state as beautiful as this one?

c. These oranges are four for a dollar; the <u>others</u> are two for sixty cents.

1. She was holding a baby in one arm and groceries in the _____.

2. It's six o'clock in the evening; _____ day has gone by.

3. These grapes are a little sour, but the _____ are quite sweet.

4. Why aren't they talking to each _____ ?

5. Two messages have just arrived; one is for me, the _____ is for you.

6. Danny, you've already had three pieces of fried chicken, and now you want _____; you really must be hungry this evening.

7. Yes, I'm going to be at the meeting, but my sister has _____ plans.

8. Some students in a class may never do any studying, while _____ may be studying all the time.

9. This pen isn't working right; may I try _____ one?

10. Those were difficult questions to answer, Professor. Do you have some _____ that I may answer more easily?

score _____ (20 points each)

REVIEW QUIZ I

In each group of sentences, <u>one</u> *sentence is correct; the other two contain* <u>one</u> *mistake each. Circle the letter corresponding to the correct answer, and then make the appropriate correction in the two remaining sentences.*

Example: A. a. ~~You're~~ children are at school today.   *Your*

b. ~~Your~~ making a lot of money now, aren't you?   *You're*

ⓒ. Your wife is doing well in her company, isn't she?

1. a. They are married for seven years.

b. They have been in Bangkok two weeks ago.

c. They have known each other since they were children.

2. a. That cost a great deal, doesn't it?

   b. The color of her eyes are blue.

   c. One of the students lives at the YMCA.

3. a. Never I have been at the North Pole.

   b. Only once did I go swimming last year.

   c. Seldom do she eat out in a restaurant.

4. a. Fortunately, we didn't have any problems so far.

   b. They're going to the movies once in a while.

   c. He's driving his son's car for the time being.

5. a. Let's go out to dinner tonight, do we?

   b. Let's not take a break, shall we?

   c. Shall we take a break? Let's.

score _____ (20 points each)

REVIEW QUIZ J

Follow the same procedure as in Review Quiz I.

Example: A. a. She never studies, but she does get good grades.

   b. Never in her life she has been seriously sick.

   c. Seldom has fish cost as much as it does now.

1. a. We went at a party and danced all night.

   b. I put the bowl of potatoes on the middle of the table.

   c. Only a few people were sitting in the first row of seats.

2. a. Time goes fast, don't it?

   b. He's had a great deal of luck lately, didn't he?

   c. You've got to go to the dentist today, haven't you?

3. a. Neither of us have the desire to be rich or famous.

   b. Not many fish live in that lake.

   c. How smooth your mother and father dance!

4. a. How strange that young man behaves when he's nervous!

   b. I want to go and to see that movie.

   c. Their attendance is poor, but they do do the homework.

name _____

5. a. None of this laundry are clean.

b. I never cheat, and no one else in the class doesn't either.

c. How beautiful she looks today in her new blue dress!

score _____

REVIEW QUIZ K

Place in each blank the letter corresponding to the correct answer. Either *means both a and b are correct.*

Example: a. The Pope _c_ is going to say mass at our church.
a. himself   b. X   c. either

1. _____ though the sun is shining brightly, it's quite cold, isn't it?
a. Even   b. X   c. either

2. Have you got _____ to lend me a little?
a. money enough   b. enough money   c. either

3. The sun rose yesterday morning _____ 6:37.
a. at   b. on   c. either

4. Please divide this money evenly between you and _____.
a. I   b. me   c. either

5. There _____ some very good news in this report from the Middle East.
a. is   b. are   c. either

6. We're going to stay _____ the Canary Islands for a month.
a. in   b. on   c. either

7. Our son likes to play baseball, but our daughter doesn't _____.
a. like   b. like to   c. either

8. Money _____ itself isn't important; it's what it buys.
a. by   b. X   c. either

9. These are expensive, aren't _____?
a. these   b. they   c. either

10. This is delicious. _____ you like some?
a. Do   b. Would   c. either

QUIZ 114   the past perfect tense

handbook p. 112

Supply in the blanks appropriate verb phrases in the past perfect tense.

cool off	die down	have
deal out	give out	lie down
decide	grow out of	put

Examples: a. Although I *hadn't put* any salt in the stew, it tasted delicious.

b. By the time we got into the game, the dealer *had dealt out* all the good cards.

1. Grandpa was a little tired yesterday evening because he _____ for his usual afternoon nap.

2. Because it _____ a lot in the early evening, we didn't have to use our airconditioner last night while we were sleeping.

3. By the time we got home, the storm _____, but it was still raining.

4. Even though he _____ a whole chicken for dinner, he was still hungry later on.

5. Since I _____ time to go shopping on Saturday, the refrigerator was bare all day Sunday (the stores are closed then).

6. They were happy because their sixteen-year-old daughter_____ _____ not to drop out of high school.

7. My neighbor upstairs in the back went to a lawyer because she_____ _____ some kind of trouble with the landlord (I think he wanted to kick her out).

8. My grammar teacher _____ an assignment yesterday morning, so I didn't have any homework to do last night.

9. Because Tony _____ those shirts, his mother gave them away.

10. Though she _____ many proposals of marriage, she was still single at the age of forty.

QUIZ 115 adverbs with the past perfect tense

handbook p. 115

Fill in each blank with an appropriate verb phrase in the past perfect tense.

come out	fill out	get out of	lie down	take on
die (pass away, pass on)	flee	have	run out of	walk out on

Example: a. (just) Grandma *had just gotten out of* bed when the earthquake suddenly occurred; she got right back in again.

1. (already) The thieves _____ when the police finally got to the scene of the crime; they got all of poor Mrs. Richhouse's jewelry.

2. (just) I _____ my dinner when a friend called and asked me out to one of the best restaurants in town.

3. (just recently) When I first met Hope Onslow-Ford, her tenth romantic novel _____ .

4. (just) When the phone rang, I _____ for my usual afternoon siesta (Spanish for <u>nap</u>).

5. (already) When Paula Manners entered the university at the age of eighteen, she _____ twelve years of education.

6. (finally) After about three hours, I _____ the application form for getting into the University of Illinois at Urbana.

7. (just recently) When I last spoke to the president of that company, she said business was extremely good; they _____ 300 workers.

8. (already) When the family doctor finally got to the hospital, Mr. Crews _____ .

9. (already) After only a half hour of shopping, I _____ money.

10. (just) When I spoke to Virginia on the phone a few hours ago, she sounded very upset; her boyfriend _____ her and slammed the door.

QUIZ 116   *never*, *before*, and *ever*

handbook p. 115

Place in each blank an appropriate verb phrase in the past perfect tense.

be	go out with	see	take advantage of
eat	have	study	

Examples: a. (ever) When she went out with Roberto Crespo, a man from Colombia, she *hadn't ever gone out with* a man from Latin America before.

   b. (never before) When Mohammed, a friend of mine from the Middle East, first went to the United Kingdom to attend the university, he*'d never before studied* with women in the same class as his.

1. (ever) When I lost my temper (got angry) at my boss's meeting yesterday afternoon, no one in the office _____ me get so angry before.

2. (never) Before I went to the reception at the Russian Embassy, I _____ caviar before; it was very salty.

3. (never before) When Sheridan Richhouse borrowed some money from his parents recently, he _____ their great wealth.

4. (ever) When our son fell in love with the girl next door, he _____ _____ in love before.

5. (never) When Betty Weavers inherited that great fortune from a distant cousin (whom she hadn't ever even met), she _____ _____ any money before; consequently, she didn't know how to spend it and eventually lost it all.

QUIZ 117   *still* in the simple past tense; *anyhow* and *anyway*
handbook p. 116

Put in each blank an appropriate verb phrase with <u>still</u> *in the simple past tense.*

cross up	lock up	run away	take advantage of	his wife
cut out	pass up	run out of	take out	me
go	put up with	stand up	understand	them
have				it

Examples: a. Although he hadn't received an invitation, he <u>still went</u> to the party any-how.

             b. The company had offered him a golden opportunity, but he <u>still passed it up.</u>

1. He'd always had a reputation as an honest man in the business world, but
he _____ in our last business deal.

2. I _____ the formula even though the teacher had
given me a long and detailed explanation.

3. Even though he didn't have much money, he _____
to dinner.

4. They were pleased; they _____ quite a bit of money
in their pockets even though they'd been traveling for more than six
months.

5. He'd asked his parents for money many times, and they'd done a great
many favors for him, but he _____ again anyhow.

6. His parents had always been good to him, but the little boy_____
_____.

7. It wasn't a very good picture of me in yesterday's newspaper, but I _____
_____ anyway.

8. Although the bracelet wasn't very valuable, he _____
_____ in the safe anyhow.

9. She'd promised me at least five times to meet me, but she_____
_____.

10. We'd made a lot of extra ice for the party, but we _____
_____ anyway.

QUIZ 118   *still* with the past perfect tense
handbook p. 117

Insert in each blank an appropriate negative verb phrase with <u>still</u> in the past perfect tense. If an object is needed, choose one from the right below.

call back	deal out	grow out of	slow down	a present	me
call on	decide upon	lay off	sort out	anyone	the joker
cut out	get out of	pick out	take care of	it	

Examples: a. Though I'd told Andrew to stop teasing the kitten so much, he <u>still hadn't</u> <u>cut it out.</u>

b. Even though the Prime Minister and her husband had been formally invited, they <u>still had not called on</u> the Royal Family.

1. What a serious problem it was! And when I called my lawyer, he _____ _____.

2. (even) When I called him up at 11:30 yesterday morning, he_____ _____ bed.

3. I'd told him several times he was running that machine too fast, but he _____ when it suddenly broke down.

4. The company hadn't had much business for months, but they _____ _____.

5. Barbara had been in the store for more than three hours, but she _____ _____ for her neighbor's husband's birthday.

6. The pile of mail got bigger and bigger, but my secretary _____ _____.

7. I'd called that customer six or seven times, but she _____ _____.

8. The baby was almost a month old, and her parents _____ _____ a name.

9. Someone had already gotten the ace of spades, but the dealer _____ _____ .

10. (even) When their little boy was three, he _____ diapers.

QUIZ 119 the past perfect continuous tense
handbook p. 118

Fill in each blank with an appropriate verb phrase in the past perfect continuous tense.

climb	listen in on	put by	stand up
figure on	pick on	rain	turn out
get along	pick up	snow	work on

Examples: a. When he finished the sculpture, he'*d been working on* it for at least a year.

b. They *hadn't been getting along* for months when their relationship suddenly changed, and they fell in love again.

1. Since it _____ for more than a month (it was the monsoon season), everything in the house felt damp.

2. When we reached the summit, we _____ for almost a week.

3. We _____ 200 people attending the conference, but more than 300 showed up; we ran out of chairs.

4. When we arrived at our friends' farm up in Vermont, it _____ _____ for a couple of days. The place looked as if everything had been covered with a white blanket; it was very beautiful.

5. The spy _____ the director's phone calls to the CIA in Washington for almost six months before she was finally caught by FBI agents.

6. He _____ his girlfriend for hours when she finally got angry and walked out on him.

7. Our company _____ approximately 5,000 washing machines a month when the market suddenly boomed and sales increased dramatically.

8. He _____ part-time jobs here and there for at least a couple of years before he finally found a full-time position at a bank.

9. They _____ money for their old age, but inflation wiped them out.

10. The doctor's feet were aching because he _____ for more than ten hours.

QUIZ 120   the past perfect tense with *yet*

handbook p. 119

Place in each blank an appropriate negative verb phrase in the past perfect tense with yet.
Provide objects when needed.

ask out	figure out	run away	her	them
attend to	hand in	thicken up	him	the stew
call down	hand out	try out	it	
cross out	pass out			

Example: a. I'd asked him several times to omit my name from that list, but when I last
saw the list, he *hadn't crossed it out yet.*

1. Lucky for us (fortunately), when the police arrived, the thieves
_____.

2. He had drunk almost two gallons of beer, and he _____
_____.

3. He'd been showing up late at the office for more than a month; however, no
one _____ , not even his boss.

4. The teacher had assigned the composition three weeks before, and I
_____.

5. We'd been sitting in the classroom for almost three hours waiting for the
professor to give us our final grades, and she _____.

6. Everything on the stove was ready to serve, but I _____
_____.

7. The problem had been bothering me for days, and I _____
_____.

8. They'd had their car for more than a month, and they _____
_____.

9. I'd been working on the puzzle for at least a week, and I _____
_____.

10. Bob was afraid of being rejected; he'd been wanting to go out with the new
girl ever since she arrived at the school, but he _____
_____.

QUIZ 121 questions with the past perfect (continuous) tense
handbook p. 120

Complete the following yes–no and information questions with appropriate verb phrases in the past perfect tense or the past perfect continuous tense. Provide subjects.

Tim and Tinka	your friend	arrive	go with	listen in on
you	your grandfather	be	have	smoke
your father	your mother	get into	leave	work

Examples: a. (just) <u>Had you just gotten into</u> the shower when I called last night? Yes, I had.

b. How long <u>had your father been smoking</u> when he finally decided to give the habit up? . . . For more than thirty years.

1. How many times _____ an interview with the company before she finally got the job in the accounting department? . . . Three.

2. (already) Who _____ when you got to class yesterday morning? . . . Only Kim and Maria.

3. (ever) When you bought your house in Puerto Rico two years ago, _____ _____ a house before? . . . Yes, several.

4. How long _____ each other before they finally got married? . . . Quite a while.

5. How long _____ when he finally retired? . . . Since 1933.

6. (already) _____ dinner when I called last night? . . . No, only a little snack.

7. How long _____ her boss's phone calls before he finally found out and fired her? . . . More than a year.

8. (already) Who _____ the house when you got up this morning? . . . No one.

9. (already) How many children _____ when she had you? . . . None.

10. (already) How many times _____ in Switzerland when he went there this last time? . . . At least ten.

QUIZ 122 *lay* and *lie*

handbook p. 121

Fill in the blanks with appropriate affirmative or negative verb phrases. Use only forms of
<u>lay</u> *or* <u>lie</u>.

Examples: a. (usually) A hen usually <u>lays</u> only one egg a day.

               b. While the police were looking for them, the terrorists <u>were lying</u> low (hiding) in a cabin up in an isolated part of the mountains.

1. Even though he _____ down for several hours, he was still very tired when he got up.

2. I'm afraid I scratched the top of the table when I _____ some tools on it.

3. (ever) Even though our neighbors' little boy sometimes steals (he's a good boy actually), he _____.

4. For the time being, my favorite Persian carpet _____ on the floor of a friend's apartment because I haven't got an apartment of my own.

5. The men from the store were going to put linoleum on the kitchen floor early this morning, but they _____ it yet, and it's almost five o'clock in the afternoon.

6. (just) When I called Grandpa up, he _____ down for a nap. I'm afraid I disturbed him.

7. (often) When it gets very cold in the winter, our old dog _____ in front of the fire in the living room to keep warm.

8. For the time being, we _____ the firewood outside on the front porch; we need a better place to store it, but we can't find one.

9. Although Alexandra _____ to Edward many times, he still loved her desperately. He was her slave.

10. Where are my shoes, Mommy? They _____ on the floor under your bed, Buddy. I saw them there a few minutes ago.

QUIZ 123   set and sit
handbook p. 122

Fill in the blanks with appropriate verb phrases. Use only forms of set or sit.

Examples: a. I woke up late the day before yesterday because I *hadn't set* my alarm clock the night before.

b. Abraham Lincoln *was sitting* with his wife in a box at Ford's Theater in Washington when he was assassinated by an actor named Booth.

1. Because he _____ down by accident in a puddle of water, the little boy's pants were all wet.

2. Almost 400 passengers _____ on the plane for more than 3 hours before it finally took off.

3. (still) Although she has naturally curly hair, she _____ it every night before she goes to bed.

4. Watch out! Don't walk on the sidewalk; that's fresh concrete (it was just poured an hour ago), and it _____ yet.

5. (still) Yes, we can go swimming, the sun _____ .

6. The climbers _____ out yesterday morning for the summit and reached it just as the sun was setting; they camped at the top for the night.

7. I've just made some Jello, but it _____ yet.

8. Since I had to get the 7:30 train this morning, last night I _____ my alarm for six o'clock.

9. The table at my dinner party last night looked lovely even though I _____ _____ it in a hurry.

10. (still) They want to get married soon, but they _____ a date.

score _____

QUIZ 124   raise and rise
handbook p. 122

Fill in the blanks with appropriate verb phrases. Use only forms of raise or rise.

Examples: a. They *raised* lettuce, tomatoes, radishes, corn, strawberries, and blueberries in their garden last year.

b. Oil and gas are getting more expensive all the time, food costs more than ever, and the price of clothes *rises* from week to week, but my salary remains the same.

1. Jack, please hurry up; the temperature _____ by the minute, and we want to get to the swimming pool fast.

2. *The Sun Also* _____ is a famous novel by the late American writer, Ernest Hemingway.

3. I baked some bread yesterday, but for some reason it _____ .

4. The lights lowered, the audience quieted down, the curtain _____ _____, and the play began.

5. (just) When a friend of mine and I were on a trek in Nepal, one morning the sun _____ when we woke up; the snows of the high Himalayas surrounding us were a brilliant pink. What an extraordinary sight it was!

6. (always) He _____ his hand when the teacher asks the class a question; he rarely has the correct answer, however.

7. Children, please come in out of the water now, the tide _____ .

8. Certainly, in the past few years, the rate of inflation _____ faster than workers' salaries.

9. Because we thought it would be better for them than the city, we _____ _____ our children in the country.

10. According to the New Testament, Christ was crucified on The Cross and _____ from the dead three days later.

score _____

QUIZ 125   the passive voice

handbook p. 123

Supply in the blanks appropriate verb phrases in the passive voice.

Examples: a. (speak) English *is spoken* almost everywhere in the world.

b. (eat up) All the food at the party *had been eaten up*; there was nothing left over for the cat's or dog's dinner.

1. (release) Twelve political prisoners _____ from prison tomorrow in exchange for the twelve hostages being held by the counterrevolutionaries.

2. (bear) Everyone in my family, except my grandfather, _____ _____ in a hospital.

3. (serve) We're waiting for our last guest to arrive, so dinner _____ _____ yet.

4. (accomplish) By the end of last week, absolutely nothing of importance in the office _____, so the boss wasn't in a very good mood.

5. (lay) A new wall-to-wall carpet _____ on the living room floor tomorrow.

6. (bear) When we were living in Korea, our son _____ yet.

7. (paint) Our house _____ since we bought it almost ten years ago, and it still looks brand new.

8. (set) When I last spoke to Dawn and Adam, their marriage plans _____ _____ yet.

9. (correct) Our compositions _____ by the professor last night.

10. (give) The final examination for the course _____ on the last day of class. That's next week.

score _____

QUIZ 126   the passive voice with adverbs

handbook p. 124

Supply in the blanks appropriate verb phrases in the passive voice.

Examples: a. (build / just) When we moved into our house, it *had just been built.*

b. (send out / already) So far, seventy-five invitations to my sister's wedding *have already been sent out*.

1. (water / always) The garden _____ in the mornings; it's sometimes done in the early evenings.

2. (ban / probably) Because of its explicit sex scenes, that movie, which hasn't come out yet, _____ by the government.

3. (hang / finally) The murderer _____ for his crime at midnight last night.

4. (publish / just) That author was one of our company's most important writers; her recent book _____ when she suddenly signed a contract with another publisher. We were surprised.

5. (find / eventually) We all hope that peace _____.

6. (invent / yet) A perfect mousetrap _____ .

7. (take care of / still) Mr. Watson, I've asked you at least ten times to deal with this situation, and it _____.

8. (do / already) When I started work on that project, there was really nothing for me to do because everything _____.

9. (solve / finally) At last! Our problems _____. We don't have a thing to worry about.

10. (baptize / probably) Their baby _____ this coming Sunday.

score _____

QUIZ 127   transforming active verb phrases into passive verb phrases

handbook p. 125

Transform the following sentences, changing the verb phrases from the active to the passive voice. <u>Omit the performing agents.</u>

Examples: a. Unfortunately, we haven't found a solution yet.
Unfortunately, a solution hasn't been found yet.

              b. I'll probably fix the toaster by tomorrow.
The toaster will probably be fixed by tomorrow.

1. My lawyer didn't do anything about the problem.

   _____

2. The people of the nation elected the best person in the last election.

   _____

3. The professor has given several students low grades on the final exam.

   _____

4. My secretary doesn't ever sort the mail in the afternoons.

   _____

5. No one had declared war yet when we left the country.

   _____

6. They named their little baby girl after her grandmother.

   _____

7. They didn't build Rome in a day.

   _____ (old saying)

8. In China, people usually eat food with chopsticks.

   _____

9. Our teacher sometimes holds our grammar class in the park near school.

   _____

10. Construction companies don't build houses of wood much these days.

   _____

QUIZ 128 the present continuous tense and the passive voice
handbook p. 125

Supply in each blank an appropriate verb phrase in the present continuous tense. Use only the passive voice.

censor	install	sing	take care of
deal with	pay	spend	tear down
fix	punish	split	tow away

Examples: a. Fortunately, a new phone *is being installed* in my office this morning.

b. The man has been found guilty of stealing a million dollars, but the newspapers say he *isn't being punished* for his crime.

1. Look! Your car _____. Try to stop them.

2. Mr. Smith, I'm worried; this customer _____ properly.

3. I'm not wearing my watch today because it _____.

4. Those people _____ much for their work; they're unskilled labor.

5. This money _____ in three ways: some for you, a little for him, and the rest for me.

6. Not enough money _____ for education in our community.

7. A lot of my favorite songs _____ at the concert next week.

8. That beautiful old building _____ soon. How sad!

9. This situation is serious, but it _____ in the right way; everyone in the nation has confidence in the President.

10. Someone says my letters _____, but I don't think so.

QUIZ 129   the past continuous tense and the passive voice
handbook p. 125

Supply in the blanks appropriate verb phrases in the past continuous tense. Use only the passive voice.

coach	lay off	look after	question	take care of
give	lie	present	take	work on

Examples:
   a. When I got to the meeting late, the plans for the project *were being presented* to the clients.

   b. My car *wasn't being worked on* when I got to the garage.

1. While I _____ the injection, the nurse was holding my hand.

2. I quit my job because I _____ a fair deal.

3. He knew he _____ soon, so he wasn't working very hard.

4. Our team was doing poorly during last season because it _____ _____ well.

5. Unfortunately, I _____ seriously at the meeting, so I left.

6. I was annoyed because I knew I _____ to.

7. This situation _____ by the security guards in my office building, so I called the police.

8. I _____ a promotion and raise in salary, so I quit my job and found another one right away.

9. We were very nervous while we _____ by the examiners.

10. Ann's children _____ by their grandmother while Ann was away with her husband on an important business trip to Seattle.

QUIZ 130 yes-no questions in the passive voice
handbook p. 126

Complete the following yes–no questions with appropriate verb phrases in the passive voice. Provide subjects from the list on the left.

a meeting	textbooks	bear	give out	pay
a test	you	deliver	hold	write
new material	your apartment	fix	listen to	
some students	your car	give	paint	
mail	your house			

Examples: a. *Were you being listened to* at the last meeting?
Yes, everyone was paying attention to what I had to say.

b. *Has your house been painted* since you moved into it? Only once.

1. _____ in your class every day? Yes, usually.

2. (already) _____ when you moved into it?
Yes, fortunately.

3. _____ when you got to class yesterday?
Yes, some of the students were almost finished.

4. _____ at home or in a hospital? Neither; I was born in a taxi on the way to the hospital.

5. _____? Yes, that's why I'm taking the bus today.

6. (ever) _____ on Sundays? Yes, but only special delivery.

7. (usually) _____ once a month? No, once a week.

8. (probably) _____ in this room next Saturday afternoon? Yes, for almost three hundred people.

9. (usually) _____ by teachers? Yes, they are.

10. _____ an examination in the other room?
Yes, that's why it's so quiet in there.

QUIZ 131   information questions in the passive voice
handbook p. 126

Make information questions. Observe only the informal style.

Examples: a. *Why wasn't the project completed*?
Since there wasn't enough time, the project wasn't completed.

b. *Who will the prize most probably be given to*?
The prize will most probably be given to *John Smith*.

1. _____

You're being introduced to *your new boss* at 10 o'clock.

2. _____

Animals like that are *seldom* seen in captivity.

3. _____

You'll probably be given a raise *in six months*.

4. _____

I'm not being transferred to another department *because I'm not ready to go*.

5. _____

The windows are usually washed *once a month*.

6. _____

My boyfriend and I will probably be married *by the end of the year*.

7. _____

Beautiful weather has been forecast for today.

8. _____

He'll never be laid off; *he owns the company*.

9. _____

You're not being given a raise *because you don't deserve one*.

10. _____

You and your wife have been given *a Rolls-Royce automobile* as a prize.

QUIZ 132   passive versus active verb phrases
handbook p. 126

Supply in each blank an appropriate verb phrase (passive or active) in the present (continuous) tense, the past (continuous) tense, the future tense, the present perfect tense, or the past perfect tense.

Examples: a. (record) No, this conversation *isn't being recorded* .

b. (begin) When we got to the theater, the movie *hadn't begun* yet.

1. (give) Everyone in the class _____ a new dictionary yesterday.

2. (permit / never) The serving of alcohol _____ in our club.

3. (do) We _____ anything special last night.

4. (rob) Just as I looked out of my bedroom window, someone _____ _____ down on the street.

5. (die) My neighbor's father _____ just a few days ago.

6. (buy / ever) When my boss goes to the wholesale market, he _____ _____ the right kind of merchandise for the store.

7. (play) A very important game between our school and yours _____ _____ out on the field right now.

8. (smoke) My roommate _____ only once in a while.

9. (sell) So far, 26,000 copies of the book _____ since its publication last year.

10. (destroy) The people of the village had to sleep in tents for several weeks because their homes _____ by a tornado.

REVIEW QUIZ L transforming passive verb phrases into active verb phrases

Transform the passive verb phrases in the following sentences to active verb phrases. Supply a performing agent. Provide objects when necessary. Use the when needed.

company	no one	president	speaker	you
government	people	secretary	surgeon	watchmaker
lawyer	police	someone	teacher	

Examples: a. The patient wasn't operated on because there was no need for it.
The surgeon didn't operate on the patient because there was no need for it.

b. Nothing has been done about the high crime rate in the city.
No one has done anything about the high crime rate in the city.

1. What time was the speech given last night?

_____

2. It's being fixed today; it was broken last week.

_____

3. English isn't spoken much in that part of the world.

_____

4. I'm not being given a fair deal.

_____

5. This kind of information isn't ever revealed to the public.

_____

6. Nothing is being done about the gophers in the garden.

_____

7. Material wasn't being handed out when I got to class.

_____

8. Why wasn't an explanation given to the detective?

_____

9. Why isn't the mail ever sorted in the afternoon?

_____

10. My boss probably won't be given a raise.

_____

QUIZ 133 passive infinitives
handbook p. 127

Supply in the blanks appropriate infinitives (passive or active).

call down	eat up	lay off	put up
chop up	hand in	look after	run out of
cross out	hang up	put by	turn down

Examples: a. I wouldn't like *to be laid off* this time of year; it's hard to find a job.

b. It's necessary *to put by* money for a rainy day (a day when one might need money).

1. Are these compositions going _____ to the teacher?

2. I can tell you one thing; I don't want _____ by the boss.

3. I'm afraid there are a lot of mistakes in this composition for me _____

_____ .

4. I'd like my children _____ by their grandmother every day.

5. I don't want _____ ice when I have the party tomorrow night.

6. When he offers someone something, he doesn't like _____ .

7. The government is going _____ the money for the dam project on the river near our town.

8. I want these clothes _____ in the closet immediately, children.

9. Sandy and Andy, I want all the food on your plates _____ .

10. All these vegetables need _____ before they're cooked.

QUIZ 134 the future perfect tense
handbook p. 127

Put in each blank an appropriate verb phrase in the future perfect tense.

| do | fix | have | iron out | put up |
| drive | go | invent | put down | tear down |

Examples: a. (probably) When your father gets home, you *probably won't have gone* to bed yet, so you'll be able to see him.

b. By the end of this century, many new things *will have been invented*.

1. By the time we get to San Francisco, we _____ a little bit more than 3,000 miles, and I've done all the driving so far.

2. The newspapers say all the rebel forces in the southern part of the country
   _____ by the end of the year. It sounds like
   propaganda.

3. (probably) When we get to the garage, our car _____
   yet.

4. (already) We _____ our dinner when you get
   home tonight, but there will be some leftovers in the refrigerator for you.

5. I really do promise. All of these problems _____
   by the end of the day.

6. (probably / already) My roommate _____ his
   homework when I get home, so we'll be able to go to the movies together.

7. We are meeting together, Ladies and Gentlemen, on an important occasion.
   By the end of this convention, a candidate from our great party _____
   _____ for election as the President of the na-
   tion.

8. Yes, I'll be hungry by then; I _____ anything to
   eat all day.

9. When we finish this book, we _____ hundreds
   of quizzes.

10. (still) Look at that funny old building; it's almost falling down. I'm afraid it
    _____ when we return ten years from now.
    They do things very slowly in this part of the world.

score _____ (20 points each)

QUIZ 135   the future perfect continuous tense

handbook p. 128

Place in each blank an appropriate verb phrase in the future perfect continuous tense.

> rain   stand   travel   work
> sit   study   use

Examples: a. (probably) By the time we get up tomorrow morning, it *will probably have been raining* all night long.

b. When you come back to school in September after summer vacation, you'll have to get used to the old routine of school again; you *won't have been studying* for more than three months.

1. When we have our new computer installed next week, we _____
   _____ our present computer for only two years.

2. When he returns to New York from his trip around the world, he's not going
   to have much money; he _____ for more than a year,
   and traveling is expensive.

3. (probably) By the time we get to the ticket office, we _____

_____ in this line for at least five hours; I hope the

show is good.

4. When my Uncle Howard retires from his job this September, he _____

_____ at the same company for thirty-seven years;

they'll probably give him a gold watch.

5. (probably) When I finish my homework this evening, I _____

_____ at my desk in the library for at least a couple

of hours. I've got a lot of quizzes to do.

score _____ (20 points each)

QUIZ 136   questions with the future perfect (continuous) tense
handbook p. 129

Complete the following yes–no and information questions with appropriate verb phrases in the future perfect tense or its continuous form. Provide subjects, when needed, from the list on the left.

he	the earth	drive	rain	spend
it	you	have	rotate	visit
		live		

Examples: a. (already) <u>*Will you already have had*</u> dinner when you get home from work tonight?

b. Mr. Wilson, when you move from your old house to the new one, approximately how long <u>*will you have been living*</u> in the old one?

1. Professor Powers, how many countries _____

by the time your trip through Asia comes to an end?

2. (already) Ma'am, when this project finally comes to its third phase toward

completion, approximately how much tax money _____?

3. _____ much when we get to Southern Califor-

nia? I certainly hope so; then the gardens and parks will be all green and

lovely.

4. According to your calculations, Professor, how many times _____

_____ on its axis by the year 3000?

5. When your husband buys his new car, how long _____

his present one?

QUIZ 137   modal auxiliaries; *can*

handbook p. 129

Supply in the blanks appropriate verb phrases with <u>can</u> *or* <u>can't</u> *(*<u>cannot</u>*).*

be	figure out	fix	make	read	tune
do	find	introduce	play	survive	

Examples: a. One <u>can't be</u> too careful with the people one meets these days.

   b. These things <u>can be fixed</u>, but it's going to cost you a lot.

1. No one _____ without water.

2. My wife and I are working hard so that a better life in the future _____ _____ for our children.

3. Yes, my husband will be at the meeting, but I _____ , unfortunately.

4. Please don't be in such a rush; not everything _____ at once, you know—Rome wasn't built in a day.

5. Our son _____ well; nor can our daughter. They both need special tutoring, Mrs. Scott.

6. I'm sorry, your piano _____ today; I forgot to bring my tuning forks.

7. A Pepsi-Cola or Coca-Cola sign _____ almost everywhere in the world.

8. We _____ these forms ourselves; we've got to go to a special tax accountant.

9. You _____ outside now, Betsy, and neither can your baby brother; it's raining cats and dogs out (it's raining hard).

10. No one_____to the King until he or she has been given a security clearance and a thorough body search.

QUIZ 138 questions with *can*

handbook p. 131

Complete the following questions with verb phrases containing <u>can</u> or <u>can't</u>.

I	do	get	pick up	send
we	explain	give	quiet down	squeeze in
you	figure out	iron out		

Examples: a. What <u>can be done</u> about the energy shortage, pollution, and corruption in our town? . . . Well, something must be done soon.

b. <u>Can you explain</u> the meaning of this word to me? . . . Of course.

1. What kind of flowers _____ to my mother for Mothers' Day? . . . How about some lovely orchids?

2. _____ the children for me at school this afternoon? . . . I'm afraid I'm busy then.

3. What time _____ to my meeting tomorrow? Will you be there on time or a little late? . . . I'm sorry, but I can't make it.

4. What _____ to the baby or done for her to make her stop crying? . . . Take her in your arms.

5. Why _____ the dishes now? Is it because you don't have any soap? . . . I don't have any water.

6. _____ this complicated application form for me? . . . I don't know; let me see.

7. What _____ to solve the problem of overpopulation in the world today? . . . Family planning.

8. Why _____ , children? Daddy is taking a nap. . . . We're playing.

9. Sir, _____ these tax problems for me? . . . I've got problems of my own.

10. Miss Brooks, don't you think this classroom is becoming too crowded? Just how many more students _____ ? . . . Talk to the Director.

score _____ (20 points each)

QUIZ 139 *could*

handbook p. 131

Supply in the blanks appropriate verb phrases with <u>could</u> or <u>couldn't</u>. Provide objects when needed.

buy	get rid of	keep out of	send out	him
figure out	keep away from	keep up with		them

name _____

a. He _could figure out_ the first quiz, but the second one was a complete puzzle to him.

b. When our son was a little boy, he _couldn't keep out of_ the cookie jar.

1. Yes, I _____ the other students in the class, but I found it next to impossible to follow the professor's lectures.

2. (never) I _____ candy when I was younger, and I still can't.

3. A traveling salesman came by our house the other day; he was standing on the porch with his foot in the door for hours trying to sell me a vacuum cleaner—I _____ .

4. Mr. and Mrs. Walters had written out the invitations to their daughter's wedding, but they _____; their daughter hadn't yet decided whether she wanted to get married or not.

5. No, we _____ or drink alcohol when we were in Saudi Arabia. It was strictly forbidden.

score _____

QUIZ 140   be able to

handbook p. 132

Fill in each blank with an appropriate verb phrase using _be able to_:

be	get into	lock up	slow down
get	go	make	stand up for
get along with	go out with	sit down	throw away

Examples: a. We _weren't able to lock up_ the house yesterday morning; we'd lost our keys.

b. (ever) My neighbor is very old; she _isn't ever able to go_ anywhere by herself.

1. Yes, I agree; John is a very complicated person—that he _____ _____ people is his main problem.

2. Fortunately, I _____ many new friends since I arrived in this town almost two years ago.

3. He _____ his girlfriend tomorrow night; he's got to take care of some things at school.

4. (never) I'm always busy at my job; I _____.

5. No one _____ that building since it was locked up several months ago.

6. Unfortunately, neither my wife nor I _____ at your picnic next Saturday afternoon—we're going to our son's graduation.

7. (ever) Your neighbor certainly has a lot of junk in her house, doesn't she? Yes, she _____ anything since she moved in ten years ago.

8. Unfortunately, I _____ you in court tomorrow, I think you're guilty of the crime you've been accused of.

9. Yes, I hit the car in front of me because I _____.

10. He _____ to work on time yesterday; he'd had a flat tire, and his spare had been stolen.

score _____

QUIZ 141 *could have*; past opportunity not realized

handbook p. 132

Put in each blank an appropriate verb phrase containing could have. *Provide objects when needed.*

buy	do	look over	sort out	it
cross up	give	put up	take place	me
dance	lay	see off	vote	

Examples: a. She *could have married* a Rockefeller, but she married the boy next door instead.

b. Yes, all that work *could have been done* yesterday, but I was too tired to do it.

1. I _____ all night, but the party eventually came to an end around four.

2. The customers' new carpet _____ yesterday, but they weren't there when the workers got to the house, so the workers weren't able to get in.

3. He's got a lot of money; he _____ a Rolls-Royce, but he decided to buy a pickup truck instead.

4. Those things on the desk _____, but there were some other things to attend to that were more important.

5. I'm a little disappointed with a friend of mine; he _____ at the airport (he had nothing else to do), but he never showed up.

6. A friend of mine _____ while I was in Vancouver, but I decided to stay in a hotel instead.

7. The wedding _____ in the garden even though it wasn't a very nice day, but we at last decided it would be better to have it in the house.

8. There are a great many mistakes in this composition, Mr. Thomason; surely, you _____ before you handed it in.

9. I _____ in the last election (I'd registered), but I forgot to.

10. Yes, Nick Dixon _____ in our last business deal, but he remained an honest man instead and didn't try to take advantage of me.

score _____

QUIZ 142 *could, could have*; probability and conjecture

handbook p. 132

Put in the blanks appropriate verb phrases using could have. *Provide objects when needed.*

call off	fool around	pass out	stand up	him
cross up	get *away* with	run out of	throw away	it
fall in	leave out	show up	throw out	you

Examples: a. Why is the car stalling? We *could have run out of* gas, but I don't think so.

b. Where is that important letter? You *could have throw it away* by mistake, perhaps.

1. Why aren't there any people in Room 9? There's supposed to be a meeting going on there right now; it _____ , but I don't know.

2. Why hasn't Bully Baxter been around school lately? Well, the principal _____ , but no one really knows.

3. We're selling a lot of goods in our store, but our profits are not so high as they should be. Perhaps, your accountant _____ (he doesn't look honest to me).

4. She wasn't there when I got to the airport to see her off. You _____ too late, perhaps, or the plane may have already taken off ahead of schedule.

5. Why haven't they called out my name from that list yet? It _____ _____ .

6. Why isn't my boyfriend here yet? He was going to take me out tonight. I know you don't want to think so, but he _____ .

7. I hear the thief was caught. Yes, he _____ the crime, but his mother and father turned him in to the police.

8. Why has Cliff Winters been acting so differently lately? Well, he _____ _____ love, perhaps; or something else might be bothering him.

123

9. Why did he suddenly faint? Well, he _____ be-cause he'd drunk too much alcohol, but I don't really think so. I think he was sick.

10. Why did Dave lose his job? Well, he _____ too much at the office.

score _____

QUIZ 143   couldn't have; impossibility

handbook p. 133

Fill in the blanks with appropriate verb phrases with <u>couldn't have</u>.

be	do	run into
betray	have	see
cook	invent	write

Example: a. You're mistaken, I'm afraid; you <u>*couldn't have seen*</u> me at the last meeting—I wasn't even there.

1. Listen, Mr. Smith, please; that job _____ in just a day—I had absolutely no one here in the shop to help me out.

2. No, impossible! You _____ old Tom Mathews on the street yesterday—he's been dead for years.

3. What a wonderful movie it was last night! It _____ better.

4. We had rain, snow, blizzards, and tremendous winds during the whole of our last vacation; the weather _____ worse, but we had a wonderful rest.

5. We went to an absolutely wonderful party last night; we _____ _____ a better time anywhere else in town.

6. No, Ronnie, that machine _____ by Edison; he didn't know anything about transistors in his time.

7. No, Shakespeare _____ that play; he hadn't even been born yet when it was first produced on a London stage.

8. Yes, it was very easy to move into our new house; our neighbors _____ _____ more to help us.

9. Mrs. Butler, you _____ a better meal; everything is delicious.

10. (ever) No, John Hancock _____ his country; he loved it too much.

QUIZ 144   questions with *could have*

handbook p. 134

Complete the following questions with appropriate verb phrases using <u>could have</u>.

he	it	catch up	go off to	put on
I	you	do	put	throw away

Examples: a. What <u>could have been done</u> about that problem with the troublemaker?
. . . Absolutely nothing.

b. This coat is way too large for me. <u>Could you have put on</u> someone else's by mistake? . . . I believe I've put on yours.

1. _____ my foot in my mouth when I made that remark to James about his former wife? . . . I don't think he even heard you.

2. Yes, I was absent from class for almost seven weeks. (ever) How _____ _____ ? . . . I did nothing but study for a month.

3. Where's Baby Bobby? Where _____ ? . . . Is he outside?

4. Where's that certified check from the bank? _____ by mistake? . . . No, I just saw it a few minutes ago.

5. Someone took all the money out of my wallet. Who _____ _____ it? . . . Don't look at me.

score _____

QUIZ 145   asking for permission with *may* and *can*

handbook p. 134

Complete the following questions. Provide an object in each.

cross out	kick out	try on	him
cut up	pass out	try out	it
deal out	take off	turn down	them
help out	throw out	turn up	you

Examples: a. My feet are tired and sore; my shoes are killing me. May I *take them off*, please?

b. What old magazines these are! Can I *throw them out*?

1. Isn't the radio a little loud? May I _____ ?

2. What a beautiful typewriter! Can we _____ ?

3. Have these tests already been corrected, Professor? May I _____ _____ ?

4. Aren't these pieces of meat a little large for a stew? Can I _____?

5. What a lovely diamond ring that is! May I _____?

6. Are you ready for your cards, Ladies and Gentlemen? May I _____ _____?

7. You really look busy today. Can I _____?

8. Several statements in this report are incorrect. May we _____?

9. Sir, that man is making a lot of noise and disturbing the other customers; he's become quite drunk. May I _____?

10. The radio isn't loud enough, is it? Can I _____?

score _____

QUIZ 146 *may* and *might*; conjecture

handbook p. 135

Put in the blanks appropriate verb phrases using *may* or *might*. Provide objects when needed.

be	look over	send out	tear down	it
have	put in	spread around	test out	me
joke around	sell out	stand up for	turn up	them

Examples:

a. Why is Cynthia Groves always at home? She <u>may have</u> no one to go out with.

b. Why are the students' composition so often full of spelling errors? They <u>might not look them over</u> enough before handing them in to the teacher.

1. Why don't they get more Christmas cards every year? They _____ _____ many.

2. Ma'am, wouldn't you like to drive our new sports model? Yes, I _____ _____, but that doesn't mean I'm going to buy it.

3. Yes, I'm going on trial in court tomorrow for grand larceny; my old boss _____, but I'm afraid he'll chicken out at the last moment.

4. Why doesn't my roommate get better grades? He _____ _____ at school too much.

5. That building is almost ready to fall down, isn't it? Yes, it _____ _____ any day now, in fact.

6. Why are my salad dressings never very good? Well, you _____ _____ enough spices—try a touch of garlic.

name _____

7. Our company's new product is doing well in your store, isn't it? Yes, it certainly is; it's doing so well, in fact, that it _____ before Christmas.

8. Why are my neighbors complaining? You _____ your stereo too much at night.

9. Doctor, why isn't this ointment working? You _____ enough.

10. Why can't I open this door? You _____ the right key.

score _____

QUIZ 147   *may have* and *might have*; conjecture about the past
handbook p. 136

Supply appropriate verb phrases with <u>may have</u> or <u>might have</u>. Provide objects when needed.

bring up	have	test out	her
get rid of	lay over	turn in	him
give	leave out	turn off	it
hand out	stand up	wear out	them

Examples: a. Why did he throw his watch away? Well, it *may have worn out*.

b. How did those hikers get lost in the forest? They *might not have had* a compass.

1. Why doesn't he want to buy a new car now? He _____ his old one yet; I don't know.

2. Professor, why don't we have page 83 of the material? Well, I _____ _____.

3. Why don't they call me? You _____ your phone number.

4. Why isn't my name on this list? It was before it went to the printer's. Well, it _____.

5. He and his brother appear to be unhappy young people, don't they? Yes, they _____ in a happy home, but I really don't know the reason.

6. How did the police catch the kidnapper? Well, his neighbor across the street _____.

7. Why isn't that textbook effective in the classroom? Well, the author _____ _____ in the classroom before it was published.

8. Their plane is very late, isn't it? Yes, it _____ in London for a while; weather conditions over the Atlantic have been poor for the past few hours.

9. Why didn't my grandparents like that movie? Well, the explicit sex scenes _____.

10. Why is Ann crying? Well, her date (a person with whom one has an appointment) _____.

score _____ (20 points each)

QUIZ 148 *may have* and *might have; that* noun clauses

handbook p. 136

Put in the blanks appropriate verb phrases using may have *or* might have. *Provide objects when needed.*

burn up	pass up	talk over	it
get off	split up	throw away	them
goof up			

Examples: a. Do you think that I *might have passed up* a good opportunity when I turned that company's offer down?

b. You don't think I *may have goofed up* when I did what I did, do you?

1. Does your father think you _____ the problem with the wrong person? Perhaps, you should have gone to a lawyer.

2. A: One doesn't see Wanda and Jerry together much anymore, does one?

   B: Yes, I've noticed that recently. Do you think they _____ _____?

3. Where is my composition? You don't think I _____ by mistake (accidentally) along with those other papers, do you?

4. How did my shoes get into the incinerator? Do you think little Carlitos (he's always getting into trouble) _____ on purpose (intentionally)?

5. Why hasn't Phillip arrived on this train? This is the one he said he was going to be on. You don't think he _____ at the station before this one by mistake, do you?

QUIZ 149   *must;* necessity, prohibition, deduction, and recommendation

handbook p. 137

Put in each blank an appropriate verb phrase using <u>must</u>. Provide objects when needed.

chicken out	clear up with	give away	live	it
clean up	cut out	go out with	make out	them
clear away	do over	goof off	make up	

Examples: a. We *mustn't live* to eat; we must eat to live.

b. This report is full of grammatical errors, Miss Quick; the whole thing *must be done over*.

1. This is an extremely important matter; I _____ my lawyer at once.

2. Mr. Wheaton, I'm sending you to a surgeon; the cyst on your leg _____ _____ as soon as possible—it's growing fast.

3. Yes, please do come and climb to the top of the mountain with me, but you _____ during the climb because I'll need your help to get to the summit.

4. Sandra, you _____ the boy next door; he's not any good for you.

5. Why are these things spread out all over my desk? Someone _____ _____ at once.

6. I _____ well in my next project; my last two were complete failures.

7. Her apartment looks like a cyclone has hit it. Yes, she _____ _____ much.

8. Now, listen to me, Robbie; you _____ at school. Your teacher has complained that you're always fooling around and wasting your time and the time of others.

9. They're very rich and generous people; they _____ a lot of money to various organizations that help the poor and the forgotten.

10. You _____ stories, Janie; always tell the truth.

QUIZ 150   *must have; deduction*

handbook p. 138

Place in the blanks appropriate verb phrases using <u>must have</u>. *Provide objects when needed.*

call off	give back to	grow up	make out	it
catch on to	give up	kick out	run over	them
give away	goof up	knock out	squeeze in	

Examples:
   a. Why is that dog lying at the side of the road? It *must have been run over*.

   b. When I got to Room 7, no one was there; the meeting *must have been called off*.

1. What a happy woman she is! Yes, she _____ in a happy home.

2. Look! Those people are carrying a white flag and coming toward us with their hands up in the air; they _____ .

3. Look! The fighter in the white shorts isn't getting up; he _____ .

4. Rod Witter is going around looking worried and disappointed. Yes, he _____ well on that business deal he was always talking about.

5. Look! Here are those missing compositions. I _____ the class.

6. He didn't laugh a bit when I told him the joke; he _____ it.

7. Did you notice Mrs. Dowling no longer has that beautiful coffee table that used to be in the living room? Yes, she _____ to one of her daughters, or else she must have sold it.

8. My boss is unbelievably angry at me. I really _____ .

9. Why are he and his wife no longer in that club? They _____ ; they never got along very well with the other members.

10. My algebra class is really getting large; they _____ at least ten more students yesterday.

QUIZ 151   the idiom *have to;* necessity and lack of necessity

handbook p. 138

Fill in each blank with a verb phrase in the simple present tense using *have to*.

> catch up   defrost   look for   pull out   spank
> cross out   go over   mop   shave   work

Examples: a. (ever) Our little boy *doesn't ever have to be spanked* because he's always so good.

         b. I *have to go over* these reports very carefully; they're very important.

1. (never) Our refrigerator is automatic, so it _____.
2. Even though I _____ on Sundays, I often do—for the extra money.
3. The kitchen floor _____ ; it looks dirty.
4. His wife _____ a job, but she wants to.
5. He's fallen behind in his class, and he _____ .
6. No, you don't have to rewrite this composition; just a few mistakes _____ .
7. (often) A doctor _____ seven days a week.
8. (always) Our son _____ every day, but he usually does.
9. Three of Grandpa's teeth _____ .
10. (ever) He's really very rich—he _____ , but he does because he wants to make much more money than he already has.

score _____

QUIZ 152   *must not* versus *do not have to;* prohibition versus lack of necessity

handbook p. 139

Supply appropriate verb phrases using *must not (mustn't)* or *don't (doesn't) have to:*

Examples: a. (slam) Roland, there's a cake baking in the oven, so you *mustn't slam* the kitchen door.

         b. (slam) Well, I know you're mad at me, but you *don't have to slam* the door in my face.

1. (play) Now, listen, Baby Janie, you _____ with matches.
2. (put) This story _____ in the newspaper; everyone in town has already heard about it through the local gossip.

3. (waste) I've got a lot of chores to do around the house and errands to run downtown; I _____ a minute today.

4. (clean) She _____ her apartment herself because she can afford to have a cleaning person come in every day for a few hours.

5. (eat) A person with ulcers _____ rich and spicy food.

6. (believe) In the Hindu religion, a person _____ in only one God; however, many Hindus do.

7. (live) My priest is always telling me that man _____ _____ by bread alone.

8. (go) A Moslem _____ to a mosque to say his prayers, but he believes they are more meaningful when he says them there.

9. (do) Class, you _____ your homework every day, but it's a good idea in the long run (for now and the far future).

10. (tease) You _____ the bees in the hive, James; they might get angry, and you might get stung.

score _____

QUIZ 153   *have to;* contrasting verb tenses

handbook p. 140

Put in the blanks appropriate verb phrases using have to.

brush	go	paint	take	sit down	work
do	have	pay	tear down	wind	

Examples: a. It was such a funny joke; I was laughing so hard, I *had to sit down*.

b. Mr. Dunlap, you *won't have to pay* any income taxes next year; you're not going to be making any money.

1. (ever) She's lucky; she _____ to the dentist; she's got wonderful teeth.

2. Robin Taylor _____ three meetings with the president since the beginning of the week.

3. (never) My watch is automatic; it _____ .

4. (ever) Alice Capwell _____ again after she's fifty; she's making and saving a lot of money now.

5. Since it wasn't raining, I _____ my umbrella yesterday morning.

6. We've been lucky; our house _____ since we bought it five years ago.

7. (never) Since the Count Luis de San Obispo _____ a day in his life, as he grew older he became fat, slovenly, and lazy.

8. Fortunately, that beautiful old church _____ when the new highway was built nearby; we were able to save it.

9. Yes, Buddy, you _____ your teeth before you go to bed.

10. No one _____ the homework, but it makes a big difference when one does.

score _____

REVIEW QUIZ M   yes-no questions with *have to*

Complete the following yes–no questions with appropriate verb phrases using <u>have to</u>.

Anna	you	call	have	take
Bob	your TV	do	look after	travel
		fix	run	work

Examples: a. <u>*Has Bob had to have*</u> many conferences with you since the beginning of the project? . . . Only one.

b. <u>*Will you have to take*</u> a lot of clothes when you go on your trip to Tahiti? . . . Only my bathing suit.

1. _____ when he's sixty-five years old? . . . I don't think so.

2. (often) _____ homework for his classes this semester? . . . Rarely.

3. (ever) _____ since you bought it five years ago? . . . Not once.

4. _____ many chores yesterday afternoon? . . . No, I just relaxed.

5. _____ the police when your cat was up in the tree and wouldn't come down? . . . We called the Fire department.

6. (usually) _____ a lot of errands every day? . . . Yes, I'm running around all day long.

7. (ever) _____ a lot while he was working for International Express? . . . All over the world.

8. (ever) Mr. Crowley, _____ a surgical operation at any time in your life? . . . Never, fortunately.

9. (usually) _____ your sister's children when she goes away on a business trip? . . . Yes, and she takes care of mine while I'm away.

10. (ever) _____ an English lesson since he arrived in the United States? . . . Not once.

score _____

REVIEW QUIZ N information questions with *have to*

Complete the following information questions with appropriate verb phrases using have to, *and appropriate subjects when necessary.*

the patient	your baby	call off	feed	pay
the turkey	your house plants	cook	get up	speak
we	your piano	do	go	tune
you		drive	have	water

Examples: a. (usually) What time *do you usually have to get up* in the morning? . . . Early.

b. How many quizzes *have we had to do* this week? . . . About fifteen.

1. Who _____ to when you went there? . . . The president.

2. About how often _____ ? . . . Every six months.

3. How many times _____ to the dentist this year so far? . . . Not once, fortunately.

4. Next week on Thanksgiving Day, how long _____ _____ ? . . . Not more than six hours.

5. How many times _____ a conference with your supervisor in the past month? . . . Only once.

6. How much _____ for your plane ticket to Boston last week? . . . I can't remember.

7. What kind of special food _____ ? . . . No salt.

8. How often _____ during the winter? . . . Only once or twice a week.

9. How many meetings _____ this week so far? . . . Only three.

10. On our trip tomorrow, how long _____ ? . . . About ten hours.

QUIZ 154 *should* and *ought to;* advisability, expectation, obligation, and recommendation

handbook p. 140

Place in the blanks appropriate verb phrases using <u>should</u> *(or* <u>ought to</u>*).*

come up with	*pass up*	*put down*	*stand up*
figure on	*point at*	*put off*	*turn away*
get through with	*put*	*put up*	*work out*

Examples:

    a. Sir, you <u>*should work out*</u> in a gym at least once or twice a week; it's good for your body as well as your spirit.

    b. Gail, you <u>*shouldn't put*</u> your elbows on the table when you're eating; it's not good table manners.

1. Oh, yes, Matt Livingston will be a good person to work with on your next project; he's a clever fellow, and he _____ some good ideas.

2. Because of the bad weather conditions, I think this meeting _____ _____ until either tomorrow or the day after.

3. "Father, you _____ poor people who need food from our door."

4. Yes, approximately 300 people will probably show up for this evening's meeting, but we _____ 350 when we're putting out the chairs—just in case we need more.

5. Jason, you _____ your friends in that way; they all love you very much.

6. What wonderful strawberries we have in our garden this year! Don't you think some _____ ?

7. Yes, I _____ this project by the end of the summer; I've still got lots of time.

8. Susie, you _____ people; it's not nice, and it's also rude.

9. Mr. Russell, you _____ this opportunity; it'll make you rich and famous.

10. Ladies and Gentlemen, we _____ now; Her Royal Highness is entering the room soon.

QUIZ 155   *should have* and *ought to have*; advisability and obligation in the past

handbook p. 141

Put in the blanks appropriate verb phrases using should have *(or* ought to have). *Provide the object* it *when needed.*

call out	grind up	point out	take out of
cross out	look over	show off	talk over
cut out	pick out	squeeze in	tear up

Example: a. A few students *should have been taken out of* the class; the administration *shouldn't have squeezed in* more.

1. I'm still waiting for the doctor; my name _____ by now.

2. Darn it! I'd like to read that letter again, but I can't; I _____
   _____ .

3. I'd like to have that photograph of Mt. Everest I saw in a magazine the other day; I _____ .

4. Why did my girlfriend give me a pink bathrobe for my birthday present? She _____ a different color.

5. I got my new car yesterday; I _____ to my neighbors, but I did—I couldn't resist it.

6. Carrie, that meat _____ ; it wasn't meat for a hamburger—it was an expensive steak.

7. Why is my name still on that list? Someone _____
   _____ by now.

8. Why did the tourist guide not tell us about the large stained-glass window in the apse of the Cathedral? She _____ to us during our tour.

9. That was an extremely important contract, Mr. Waters; you _____
   _____ with your lawyer before you signed it. Why weren't you being more careful?

10. Mr. Tyler, this composition still contains a great many spelling and grammatical errors; you _____ more carefully before you handed it in to me.

QUIZ 156   questions with *should* and *should have*

handbook p. 142

Complete the following yes–no and information questions with appropriate verb phrases using <u>should</u> *or* <u>should have</u>. *Provide subjects from the group on the left.*

a baby	the telegram	arrive	elect	grind	turn in
I	this shirt	call up	feed	send	use
it	we	do	go	take over	wash

Examples:
   a. I know he's guilty of committing a serious crime, but <u>should I turn in</u> my own brother to the police? . . . It's your duty.

   b. What time <u>should I have arrived</u>, eight instead of seven? . . . Five, that's why I'm annoyed.

1. Who, instead of Jason Jaspers, _____ the president's job when old Harry Whitehouse retired and moved to Florida with his wife? . . . I was the person for the job.

2. _____ your boss and tell him you're not coming into the office today? . . . Please, but don't tell him why.

3. Where, instead of there, _____ on our trip last year? . . . I can think of a thousand places.

4. Sir, instead of Martin Pritchard, Jr., to whom _____
   _____ ? . . . His father Martin, Sr.

5. _____ in hot water instead of cold, or will it shrink? . . . Perhaps it should go to the drycleaner's.

6. What kind of meat _____ in that stew last night instead of veal? . . . Beef.

7. Yes, Ma'am, two pounds of coffee—what kind of coffee pot _____
   _____ for? . . . Drip, please.

8. Excuse me, Professor, what _____ by the government about the present political and social situation here? . . . Many, many things.

9. How many times a day _____ ? . . . At least four.

10. Who, instead of Don Grimes, _____ the captain of the team? . . . T. J. Matson, the greatest hitter ever in the history of baseball.

QUIZ 157   should and should have with have to
handbook p. 142

Place in the blanks appropriate verb phrases with <u>should</u> or <u>should have</u> and <u>have to</u>.

be   do   go   tune
cook   do over   pay

Examples: a. A: I get my car tuned every 10,000 miles, Jake. B: You car *shouldn't have to be tuned* so often, Mr. Knox.

             b. A: I really didn't want to discuss the problem with the administration, but I finally decided to. B: You *shouldn't have had to go* to them; it wasn't that serious.

1. A: We _____ so much homework, Professor. B: You don't have to do it, but it'll help you to learn.

2. Yesterday my boss asked me to redo a five-page letter which he thought was poorly written. I didn't want to, but I redid it anyway; it _____ .

3. A: Oh, I usually fry chicken for about two hours. B: What! You _____ it that long.

4. A: Dad, I had to pay $10.00 to get into that movie last night. B: That's terrible, Ted, you _____ so much, but that's inflation.

5. A: The turkey had been in the oven for more than eight hours, and it still wasn't quite done. B: It _____ in the oven for so long (the bird weighed only 20 pounds, didn't it?). Something must have been wrong with the oven.

QUIZ 158   should and should have with be able to
handbook p. 143

Put in the blanks appropriate verb phrases with <u>should</u> or <u>should have</u> and <u>be able to</u>. Provide objects when needed.

get out of   pass out   squeeze out   wipe out   it
make   squeeze in   try out   them

Examples: a. A: They wanted me to buy the car without taking it out for a drive first. B: You *should have been able to try it out* before you bought it.

             b. A: The patient *should be able to get out of* bed by now. B: She hasn't made as much progress as she should have.

1. A: But, Mr. Roberts, my classroom can take only so many students; we can't take any more. B: Now, Mrs. Crawford, don't you think we _____ _____ only two more students?

2. A: I wanted to distribute these political pamphlets, but the police wouldn't let me for some reason. B: You _____—the police haven't got the right to stop you.

3. A: No, Mom, I don't think there's any more juice in this lemon. B: Oh, I think we _____ a little bit more.

4. A: The champion _____ the other guy last night. B: Yes, perhaps, but isn't he getting a little old now and out of shape?

5. A: Randy Davis _____ more money than he does; he's a very bright and clever man with great potential. B: I agree; why doesn't he ask his boss for a raise?

score _____ (20 points each)

QUIZ 159   must and must have with have to

handbook p. 143

Supply in the blanks appropriate verb phrases with <u>must</u> or <u>must have</u> and <u>have to</u>.

come up with	finish up	put up with	work on
deal with	make up	spend	

Examples: a. A: Mr. and Mrs. Richhouse went on a trip around the world last year. B: My, they *must have had to spend* a lot of money.

b. A: He always gets home late every night—quite often after dinner. B: He *must have to make up* a lot of alibis for his wife.

1. A: Yes, I'm a specialist in public relations. B: How fascinating! You _____ _____ all kinds of difficult people in your line of work.

2. A: When I saw him the other morning, he looked completely tired out. B: Well, he _____ late at the office the night before.

3. A: I'm an art director in a New York advertising agency. It's a challenging job. B: Yes, I can imagine—you _____ some fantastic new idea every day.

4. A: They were living in that country before, during, and after the revolution. B: How interesting that must have been! A: Yes, but they _____ some difficult times and face quite a few dangers.

5. A: Her last writing project for Hollywood was a tremendous success. B: Yes, she _____ it for a long time.

QUIZ 160   must and must have with be able to

handbook p. 144

Supply appropriate verb phrases with _must_ or _must have_ and _be able to_. Provide objects when needed.

blow up	get to	quiet down	it
figure out	put up with	squeeze out of	them
get rid of			

Examples: a. I _must be able to get to_ Toronto as soon as possible—my wife is expecting a baby any hour now. When is the next flight?

   b. I saw him going into an accountant's office carrying an income tax form in his hand; he _mustn't have been able to figure it out_.

1. A: Someone told my neighbor (and she has told me) that Gavin Arthur is leaving his wife, Kathleen. B: I've heard that, too; he _____ _____ her anymore. What a difficult person she is to get along with!

2. Clark Drew was trying to borrow some money from his parents, but I don't think he got any; he _____ them.

3. The children in the class above ours are always making so much noise and stomping their feet on the floor—the teacher _____.

4. The little boy was holding a deflated balloon in his hand and crying; he _____ .

5. I see my neighbors are still spraying around the foundation of their house; they _____ the termites yet.

score _____

QUIZ 161   modals and present continuous forms

handbook p. 144

Place in each blank a modal + _(not)_ + _be_ + a present participle.

have	land	play	wear
horse around	live	rise	worry
kid	make	stay	

Examples: a. (may) My wife and I _may not be living_ in a palace, but our house is our home and we love it.

   b. (must) No, Ellen, your teacher _must be kidding_—she can't work miracles.

1. (should) Fasten your seat belts, please; we _____ in Honolulu any minute now. Thank you for flying with us; enjoy your stay in Hawaii. Aloha (good bye).

2. (should) Bill Clinton! You _____ out here in the hall. Why aren't you in your classroom where you belong?

3. (ought to) Why are you so concerned about my problems? You _____ _____ about your own.

4. (could) Your architect _____ a mistake in this matter. Why don't you consult with another one?

5. (might) I _____ a fool out of myself in this situation, but I don't really think so.

6. (may) We _____ good weather during this vacation, but we're having a good time.

7. (ought to) A: Really, Clara, you _____ stockings. B: Oh, Mother, please don't be so old-fashioned.

8. (might) We _____ in a first-class hotel, but we do have good hot water and ice (and the beds are turned down in the evenings).

9. (ought to) Jerry, you _____ with your brother's toy cars outside; you might lose one.

10. (could) The patient's temperature _____ , nurse; please take it again.

score _____

QUIZ 162   modals and past continuous forms

handbook p. 144

Put in each blank an appropriate verb phrase using a modal in its past continuous form.

dial	make	sleep	think
do	make up	slurp	use
live	pull	talk	

Examples: a. (may) Gordon Howard *may have been pulling* your leg (joking with you) when he told you he was a millionaire; he often likes to kid people.

b. (could) No, Grandpa, I think you're a little mixed up. I *couldn't have been living* in New Orleans during the '40's; I hadn't even been born yet.

1. (ought to) Meredith Savage _____ more about her future when she was younger, but she was having too good a time to worry about it.

2. (must) The director _____ his head when he made that crazy decision.

3. (might) Yes, it was an excellent alibi; he _____ a story.

4. (ought to) You _____ with your neighbor during the examination, Thomas Blake.

5. (must) Tad, you _____ your dictionary while you were writing the composition. Just look at all the spelling errors.

6. (should) Someone _____ something about the situation before it became so serious that the FBI had to be called in.

7. (may) I was very nervous at the meeting; I _____ a good impression, but everything seemed to go well.

8. (must) I _____ in the wrong position last night; my back aches this morning.

9. (should) Douglas, you _____ while you were eating your soup—it's not really good table manners.

10. (might) Well, Operator, I've gotten the wrong number twice. I _____ the correct number, but I don't think so.

score _____

QUIZ 163   had better; advisability

handbook p. 146

Complete the following verb phrases with appropriate verb phrases using had better. *Provide objects when needed.*

check out	give away	keep away from	stand up	it
figure on	give back to	nibble on	tow away	me
fool around	goof up	quiet down	watch out for	

Examples: a. You*'d better not fool around* at work; you*'d better watch out for* the boss.

1. (just) I don't think I can sell this chair; I _____ .

2. We still have our neighbor's lawnmower; we _____ him before he comes over asking for it.

3. Listen, Jim, I'm beginning to get a little annoyed; you _____ ; otherwise, you'll be starting an argument.

4. (just) We _____ a little something before we go to the party this evening; dinner isn't being served until very late, the host told me.

5. Why hasn't my date shown up yet? She _____ once again, or else.

6. Yes, son, you may borrow my car for this evening, but it _____ . That's already happened twice, and I don't want it to happen again.

7. Ten people are coming to dinner tonight, but I _____ twelve; we don't want to run out of food and drink.

8. You _____ on this project, or else you might be kicked out of the company.

9. This information doesn't look correct; it _____ right away.

10. Dear, you _____ the stove; I'm doing some deep-fat frying, and I don't want any of the hot oil to splatter on you.

score _____

QUIZ 164   would rather; preference

handbook p. 147

Complete the following statements and questions with appropriate verb phrases using would rather. *Supply subjects and objects when needed.*

you	be	lay off	put off	try on	it
	find out	look over	put up		them
	go over	pick up	take up		
	hold up	put down	talk over with		

Examples: a. *Would you rather take up* medicine or study law at the university?

b. Of course, Ma'am, I *'d rather not be laid off*, but have I got a choice?

c. This is to be an important meeting; I *'d rather put it off* until tomorrow, Ladies and Gentlemen, but there are some things that must be discussed at once.

1. No, thank you, I wouldn't like you to read my palm and tell me my fortune; I _____ anything about future events in my life.

2. Madam, _____ a silver bracelet or a gold chain?

3. A: Would you like to see the report now, Mr. Pearson? B: No, I _____ _____ a little bit later, thank you.

4. I _____ by a stranger than a friend.

5. I'm sorry, I can't discuss that situation now; I _____ _____ my lawyer before I reveal any information to the police or the newspapers.

6. Hello, Mrs. Grant? This is the Ajax Pillow Company. The ten pillows you ordered have just arrived. _____ yourself or have them delivered?

7. Friends, I _____ as a candidate for public office; I'm not qualified, nor would I be able to get any votes in the next election.

8. _____ an architect, a lawyer, or a person in the business world?

9. No, I don't want to go to that dangerous part of the city at night; I _____

_____ .

10. This bill is probably correct, but I _____ the figures again.

score _____ (20 points each)

QUIZ 165 *would rather have*

handbook p. 148

Fill in the blanks with appropriate verb phrases using would rather have. *Provide subjects when needed.*

you	deal with	go out	have	roast
	give	grow up	marry	

Examples: a. I fried this meat on the top of the stove; I *'d rather have roasted* it in the oven, but I wasn't able to get the oven door open for some reason.

b. *Would you rather have grown up* in the city? Didn't you enjoy your childhood on the farm?

1. She and her husband _____ at home, but her parents and his wanted to have the ceremony in a church.

2. _____ your dinner party last night at a restaurant instead of here at home? Look at all those dirty dishes you and I are going to be doing for the rest of the week.

3. We _____ that lawyer during our case, but we had no choice. We had to stick with her even though we didn't want to.

4. _____ the final examination yesterday instead of today? You told me that you didn't want to have it yesterday. I suppose all of you would rather not take it at all.

5. We _____ last night, but our daughter was giving a party, and my husband and I didn't want to be there.

QUIZ 166   be supposed to

handbook p. 148

Fill in the blanks with appropriate verb phrases using be supposed to. Provide subjects and objects when needed.

you	blow up	clean out	go out with	leave out of	them
	break out	finish up	hang around with	see off	
	carry out	get on	introduce	sit	

Examples: a. The Rogers' flight left on time, but I wasn't at the airport. *Were you supposed to see them off?*

          b. Helen, you know you *'re not supposed to be sitting* at your boss's desk.

1. We _____ early last night, but we ended up getting out of the office much later than we'd expected.

2. She _____ her neighbors' son, but she often does.

3. I'm sorry, Mr. Conway, _____ to the President at the reception last night? Someone must have forgotten to do it.

4. A revolution _____ in that country soon—the people are ready to take over.

5. Cliff, what difficult orders those are! _____ _____ by tomorrow?

6. What a silly mistake I made! I _____ the number 1 bus, not 7.

7. Their son _____ those troublemakers down at the pool hall on the corner, but he often does, and his parents don't like it a bit.

8. You crazy idiot—what a terrorist you are! You _____ _____ the Ambassador's car, not ours.

9. Hey, Lazy Bones, you _____ your closet this morning, and you're still in bed. Get up and at it right away, young man.

10. That material _____ the report. What happened? Did someone at the printer's make a mistake?

QUIZ 167   dare
handbook p. 149

Supply appropriate infinitive phrases without to in the blanks. Provide objects when needed.

doublecross	listen in on	put down	take advantage of	him
fall in	lock up	spread around	tell	me
hand in	mess up	stand up	wake up	

Examples: a. I swear my father is an innocent man. How dare the police *lock him up* in jail.

   b. How dare he *take advantage of* my good nature—I'm really upset.

1. I certainly don't want to make a date with him again. How dare he _____ _____ (I'd been waiting for almost three hours).

2. What! Are you forgetting that you're talking to your boss? How dare you _____ to shut up.

3. I'm really surprised at my neighbors next door. How dare they _____ _____ town gossip about me. What two old gossips they are!

4. Do you realize what you've done? How dare you _____ my life.

5. I'm so furious at my teacher. How dare he _____ in front of the class.

6. Some charity organization called me up around midnight last night asking me to donate some money. How dare they _____ in the middle of the night.

7. I can't begin to tell you how angry I am at my business partner. How dare he _____ . But I'll eventually get even with him.

8. I'm quite surprised at my roommate. How dare he _____ _____ the extension to my private phone conversations with my girl-friend.

9. I'm disappointed in Sandra Jones. How dare she _____ my composition with her name on it and tell the professor it's hers.

10. What! Aren't you my best friend? How dare you _____ love with my wife.

QUIZ 168   *need*

handbook p. 150

Write in the blanks appropriate verb phrases using need *as a modal auxiliary. Provide subjects when needed.*

I	buy	leave	tear down
we	call down	put	use
you	do over	put off	

Examples: a. No, I disagree—Mr. Caldwell *needn't be called down* for being late all the time, but he does need to have attention called to it. Let's be diplomatic.

b. That meeting *needn't have been put off* until tomorrow; we had time yesterday.

c. *Need I do over* this composition, Professor? Isn't it perfect enough yet?

1. No, Sir, that beautiful old residence _____ ; it can be renovated at a reasonable cost, and it'll look more beautiful than ever.

2. Can't we use first names? _____ last names? Let's be friendly.

3. A: Do you need anything else today, Ma'am? B: No thanks, I don't need anything else. I _____ as much as I did—I've run out of money. I do need someone to help me carry all these things out to the car, however.

4. _____ me now, John? Can't you stay with me a few minutes longer?

5. A: I was able to do most of the talking at the last meeting, wasn't I? B: Yes, Louella, you were able to do most of the talking, but you _____ _____ your foot in your mouth. You made everyone there furious.

QUIZ 169   perfect infinitives
handbook p. 150

Write in the blanks appropriate perfect infinitives.

       be   have   see   vanish
       go   leave   tear down

Examples: a. Whatever happened to that old yellow house on the corner? It was there
              yesterday, wasn't it? Why, it appears *to have been torn down* , doesn't it?

          b. A: Did you hear that one of your neighbors was arrested by the police? B:
              Yes, I'd love *to have seen* it; he'd been making trouble in the neighborhood
              for years.

    1. Oh, that sounds like it was a terrible situation; I wouldn't like _____
       _____ in your shoes.

    2. Whatever has happened to Mrs. Adikari? She seems _____
       _____ ; she's nowhere to be found on the ship. She must have fallen over-
       board.

    3. Why, the classroom is completely empty. Everyone seems _____
       _____ . Where could they have gone?

    4. The patient appears _____ a heart attack; he will
       need intensive care and complete rest. He must not be disturbed.

    5. A: I had a wonderful time at the beach last weekend. B: Really, I'd like _____
       _____ with you. Why didn't you invite me?

REVIEW QUIZ O   *too, either, so, neither, and,* and *but*

Put appropriate words in the blanks.

Examples: a. He's got to be transferred, and one other worker *has too*.

           b. (seldom) Mr. Wright always says good morning to me, but his wife *seldom
              does* .

    1. I still haven't changed my schedule, and no one else _____ .

    2. (often) Never do I have coffee in the morning, but my wife _____.

    3. I've not yet finished this quiz, and _____ anyone else in
       the class.

    4. (frequently) She hardly ever gambles when she plays cards, but her son
       _____ .

5. He'll make out well on the final examination, and _____ I.

6. These sheets have to be washed with bleach, but none of the other laundry _____ .

7. I've never been to the summit, and not many others _____ .

8. Barbara set her hair late every night, and her roommate _____ .

9. (rarely) His niece usually remembers his birthday, but his nephew _____ .

10. You'd better take advantage of this bargain, and _____ she.

11. There were no credit cards in the stolen wallet, and _____ any money.

12. He should stop smoking, and _____ she.

13. He's been studying hard lately, but not one of his classmates _____ .

14. These can never be corrected by tomorrow, and _____ those.

15. She'd rather be rich than poor, and _____ most other people.

16. He's being interviewed for a job today, and his cousin _____ .

17. You'd already left by the time I got to the meeting, and _____ he.

18. He'd like to retire to a tropical island in the South Pacific, but his wife _____ .

19. They'll not be at their daughter's graduation, and _____ we at ours.

20. Everyone in the class is ready to take a break, and _____ I.

score _____ (5 points each)

REVIEW QUIZ P   tag questions

Fill in the blanks with appropriate words. Observe either a formal or informal style.

Examples: a. I'm not being crossed up by someone, *am I?*

b. You haven't got a hobby, *have you?*

1. She's being given the good news about her husband now, _____ ?

2. Not everyone in the class has finished the quiz, _____?

3. Coach, I'm going to be able to play in the next half of the game, _____ _____?

4. This needs a little bit more salt, _____?

5. They'd better watch out for card sharks (professional gamblers) at that gambling casino, _____?

6. Let's make a toast to our great country, _____?

7. These cost less than those, _____?

8. Your Excellency, you'd like to be introduced to the Prime Minister now, _____?

9. She's recently been given a promotion and raise, _____?

10. The Smiths hardly ever entertain businesspeople at their home, _____ _____?

11. Sandra shouldn't always snoop into other people's private affairs, _____ _____?

12. You'd rather sit down than stand up, _____?

13. Harriet, there's no reason for putting me down like that, _____ ____?

14. When I said that, I wasn't putting my foot in my mouth, _____ ____?

15. She's got a reason for being so late to class, _____?

16. He'll always be living with his family on the farm, _____?

17. I'm never going to be able to remember the combination for this lock, ____ _____?

18. You've seldom had to work very hard since you started at that company, _____?

19. You have to have a good excuse to give to your teacher, _____ ____?

20. We're now going to be able to take a break, _____?

QUIZ 170 "X article" versus *the*

handbook p. 151

Fill in each blank with <u>the</u> *or "X."*

Examples: a. A strange man broke into our house the other evening. My wife saw him and screamed, and then <u>the</u> man jumped out of the window and fled into the night.

b. All her husband, a very successful banker, thinks about is <u>X</u> money.

1. Los Angeles, _____ largest city in the state of California, is my hometown.

2. How beautiful _____ air feels today—how fresh it smells!

3. A: Yes, son, _____ water cannot flow uphill. B: But the Nile River flows up, Daddy.

4. Even though _____ material in this report is complicated, it shouldn't be too difficult to figure out.

5. _____ Catholicism is the official religion of Spain.

6. _____ children often believe that Santa Claus lives at the North Pole.

7. _____ love of money is the root of all evil. (old saying)

8. He's got to go to _____ dentist's and have a lot of dental work done.

9. _____ money can't buy you love, Mr. Scrooge—why are you always wanting to make more and more of it? Life is too short.

10. _____ Christianity is the major religion of the West.

score _____ (5 points each blank)

QUIZ 171 "X article" versus *the*; geographic names

handbook p. 153

Fill in the blanks with <u>the</u> *or "X."*

Examples: a. Bombay, one of Asia's greatest port cities, is on <u>the</u> Arabian Sea; it's the gateway to <u>X</u> India.

b. *The* Equator runs through three countries of <u>X</u> South America.

1. _____ Hague is the de facto (actual) capital of _____ Netherlands.

2. _____ Khartoum, the capital of _____ Sudan, is located at a point on the map where the White Nile meets the Blue.

3. _____ Canary Islands, which lie off _____ northeastern coast of Africa, comprise two provinces of Spain.

4. Manila is the largest city and former capital of _____ Philippines; it is situated on _____ Luzon Island.

5. _____ Bay of Biscay is an inlet of the Atlantic Ocean bordered on the south by Spain and on the east by _____ France.

6. _____ Biscayne Bay is an inlet of the Atlantic Ocean, 40 miles long and from two to ten miles wide, along the southeastern coast of _____ Florida.

7. _____ Kathmandu is the capital of _____ Nepal, the only Hindu kingdom in the world today.

8. _____ Pretoria is the capital of _____ Union of South Africa, the richest country in Africa and one whose government is one of the most criticized in the world today.

9. Managua, the capital of _____ Nicaragua, is in _____ Central America.

10. Have you ever been to _____ Lake Titicaca? It's high up in the Andes Mountains (more than 12,000 feet) and between Peru and _____ Bolivia.

score _____ (5 points each blank)

QUIZ 172 "X article" versus *the;* more place names and other uses of *the*

handbook p. 154

Put in each blank the or "X."

Examples: a. X Islam is the major religion in *the* Middle East.

b. Look how full *the* moon is tonight! It goes into an eclipse at X midnight.

1. Winston Churchill (1874–1965) once said that _____ sun would never set on _____ British Empire. He turned out to be wrong.

2. _____ Hudson Bay, which covers a large area of the northern part of Canada, is always frozen over in _____ winter.

3. At the dawn of the revolution, _____ Shah of _____ Iran left his country for the last time.

4. Their son is studying at _____ University of North Carolina at Chapel Hill, and their daughter has just recently enrolled in _____ Cornell University at Ithaca, New York.

5. _____ Sears Tower in Chicago, Illinois, is _____ highest building (110 stories) in the world.

6. How nice it is to go bicycle riding in _____ Central Park in _____ New York!

7. _____ Metropolitan Museum of Art is on _____ Fifth Avenue at 79th Street.

8. Are we going to meet at _____ noon, the usual time, or later in _____ afternoon?

9. While he's looking for a full-time job, for _____ time being he's writing articles for _____ *New York Times*.

10. When I was in _____ Boy Scouts, I used to play _____ trombone in a band.

score _____

QUIZ 173   the comparative degree of adjectives

handbook p. 156

Supply in each blank an appropriate adjective in its comparative degree. Use each adjective only once.

big	far	good	hot
darling	fun	handsome	important
famous	funny	honest	low

Examples: a. In area, Canada is much *bigger than* the United States, but its population is much, much smaller.

b. Nothing in our lives is *more important than* good health.

1. Is the air anywhere _____ the air here in our mountain village?

2. No one is _____ my father, but even he sometimes tells a little fib (lie).

3. Could anywhere else have been _____ Hong Kong was on our vacation last year?

4. Hello, little baby. Can anyone in the world be _____ you?

5. Not many places can be _____ Saudi Arabia, where my father, an engineer, once worked out in the desert for several years.

6. Connie Blackwell thinks Rock Turner, her new boyfriend, is _____ _____ any other man at the university, and so do all her girlfriends, who are a little jealous.

7. The price of rice now is much _____ it was last year at this time.

8. From New York, Cairo is just a little bit _____ Buenos Aires.

9. Because Carlotta Carmel is a popular and successful television star, she is _____ her husband, who is just a hard-working businessman who also manages Carlotta's career.

10. Yes, I've often laughed at old Sam Black's stories about our town in earlier days—they're always _____ anyone else's.

score _____

QUIZ 174   *even* with the comparative degree of adjectives

handbook p. 160

Place in each blank an appropriate adjective with <u>even</u> in the comparative degree. Add <u>than</u> if necessary.

bad	cute	few	impressive
childish	easy	friendly	narrow
clever	fast	funny	wealthy

Examples: a. Yesterday's sunset was marvelous (what fabulous sunsets they have in this part of Africa!), but this evening's is even *more impressive than* last night's.

   b. Yes, the Germans have some very fast trains, and so do the Japanese, but the French have some now that are even *faster*.

1. She's always friendly to me when I see her, but her husband is even _____ _____ . He's not quite so shy as she is.

2. Ladies and Gentlemen, you may think the streets in this part of Cairo are not very wide; you must come to the part of the city where I live. The streets are even _____ these.

3. Terry is cute, but Carrie, his twin sister, is even _____ he.

4. His writing is not particularly good, and his speech is even _____ _____ .

5. Peter, your first joke was funny, but this last one was even _____ _____ .

6. G. M. Gross, Jr., is rich, but G. M. Gross, Sr. is even _____ .

7. Cindy Jones often acts like a child (she's almost 17), but Andy, her twin brother, is very often even _____ Cindy.

8. This is a good procedure to follow, and it isn't too difficult, but the other is even _____ .

9. Constance Dowling knows only five or so people in this town, and her husband knows even _____ she does.

10. A dog can be very clever, but a fox can be even _____ .

QUIZ 175   less versus *fewer*

handbook p. 160

Write in each blank <u>less</u> or <u>fewer</u>.

Examples: a. Because of the new computers in our office, more work is being done by <u>*fewer*</u> workers in <u>*less*</u> time.

b. Yes, we finally got rid of the old jalopy. The car we're now driving burns much <u>less</u> gas and requires far <u>*fewer*</u> repairs.

1. There were _____ people at the last meeting, but there was _____ boredom.

2. His roommate is smoking _____ cigarettes these days, and he's also drinking _____ alcohol; he's finally beginning to smarten up.

3. We find we're having to spend _____ time on our projects now, and we're making _____ mistakes; consequently, we're making much higher profits and the company is back up on its feet again.

4. Yes, indeed, there are _____ workers on the production line now, and there is better quality control, but we have _____ business.

5. I hear your actress friend, Carmelita Muchacha, hasn't been working much recently. Yes, she isn't performing on the stage now so much as she was, and she's making far _____ appearances on television, and, naturally, she's earning _____ money. She just asked me to lend her some the other day, in fact.

QUIZ 176   *more versus less*

handbook p. 160

Put in each blank *less* + an adjective, *more* + an adjective, or an adjective + *er*.

ambitious	comfortable	exact	important
cheap	complicated	expensive	intelligent
clever	emotional	handsome	shallow
cool			

Examples:
a. My neighbor finds that his water bed is *less comfortable* than the ordinary bed he used to have. He says his back aches every morning when he gets up.

b. Mr. Atwell, the son, is much *more intelligent* than Mr. Atwell, the father, but he doesn't have any horse sense (common sense).

c. No, this ice cream isn't necessarily better than the other kind, but it's *cheaper*.

1. Children, please swim at this end of the pool—it's _____.

2. Professor Romanoff is a brilliant scientist; however, his mind is _____ than Professor Anashkin's, who is the greater scientist of the two.

3. Many people feel that men are _____ than women, but I don't think so. Society just allows women to show their feelings more openly than it does men.

4. A person I know says he finds religion is _____ to him now than it was when he was younger and interested only in having a good time.

5. As people grow older, they sometimes become _____ than they were and lose interest in life.

6. My nephew is _____ than my niece, but he doesn't do as well as she does at school, nor does he have so pleasant a personality.

7. Yes, Ma'am, this is _____ than that, but it won't last you so long.

8. Yes, Steve Graves is _____ than Clint Astor, but Astor is a better actor.

9. Professor Clark's explanation is better than Professor Waldheim's—his is _____ and not so clear.

10. Today is _____ than yesterday, but it's warmer than it was the day before.

name _____   score _____

QUIZ 177   the superlative degree of adjectives
handbook p. 161

Fill in each blank with an appropriate adjective in its superlative degree. Use each adjective only once.

bad	exciting	high	shallow
clever	friendly	honest	short
direct	fun	little	wide

Examples: a. The police are not always the *most honest* people in town, are they?

b. The *shortest* distance between two points is a straight line.

1. Ladies and Gentlemen, we're now traveling on the Rio de la Plata, a river which extends 225 miles between Argentina and Uruguay; it is the _____ _____ river in the world.

2. Money is the _____ of a rich man's worries (if he's not losing it).

3. Yes, La Paz, Bolivia, is the _____ city in South America. While you're here you must go to Lake Titicaca; it's only thirty miles away. Why don't you spend a day there?

4. That way to get to the mountains is the fastest way as shown on the map, but, as you shall soon find out, the fastest way is not always the _____ _____ , nor is it always the best.

5. Tell me, Barby, of all the games you can play, which one is the _____ _____ ?

6. Cigarettes are one of the _____ things for your health. You must give them up.

7. Sky diving is one of the _____ (and dangerous) sports that I know of.

8. Jack and Jill, please wade and play in the _____ part of the pool; it's the safest and I don't want you to go in over your heads.

9. Yes, Barbara Benson may be one of the _____ artists in this studio, but she certainly isn't one of the most productive.

10. The people who live in this part of the country are some of the _____ _____ people I have ever met in my many years of travel.

REVIEW QUIZ Q   the comparative degree versus the superlative degree

Write in each blank an appropriate adjective in its comparative or superlative degree.

bad	curious	good
big	exact	handsome
clever	far	recent

Examples: a. *The cleverest* salespeople in my company make the highest commissions; however, they're not always the most honest people in town.

b. Professor Marconi's explanations are usually *more exact than* the teaching assistant's, but they're not so interesting.

1. Everyone says our son is _____ young man in town, and his father and I must agree with them; he's as nice as he's good-looking, too.

2. The day that Christopher Roberts entered prison for a crime he had never committed was _____ day of his long and eventful life. Fortunately, he was eventually found innocent and set free.

3. Oh, this looks good. Nothing is _____ on a cold day than a bowl of hot soup.

4. He thinks he made one of _____ mistakes in his life when he got a divorce, and his former wife feels the same way.

5. No one in the office is _____ my boss—he's really got a lot of intelligence and a quick mind.

6. Today's news from the war zone is _____ it was yesterday; we were forced to retreat another five miles.

7. Tabby, get out of that box. You're probably _____ cat I've ever seen.

8. Miss Brooks, is the planet Mercury _____ from the sun than the earth is?

9. Here it is, _____ news from the Middle East. The situation there hasn't gotten much better, has it?

10. Yes, Sir, there are other radios more expensive than this one, and we sell them, but the most expensive does not always mean _____. There is another reason you should buy this radio; we manufacture it ourselves.

name _____ score _____

QUIZ 178 the comparison of equality
handbook p. 162

Write in each blank <u>as</u> or <u>so</u> + an adjective + <u>as</u>.

aggressive	delicious	intelligent	tough
ambitious	eager	little	young
bitter	exact	tender	

Examples: a. "You're <u>*as young as*</u> you feel," my kind old doctor is always telling me.

            b. Even though the great actress Margo Young is no longer <u>*so young as*</u> she was, she still looks like a million dollars when she appears on the stage.

1. This kind of chocolate isn't _____ the other kind—it's much sweeter.

2. Veronica Lane has got an interesting job, but she makes _____ _____ I do, and that's not much these days.

3. I'm afraid my steak isn't _____ yours. Have you got a sharper knife for me to use?

4. Elliot Chase is _____ anyone else at the top in his company. He wants success, fame, and power, and he'll have them all—he's ruthless.

5. Miss, I'm sorry (I really don't want to complain), but this veal chop is not very good—it's _____ a piece of old shoe leather.

6. The person who does my income taxes every year isn't always _____ she is fast; I'm looking for another one to go to.

7. I'm _____ you are to go on a vacation; I haven't had one for more than three years. I haven't even been able to have Christmas Day off.

8. Oh, Beverly, Duane Travers is such a wonderful guy, and he's just _____ _____ he is handsome; I think I'm falling in love with him, but he doesn't even know I exist.

9. Dorothy is never _____ Archie, her twin brother, nor is she ever so selfish.

10. This food doesn't taste _____ it looks; in fact, I'm going to complain.

QUIZ 179   the comparison of equality versus the comparative degree; *the* with adjectives and adverbs in the comparative degree

handbook p. 163

Write in each blank an adjective in its appropriate form.

amusing	good	little	rich
bad	hungry	merry	stubborn
few	large	much	

Examples: a. A horse isn't <u>so stubborn</u> as a mule.

   b. My grandpa is <u>more stubborn</u> than a mule; he won't budge an inch (he's always right).

1. Yes, Conway Arthur's stories and jokes are always _____ than anyone else's, but they never seem to come to an end.

2. Never have I been _____ as I am right now. I could eat a horse.

3. Won't you all please come to my party tonight? The more, the _____ _____ .

4. With taxes the way they are these days, it seems the more money I make, the _____ I have.

5. There are _____ students in her class than mine, but she doesn't like the teacher, nor does she care much for the textbook they're using.

6. Would you like to have a lot of chocolate sauce on your ice cream, young man? Please, the more, the _____ .

7. Japan is approximately _____ as the state of California.

8. Our son's table manners are _____ than his sister's, but at least he washes his hands and face before he comes to the table.

9. Old Mr. Miser has a lot of money; the older he gets, the _____ _____ he becomes. He never spends a dime.

10. I love peanuts, but the more I eat, the _____ I want, so I don't eat them much; they're also very fattening.

QUIZ 180   certain figures of speech with *as . . . as*

handbook p. 163

Place in each blank an appropriate adjective.

bright	innocent	quiet	strong
clever	pale	sober	stubborn
dark	poor	stingy	

Example: a. What a healthy man your grandfather is! Yes, he's still as *strong* as an ox.

1. Yes, don't worry about a thing. I've got a lawyer who's as _____ as a fox.

2. The children were being as _____ as a mouse when they were upstairs in the attic, but I think they were up to something (being naughty).

3. Officer, my son didn't steal any apples off the neighbor's tree. Why, Officer, my boy is as _____ as a lamb—he couldn't hurt a fly.

4. Oh, no, Professor Higgins never drinks alcohol, nor does he ever smoke. He disapproves of such things. He's always as _____ as a judge—at least he is in public.

5. When Priscilla came to after she'd fainted, she was as _____ as a ghost. Later, she was perspiring heavily and had sporadic chills.

6. Anything that Alex Craft buys is the cheapest thing in the store, and he refuses to fix up his apartment at all (he sits on orange crates); he's as _____ as an old miser; he won't spend a dime.

7. On our walks during the day in Venice, many of the old alleys and canals were almost as _____ as night.

8. When we were in the north of Norway last summer, very often at midnight it was almost as _____ as day.

9. The little old lady upstairs in the front, Mrs. Jacobs, is as _____ as a church mouse, and she hasn't got anyone to look after her except for her neighbors.

10. My grandfather is as _____ as a mule; he won't retire, and he's 83 years old.

REVIEW QUIZ R   the comparative and superlative degrees and
as . . . as

Write in each blank an adjective in its appropriate form.

bad	fat	good	nervous
close	fun	lazy	romantic
famous	funny	little	wealthy

Examples: a. Who is *the most famous* person in the world today?

b. Because we feed her too much, our cat is much *fatter* than yours; she's also lazier.

c. People are not always *so good* as they appear—isn't that true, Mr. Nero?

1. Besides the sun, _____ star to the earth is sixteen million light years away.

2. Saudi Arabia is _____ country in the Middle East, and one of the most powerful.

3. The day isn't _____ as the night, but the day is less dangerous.

4. At times that restaurant can be the best in town or _____ —it depends on the cook's mood and how sober he is.

5. Traveling with a friend is _____ than taking a trip alone, but it's not always so easy to find a person to travel with.

6. Even though the male lion is one of _____ animals on the plains of Africa, he is still called the King of the Jungle.

7. The pollution in our town isn't _____ as it used to be, and crime and corruption have become less serious problems; things are looking up (getting better).

8. That clown is much _____ than the others, but I find he makes me feel a little sad and homesick.

9. Hope Hamilton wants to make the most amount of money for _____ _____ amount of work.

10. The patient is never _____ as she used to be, nor is she ever so hostile, but she is still a very sick woman and needs psychiatric care.

QUIZ 181   contrast and similarity; *same*

handbook p. 164

Fill in each blank with an appropriate noun.

age	height	personality	size	weight
color	language	pronunciation	weather	width
depth	length	quality		

Examples: a. This is the same price as that, but it's not the same *quality*.

b. Our swimming pool is about the same *length* as our neighbors', but it's not quite the same *depth*.

1. Yes, the English speak the same _____ as the Americans, but their _____ and intonation isn't the same.

2. She's almost the same _____ as I am, but she looks older than I do, doesn't she?

3. The _____ in California is about the same as that in my hometown, but not much else is the same.

4. I'm the same _____ and _____ as my father, and we have the same _____ .

5. Yes, young man, in a square room the _____ is exactly the same as the _____ .

6. My eyes are almost the same _____ as yours, but yours are a darker blue.

7. My left foot is exactly the same _____ as my right foot, I think.

8. My mother is about the same _____ as my roommate, but my roommate is much heavier.

9. My girlfriend's hair is about the same _____ as your girlfriend's, but it's not the same _____ .

10. He and I are carrying exactly the same _____ , but he's almost a foot taller than I am.

QUIZ 182   the comparison of adverbs

handbook p. 165

Write in each blank an adverb in its appropriate form.

bad	easy	graceful	neat
beautiful	fast	hard	reckless
careful	fluent	late	slow
early	good	long	smooth

Examples: a. He's a lucky fellow—he makes friends *more easily than* anyone else I know.

b. No one in town drives *so recklessly* as my neighbor's son; he'll kill himself someday.

c. Yes, Ching Ling Wu does her assignments *the best* of all the students.

1. Who in this class can speak English _____ the teacher?

2. Tony Arden dances _____ Yolanda, doesn't he?

3. Orlando Perez always does a quiz more quickly than the other students, but he never gets a high score. He should try to go _____ .

4. Who in your family works _____ ?

5. Emiko Hiro doesn't speak English _____ her boyfriend, Taka, but she always has more interesting things to say.

6. Juanita del Rio always does her homework _____ she can.

7. Grandpa always drives _____ than Grandma—she likes speed.

8. Did you arrive at the meeting _____ than you had planned?

9. Without a doubt, Angelina Perutti writes _____ of all the students in the class; she has great talent. She wants to be a journalist.

10. She doesn't sew _____ she knits; she doesn't like to work on a sewing machine.

QUIZ 183   gerunds and gerund phrases as subjects

handbook p. 166

Fill in the blanks with appropriate gerunds made out of the base forms in the following list.

break down	cut out	kick out of	put by
call on	deal with	lock up	put off
check out of	get up	look after	put up with
count on			

Examples: a. Our car's _breaking down_ delayed us by several hours, but we did get there.

b. _Being kicked out of_ that country wasn't an easy experience for Charles Cutter even though he was a journalist and had been in some tough situations before.

c. (have to) _Having to deal with_ those dishonest businesspeople wasn't pleasant.

1. _____ by the Prime Minister herself was an exciting experience for us.

2. (have to) _____ early in the morning is a lousy (bad) way to begin a Sunday, isn't it?

3. _____ in jail for something that he hadn't done was a horrifying experience for young Eddie Stone. He says he thought he would never get out.

4. Cynthia, _____ until tomorrow what you can do today is being foolish.

5. (have to) Mrs. Patterson, _____ your demanding boss is something that I could never do. I don't see how you can do it.

6. _____ smoking was one of the hardest things I'd ever had to do, but now I feel a thousand times better.

7. (have to) Yes, I agree, _____ your parents for money to live on isn't always so easy. I'd rather be financially independent, but I'm not yet.

8. Dear, _____ by you while I'm convalescing is making me feel better.

9. (have to) Sir, _____ this hotel so early in the morning is a great inconvenience for my husband and me.

10. _____ a little bit of money once a month, Mr. and Mrs. Johnson, is a good idea, and our bank offers several savings plans which I am sure will suit your needs.

QUIZ 184   gerunds as objects of certain verbs
handbook p. 167

Write an appropriate gerund in each blank.

call off	fill up	move over	take advantage of
chop up	keep away from	put down	take over
do over	lock out of	show off	tell off
drop out of			

Examples: a. (have to) Who enjoys *having to do over* a composition more than three times?

b. Please stop *showing off*, Sam; we all know how clever you are.

c. John, I really dislike *being put down* by you, one of my oldest friends.

1. Mrs. Sands, would you mind _____ my class while I go to the principal's office for a few minutes?

2. I can tell you I didn't enjoy _____ my apartment.

3. Would you mind _____ my glass with some more soda, please?

4. (have to) She detests _____ candy and other sweets, but she's got to—sugar is too fattening, and she's on a strict diet.

5. I try to avoid _____ by people at work, but sometimes it's almost impossible not to be.

6. I don't recommend your _____ school, Miss Taylor; you need a college education to get ahead in the world today.

7. The director has suggested _____ the meeting, but I don't think it's wise—it had better be just postponed.

8. I can tell you I don't enjoy _____ onions; it always makes me cry.

9. Would you mind _____ a bit in the pew so that I may sit down?

10. No, I didn't mind _____ by my boss; I never listen to him anyway. His bark is louder than his bite. (old saying)

name _____   score _____

QUIZ 185   gerund versus infinitive
handbook p. 168

Write an appropriate gerund in each blank. If an infinitive is also appropriate, write the abbreviation inf. alongside the gerund.

call up	make up	show off	stand up for
lie down	pick on	show up	take care of
listen in on	put off	stand up	take for granted

Examples: a. I couldn't resist *lying down* on that beautiful bed on display in the store.

b. Yes, Your Honor, I will continue *inf. standing up for* Franklin Carter; he's a good man and is innocent of the crime he's been accused of.

1. Would you mind _____ this job until tomorrow, or would you rather get it over with and out of the way today?

2. Rod, please don't neglect _____ your health. It's your most precious possession, so treat it as such.

3. Yes, the thief has finally admitted _____ that alibi about his being at his mother's house while the crime was taking place.

4. I cannot bear _____ ; it's one of the rudest things one person can do to another.

5. Mr. James, would you mind _____ a little bit early for class tomorrow? I'd like to go over your last composition with you.

6. She can no longer tolerate _____ by her roommate; she's moving out of the apartment and setting herself up somewhere else.

7. Have you finished _____ yet, young man? May your father and I now continue the conversation which you so rudely interrupted?

8. Mr. King, I cannot stand _____ . I'm a human being, too.

9. (have to) I don't like _____ my girlfriend to call off our date. She was looking forward to it as well as I was, but I have to work overtime this evening.

10. Yes, my secretary denies _____ my private phone calls, and I don't think that she does—it's just my wild imagination.

QUIZ 186   gerunds and gerund phrases as objects of prepositions
handbook p. 168

Fill in each blank with an appropriate gerund.

blow up	do	give	look after	promote	take care of	transfer
call down	find	kidnap	make	stand up for	take off	wait on
chew	find out	lie	marry	steal	take over	wear

Examples: a. Let's not show up at the meeting late; I'm afraid of *being called down* by our boss.

b. I don't believe in *giving* children everything they ask for—it spoils them.

1. She always insists on _____ first—she's a difficult customer.

2. Yes, I'm very interested in _____ where that person lives.

3. She's not really looking forward to _____ ; she wants to stay single.

4. Chris Adams is incapable of _____ —he's too honest.

5. Our little girl is responsible for _____ the canary and its cage.

6. The radio says the terrorists have been found guilty of _____ the radio station.

7. Don't worry about _____ a mistake in a quiz. You learn through your mistakes.

8. I've been thinking about _____ out of this department; I need a change.

9. Do you ever get tired of _____ homework?

10. I was planning on _____ to a new position, but I wasn't, so I quit.

11. Their company is interested in _____ ours—they're a big monopoly.

12. I suspect my neighbor of _____ fertilizer out of my garage.

13. The bad weather prevented us from _____ . The airport was fogged in (covered with fog).

14. The woman has been accused of _____ the millionaire's child.

15. Children, why don't you cut out _____ gum? It's not good for your teeth.

16. Fortunately, Mr. Popov has finally succeeded in _____ the right woman for a wife.

17. Thank you for _____ me in court. I really needed your support.

18. Mr. Wise, you're a genius. You're capable of _____ anything.

19. Thank you, Mr. Harrison, for _____ my garden while I was away.

20. He went outside without _____ a jacket and caught a nasty (bad) cold.

score _____

QUIZ 187 gerunds and gerund phrases as objects of prepositions; negative gerund phrases

handbook p. 169

Write in each blank a preposition (+ _not_) + a gerund.

about	from	on	be	go	make	show up
at	in	to	find	invite	reelect	take advantage of
for	of		get out of	kidnap	serve	

Examples: a. Jack Cranston is afraid _of not being reelected_ ; that's why he's campaigning so hard now.

b. Sir, I insist _on being served_ at once; I'm one of your store's best customers.

1. I suspect my business partner _____ completely honest. Never have I quite trusted him.

2. We're looking forward _____ at your graduation; we'll be so proud.

3. Mr. Post, thank you _____ my poor financial situation during our negotiations. You're a real gentleman, Sir.

4. I was angry _____ to my best friend's birthday party. Didn't she want me to be there?

5. My bad cold prevented me _____ bed yesterday.

6. I'm thinking _____ to church today; I'd rather sleep a few more hours.

7. At last! We've finally succeeded _____ an apartment that we can afford.

8. Don't worry _____ at the meeting tomorrow—I'll tell you all about it tomorrow evening.

9. T. W. Towers, the billionaire, is afraid _____ ; that's why he's got so many bodyguards around him all the time.

10. Sir, I'm interested _____ money. Have you got any good ideas?

QUIZ 188   gerunds in time phrases
handbook p. 169

Put an appropriate gerund in each blank.

bail out of	keep away from	put on	turn on
carry out	lock up	tow away	warm up
drop out of	move out of	turn down	work out

Examples: a. Until *being turned down* by Maria, James had never been rejected by a woman before.

   b. She looked like a million dollars after *putting on* the diamond necklace.

1. Before _____ the leftover food, wrap it up in tinfoil.

2. Darn it! My car was damaged while _____ by the police.

3. Since _____ school, Matt has been doing nothing but looking for a job.

4. After _____ cigarettes for several months, he picked up the habit again. Will he ever be able to give them up?

5. After _____ jail, the man fled the country and has never been seen since.

6. After _____ in the gym, why don't you go for a swim in the lake?

7. Before _____ any electrical equipment, be sure your hands are dry.

8. Since _____ his parents' house, he has become a happier young man; he loves his new independence.

9. After _____ the general's orders, the colonel felt he'd made a mistake.

10. After _____ in a cage for more than five years, the tiger had become quite tame.

QUIZ 189   worth, rather than, and instead of

handbook p. 169

Put an appropriate gerund in each blank.

argue over	cut down on	fix up	put off
blow up about	deal with	get out of	rely on
chop up	eat out	lay off	take up
cry over			

Examples: a. It's not worth <u>dealing with</u> those people in business—they always get the best deal.

b. Rather than <u>getting out of</u> the office late, why don't we finish up this work now?

c. Instead of <u>relying on</u> the phone, why don't you go to the airline office yourself?

1. Mr. Dickens, this matter isn't worth _____ —we'll never get anywhere.

2. Rather than _____ cigarettes, Sir, why don't you just give them up?

3. Instead of _____ tonight, let's warm up some leftovers at home.

4. Rather than _____ this meeting, why don't we just call it off?

5. This old building isn't worth _____ ; it had better be torn down.

6. Instead of _____ these workers, why don't we just cut their hours?

7. Why don't you stop worrying about the mistakes you've made. They're not worth _____ . No use crying over spilled milk. (old saying)

8. Instead of _____ this problem with a lawyer, let's go directly to our neighbor and complain.

9. Why are you getting so upset? It's not such a serious problem—it's not worth _____ .

10. Rather than _____ these potatoes for the salad, it might be better to slice them.

QUIZ 190   be used to and get used to

handbook p. 170

Supply appropriate gerunds in the blanks.

bawl out	eat out	go out with	show up
call down	fill out	lock up	take for granted
clean up	get up	look after	wait on

Examples: a. That poor little monkey is unhappy—he's not used to *being locked up* in a cage.

b. Michael Chan likes the store he works in, but he can't get used to *waiting on* people.

1. The children are excited about being in this restaurant; they're not used to

   _____ .

2. Tom, I must tell you that I'm not used to _____ , so stop doing it.

3. Frank is only eighteen, and he still isn't used to _____ girls, but he's getting used to it fast.

4. Listen, Ma'am, I'm not used to _____ by anyone, so you'd better watch your tongue.

5. Mr. Adams, you're wonderful to me; I'm not used to _____ _____ by such a good nurse.

6. Listen, Butch, you've just got to get used to _____ your bedroom every day; it's your room, and you should learn how to take care of it yourself.

7. I think the students need some more help; they're not used to _____ _____ such complicated forms as these.

8. Mohammed Abdul, a new student in the class, is doing better than Maria Gucci is, and I think she's annoyed; she's not used to _____

9. I can't get used to _____ early in the morning; I'm trying to get my morning classes changed to the afternoon.

10. Listen, Boss, I'm not used to _____ —how dare you talk to me like that! You're not my master, nor am I your slave.

QUIZ 191   used to + a base form

handbook p. 170

Fill in the blanks with appropriate verb phrases using *used to*. Provide subjects when needed.

John	be	drive	live	stand up for
people	deliver	get	run out of	wait on
you	do	go		

Examples: a. What kind of car *did you use to drive* before you bought your Rolls-Royce?

b. During the war when supplies were scarce, we *used to run out of* critical raw materials all the time.

1. _____ in a dormitory when you were at the university?

2. In the beginning of their marriage, his wife _____ him all the time—but now they treat each other as equals.

3. How _____ to work before he started taking the bus?

4. My roommate _____ such an energetic person, but now he's always involved in and working hard on some kind of project.

5. What _____ to amuse themselves before they had television?

6. Mail _____ twice a day, but the post office has cut it down to only one delivery a day. Service isn't what it used to be.

7. Mr. Smith, you were once the kind of man who _____ _____ everything that was good and decent. Now your only interest is fame, success, and money; you're not the man you used to be.

8. _____ swimming a lot in the summertime when you were younger? I always did—our house was located right on a lake.

9. Bob and Mary _____ happy together, but they went to a marriage counselor who helped them learn how to get along better with each other.

10. _____ , when you were a child, as clever as you are now?

QUIZ 192   -ing forms following sense perception verbs

handbook p. 171

Write in each blank an appropriate -ing form.

bear	crawl over	have	nest
build	give	kick	throw
burn	grab	make	try

Examples: a. The teacher saw, out of the corner of his eye, someone *trying* to pass a note to someone else.

            b. I was standing in a dark corridor (I couldn't see a thing) when I suddenly felt a hand *grabbing* my arm. I was frightened out of my wits.

1. Yes, I hear some people _____ a conversation in the other room, but I don't know who they are—I don't recognize the voices.

2. When I saw the dog on the street _____ by a big man, I became angry and tried to make the man stop (he turned out to be the dog's owner).

3. What are you doing, Professor? . . . I'm observing these ants _____ a hill.

4. When you were at the crafts fair, did you watch the pottery _____ at the ceramics exhibition?

5. While I was in the park, I amused myself by watching some young people _____ Frisbees.

6. While I was driving to work, I saw my boss _____ a speeding ticket at the intersection of Fifth Avenue and 53rd Street.

7. Don't you smell something in the kitchen _____ ?

8. Have you ever seen a baby _____ ? It must be a wonderful thing to see.

9. While I was walking through the park on my way home from work, I noticed some new birds _____ in the big maple tree that stands near the merry-go-round.

10. While I was standing in the bathroom, I suddenly felt something _____ my foot.

QUIZ 193   -ing versus -ed adjectives

handbook p. 172

Write in each blank the _-ing_ or _-ed_ adjective form of the verb given in the parentheses.

Examples: a. (interest) Yes, I'm very _interested_ in grammar—I find it a fascinating subject.

b. (bore) Some students in my class, however, find it a little _boring_.

1. (disappoint) Jerry Watson is very _____; he's not getting Christmas Day off. He's even going to have to work overtime.

2. (develop) When Tazuko Tanaka went to Nigeria, it was the first time she'd ever been in a _____ country; it was a brand new experience for her.

3. (tire) Last Monday was such a _____ day; I didn't have a moment to sit down all day long. My boss wouldn't leave me alone; he kept picking on me.

4. (bore) How _____ I am! This is a terrible movie—let's walk out.

5. (develop) What country, do you think, is one of the most _____ countries in the world today? And why have the people of that country been so successful?

6. (frustrate) Darn it! This project has certainly been _____; I'm constantly making stupid mistakes.

7. (bore) Some people find Fatima Al-Saif a _____ person, but I find she always has something interesting to say.

8. (disappoint) How _____ these sales figures are! We were hoping for bigger sales than ever this year.

9. (satisfy) Jason Macmillan is a _____ man at last—he's finally made a million dollars. He's always wanted to be a millionaire.

10. (bore) A: Mommy, I'm _____—I've got nothing to do. B: Ronnie, how can you be on such a beautiful day as this? Why don't you go out and play?

QUIZ 194   *make, let,* and *help*
handbook p. 173

Write in the blanks appropriate base forms. Provide objects when needed.

call up	put back together	stand out	him
help out	put on	take apart	it
iron out	run down	take off	them
leak out	squeeze in	turn off	you

Examples: a. Mr. Graves, please let me *help you out*—you really do need someone's assistance.

   b. Our neighbors across the street used to have a beautiful house, but they've let it *run down* so badly that it's becoming an eyesore on the block.

1. When this dining room table is assembled, it's too big to take through the front door; would you please help me _____ so we may take it through in pieces.

2. This decision, Ladies and Gentlemen, is highly confidential; I don't want any of you to let it _____ to the newspapers.

3. I know this bus is crowded, but please let me _____ ; you must be able to make room for one more.

4. I've taken this radio apart, and now I don't know where anything goes. Would you please help me _____ .

5. Oh, Mother, I hate this dress. Please don't make me _____ .

6. Please don't butt in. This is a disagreement between Richard and me and no one else—let the two of us _____ ourselves.

7. No, Father, I don't want to speak to Mr. Hanes; please don't make me _____ _____ .

8. I can't wear this red dress to the wedding; it will make me _____ too much. The bride should be getting all the attention, not her mother.

9. Mother, I love to listen to the radio while I'm doing my homework; please don't make me _____ .

10. I can't get these boots off my feet; would you please help me _____ _____ .

QUIZ 195   perfect participial phrases

handbook p. 173

Fill in the blanks with appropriate participial phrases.

be   expose   have   put down   see
eat   go over   mug   receive   study

Examples: a. <u>*Having been put down*</u> for many years by the cruel dictatorship, the people finally revolted.

b. <u>*Not having studied*</u> much, Henry really wasn't ready to take the final exam.

1. _____ and done everything that we wanted to see and do, we left New York and went on to Los Angeles.

2. _____ enough time to think about this situation, I haven't made a decision yet.

3. _____ at the scene of the crime made the woman an important witness, but she couldn't be found—she must have fled the country.

4. _____ much education, the poor man didn't know how to write his own name.

5. _____ your application for a job in this company, Mr. Jensen, I feel that this is not the job for you—you haven't got enough experience.

6. _____ any letters from him for several months, Bob and Anna were beginning to get worried about their son, who was traveling somewhere in Asia.

7. _____ there several times, Mr. Watson was afraid to walk on the street late at night in that part of town.

8. _____ to tragedy and hard times all her life, old Mary Hansen was ready to face any misfortune that might befall her.

9. _____ anything to drink for a week, the people lost in the desert were dying of thirst.

10. _____ anything yet (it was almost midnight), we were starving.

REVIEW QUIZ S

Circle the answer that is correct. Circle both choices if either answer is correct.

Example: a. Our TV isn't working ((right,) rightly), so we're going to the movies tonight.

b. How many copies of this book ((sold, were sold)) last year?

1. Never (*do*, *X*) I speak English much at home because my mother and father don't speak it.

2. Oh, yes, these shoes are (*more*, *X*) better than those; they're hand-made.

3. Yes, while I was standing in the corridor, I overheard Mr. Wilson (*to speak*, *speaking*) to your boss. They were talking about the promotion you are going to get.

4. A house is not (*a*, *an*) home.

5. I'm a good friend of yours, (*ain't*, *aren't*) I?

6. Would you mind (*to close*, *closing*) the window? It's getting a little cold in here.

7. What time did you (*lay*, *lie*) down for your nap yesterday afternoon?

8. Mr. Petersen, I suggest (*to change*, *changing*) a few things in this contract.

9. Rosemary is a woman's name, but it's also the name of (*a*, *an*,) herb.

10. Have you ever climbed to the top of (*the*, *X*) Eiffel Tower in Paris?

11. She's not a very good cook, but she (*does*, *X*) makes good apple pie.

12. How (*good*, *well*) this orange tastes! Would you like a piece?

13. The soprano at the concert last night had (*a*, *an*) unusual voice, didn't she?

14. He's not interested in that kind of job, and not one of us (*is*, *isn't*) either.

15. Our dog likes to eat this kind of pet food, but our cat doesn't like (*to*, *X*).

16. How beautifully Boris Maximov can (*to play*, *play*) the violin! He's going to be famous someday.

17. No, Sir, I don't want to have to force you (*to sign*, *sign*) this confession.

18. Never (*have*, *X*) I been studying so much as I have been since I started the course.

19. I want to go over to the park and (*to fly*, *fly*) my kite; the wind is perfect today.

20. We had (*a*, *an*) one-hour conference with the director, and we accomplished a great deal.

REVIEW QUIZ T

Write in each blank an appropriate form of the base form given in parentheses.

Examples: a. (shake) Don't you feel the earth *shaking?* It's an earthquake.

b. (love) Most everyone *loves* to take a vacation.

1. (take) His father let him _____ the family car when he went out with his friends.

2. (fix) Because it _____ , I'm not wearing my favorite watch.

3. (ride) I'm not used to _____ a bicycle in heavy city traffic.

4. (stop) Would you mind _____ at the store for a loaf of bread on your way home?

5. (be) They _____ married for seven years now, and they seem to be happy.

6. (tow away) Well! Dave, our car appears _____ . We must have been illegally parked.

7. (serve) The customer insists on _____ at once, so please hurry up.

8. (speak) He had to stop _____ to his lawyer on his way to work.

9. (lie) When I last saw the evening paper, it _____ on the sofa.

10. (quit) Barbara's dislike for her boss forced her _____ her job.

11. (guard) The police _____ that house twenty-four hours a day; it's an embassy.

12. (help) I must thank you for _____ me out so much on the last project.

13. (be) They _____ good friends ever since they met in Taipei five or six years ago.

14. (do) Please don't make me _____ something that I shouldn't do.

15. (be) Are you looking forward to _____ on the selection committee for Miss America?

16. (dance) I heard some people upstairs _____ all night long. What neighbors!

17. (call) Please don't postpone _____ your barber up to make an appointment.

18. (sign) My lawyer suggests _____ the contract at once without any delay.

19. (go) The boss let everyone in the office _____ home early yesterday afternoon.

20. (do) Your recent project for that company has been worth _____ , hasn't it?

179

name _____   score _____ (5 points each)

REVIEW QUIZ U

Write in each blank one word. Write an "X" in the blank if a word is not required. Contractions like don't and didn't count as one word.

Examples: a. _X_ though the days on the desert had become hot, the nights were still cool.

b. They live in a beautiful chalet high up _in_ the Swiss Alps.

1. About how _____ coffee do you drink every day?

2. _____ to the strike, no plane will be able to take off from this airport today.

3. His handwriting is bad, but mine is even _____ .

4. All of _____ Hudson Bay freezes over in the winter; it's far in the north.

5. What delicious wine this is! _____ you like some?

6. _____ I one of your best friends? Don't you trust me?

7. You'd _____ stop fooling around, young man, and get your homework done.

8. _____ be a nice day for the beach tomorrow—let's go.

9. Whose gloves are these? How beautiful _____ are!

10. He's not coming to the picnic, _____ does his wife want to be there.

11. Terry, I'd like you to sit _____ the third row today, please.

12. Let's take a little break, _____ we?

13. I want this top-secret information to be kept a secret between you and _____ .

14. They'd _____ be going out to the movies tonight, but they've got to work instead.

15. She was quite angry; she said not a word when she entered _____ the room.

16. Our daughter likes to play soccer, but our son doesn't like _____ .

17. I really am _____ sick to go to work today—I could never get out of bed.

18. Mom and Dad, please let me _____ out with Tom Drake. He's a very nice boy.

19. Yes, our daughter goes _____ school. She's in the second grade.

20. Yes, we can _____ on with the meeting, but we need some order here.

180

QUIZ 196   *so*, *such*, *such a*, and *such an*; adverbial *that* clauses
handbook p. 174

Write in each blank <u>so</u>, <u>such</u>, <u>such a</u>, or <u>such an</u>.

Examples: a. These are <u>such</u> delicious oysters that I can't resist ordering half a dozen more.

           b. Our son is <u>so</u> honest that he could never tell a lie.

1. Sandra was _____ angry at her landlord, she hung up on him.

2. This is _____ expensive perfume, Madam, that the store locks it up at night in a vault.

3. Janet and Bobby Baker always give _____ wonderful party that I'm usually the last one to leave.

4. It's _____ difficult research that it's driving Professor Park crazy.

5. Ladies and Gentlemen, the auction has begun. This is _____ unusual vase, I'd like the bidding to begin at three thousand dollars.

6. A: Oh, Mother, I have _____ ugly nose that I could cry. B: Now, dear, you've got a perfectly lovely nose. You shouldn't fret over (worry about) such things.

7. You've come up with _____ unique idea that I simply can't believe it.

8. Professor Clay always gives _____ marvelous lectures that I never miss one of his classes.

9. My girlfriend is _____ beautiful, I can't believe it.

10. The judge in this case, Ma'am, is _____ innocent man that a clever lawyer can sometimes take advantage of him.

QUIZ 197   clauses of purpose with *so that*

handbook p. 176

Fill in the blanks with appropriate verb phrases using can *(*could*),* may *(*might*), or* will *(*would*). Provide objects when needed.*

carry out	get rid of	lock out	pick up	herself
die	help	melt	put back together	it
fall behind	iron out	pass back	see	

Examples: a. You'd better put the ice cream in the freezer so that it *won't melt*.

b. Yes, during that time I had to study hard so that I *wouldn't fall behind*.

1. I've got to get home before three o'clock so I _____ my roommate to move a piano.

2. Grandma pinned the house keys to her dress so that she _____ _____ when she left the house.

3. Professor Robinson wants to correct this homework now so that he _____ _____ to the class tomorrow.

4. They're going to Burma so that they _____ some friends of theirs who live in Rangoon.

5. I had taken my alarm clock apart, and I had to find someone who knew about clocks so that I _____ .

6. This is a serious problem. I've got to talk it over with my lawyer so that it _____ properly once and for all (permanently).

7. We had to buy some insecticide so we _____ the insects that had invaded the apple orchard behind our house.

8. I've got to find a part-time job so that I _____ some extra money.

9. You must water these flowers every other day so that they _____ _____ .

10. The General always had to be around the camp so that his orders _____ _____ properly.

name _____ score _____

QUIZ 198   *in order* + an infinitive
handbook p. 177

Write in each blank an appropriate infinitive or gerund. Provide objects when needed.

blow away	chop up	pick up	take care of	her
break out	clear up	put off	taste of	it
call up	make up with	run away	thaw out	them

Examples: a. I've got to get to school by 3 o'clock in order *to pick up* the children.

b. They have to lock up their dog at night in order to prevent him from *running away*.

1. I've got to buy a good knife in order _____ vegetables.

2. You'd better wrap up those chopped onions when you put them in the refrigerator in order to prevent everything else from _____ onions.

3. We need to go to a good lawyer in order _____ these problems with our landlord.

4. I've got to put a paperweight on these papers in order to keep the wind from _____ .

5. Bill, have you got any change? I want to speak to my wife on the phone, and in order _____ , I've got to have a dime.

6. The government is going to impose martial law in order to prevent a revolution from _____ .

7. A: What shall I do about this rash on my leg, Doctor? B: Well, Mrs. Fraser, in order _____ , you've got to use this ointment three times a day, and don't let the rash get wet.

8. In order to keep this frozen meat from _____ , you'd better put it in the refrigerator.

9. In order _____ my wife, I'm taking these roses to her this evening—she was quite angry at me this morning.

10. In order _____ this meeting until next month, Ladies and Gentlemen, we've got to have special permission, so I suggest we just carry on.

183

QUIZ 199   despite and *in spite of*

handbook p. 178

Write appropriate verb phrases in the blanks.

| be | go out with | make out | wait on |
| check over | have | turn down | work out |

Examples: a. In spite of the fact she's worth millions of dollars, she lives like a hermit.

b. Despite the rainy weather, we *had* a wonderful vacation in Italy last year.

1. In spite of the heavy rains this spring, we _____ floods so far.

2. Despite the fact that Wanda Blair _____ Roger more than five times, he has still asked her to marry him again.

3. In spite of the fact they _____ by the best salesperson in the store, they wanted to have the manager come down and serve them personally.

4. Despite the fact the engine _____ very carefully before the plane took off, it broke down during the flight. They had to continue on with only three engines.

5. Despite her great intelligence (she's a genius), she _____ any common sense. She can't even deal with everyday problems at home.

6. In spite of the wonderful weather and good food and drinks, the picnic at the beach last Sunday _____ much of a success.

7. Despite her great beauty, Donna Bella Rolanda _____ as an actress, but she's still trying to be a star; she hasn't given up yet.

8. Mary Jane and I _____ each other a lot during that time in spite of the fact that we didn't have much in common (didn't have the same interests).

9. (never) Despite the fact that Tom _____ in a gym, he has the body of an athlete.

10. In spite of his great wealth, he _____ a happy man; he has no one to love and love him back.

QUIZ 200   adverbial *that* clauses after adjectives of feeling and emotion

handbook p. 178

Write appropriate verb phrases in the blanks.

deal with	fall in	introduce	make out
do	freeze over	lead	run around
do over	have	lock	slap
enter	improve		

Examples: a. She couldn't believe it. She was stunned that her sister *had slapped* her face.

b. He's positive he *'s doing* the right thing now; no one can change his mind.

c. I'm happy that all my friends *are making out* so well in life.

1. (already) When I went up north to Vermont in late October, I was surprised that the small lake behind my parents' house _____ .

2. I'm disgusted that the government officials _____ this difficulty without having to be bribed.

3. Before he died, my grandfather was content that he _____ _____ a good life.

4. When I got to work this morning, I was sure I _____ the door to my apartment, but I wasn't absolutely certain, so I had to go back home.

5. When I introduce Craig Hansen to my new girlfriend, he'll be jealous such a wonderful woman _____ love with me.

6. Yes, Sonny, when I met Franklin Delano Roosevelt, I was thrilled that I _____ to the President. I was so excited, in fact, that I forgot to shake his hand.

7. My husband and I are hopeful that our son _____ the university soon.

8. Oh, don't listen to him; he's just envious that you _____ _____ more money than he does.

9. (have to) I've just talked to Professor Andrews; I'm relieved that my composition _____ . I've got a lot of other homework to do.

10. Yes, the police caught the escaped convict this morning. Everyone in town is glad that he _____ free any longer.

QUIZ 201 future-possible real conditions; the simple present tense and its continuous form in *if* clauses

handbook p. 179

Put in each blank an appropriate verb phrase in either the simple present tense or its continuous form.

blow	get	make	run
elect	give	play	spank
fight	go off	promote	

Examples: a. You shouldn't laugh if a student *makes* a mistake.

b. If I'*m being promoted* to a higher position, I'll be getting a big raise.

1. If an examination _____ when you walk into the classroom, just go to the back of the room, sit down, and don't say a word.

2. If my child _____ by the teacher at school, I'll go and have a talk with the principal (director).

3. If the wind _____ this afternoon, we won't be able to go to the park and fly our kites.

4. Ladies and Gentlemen, nothing will be done about the problems in our country if I _____. Vote for me, and you'll all be better off.

5. If the power _____ , we won't be able to use all this equipment.

6. Bonnie Jane can't go out with the young man next door if her father _____ _____ his permission.

7. I'll take a bus tomorrow if the trains _____ because of a strike.

8. Fellow members of this union, if we _____ for our rights in this strike, we won't be given any.

9. We may go to a movie tonight if a good film _____ somewhere around town.

10. Clyde Warren might not stay with this company if he _____ _____ a promotion and raise. He has a large family to support.

QUIZ 202   the present perfect tense in *if* clauses
handbook p. 180

Write in each blank an appropriate verb phrase in the present perfect tense.

call	cool off	get into	run out of
come	find	make	study
complete	fix	pay	take care of

Examples: a. Where's the bus? I'll start walking home if it *hasn't come* within a few minutes.

b. Mr. Genius, if you'*ve made* a million dollars by the time you're thirty, I won't be surprised. You're as clever as a fox.

1. Jamie, remember that if you _____ trouble during the day, your father may give you a spanking when he gets home from work this evening.

2. If our car _____ by this afternoon, we'll take off this evening.

3. If this town _____ within a few days, I'm taking my car and driving up to the mountains where it's not so hot.

4. If Libby Prescott _____ a job in New York within two months, she says she'll go back home to her parents out in Indiana.

5. If this project _____ by the end of September (the first of October is the deadline), it'll surprise everyone; they all think I'm slow.

6. If this situation _____ by the end of the summer, I'm taking Mr. Cronin to court and suing him for not living up to his contract.

7. If my parents _____ me by seven o'clock, I'm going out and not waiting around here anymore—I'm getting restless.

8. Yes, Mr. Crespo, if you _____ hard during the course, you'll receive a good grade when I give them out at the end of the semester.

9. I won't be surprised if we _____ ice by the end of this party; it's a hot night, and everyone is drinking a lot.

10. Sir, if these bills _____ by the end of the month, you may very well end up in court with a lawsuit on your hands.

QUIZ 203 *should* in conditional clauses
handbook p. 181

Complete the following conditional clauses with appropriate verb phrases containing should. *Provide a subject,* there, *or* it *in each sentence. Do not use* if *in this quiz.*

I	there	be	give	snow
it	these packages	deliver	rain	wait
our rights	you	get into	sleep	

Examples: a. <u>Should there be</u> a change in the weather, we're going to go looking for wild strawberries in the woods behind our house.

b. <u>Should you be</u> late this evening, Charles, please give me a call.

1. _____ when you get home tonight, please try not to wake me up, but please do if I'm snoring—I don't want to disturb you.

2. _____ by the end of the week, we will have a very disappointed customer on our hands. He must get them by then.

3. _____ a delay with our flight, where shall we wait?

4. Jimmy, don't forget to take your snow shoes _____ when you get out of school this afternoon.

5. _____ Harvard University, I'll go to Oxford; I've already been accepted there.

6. _____ when you leave the house, take an umbrella.

7. _____ an earthquake, will there be any kind of warning?

8. Fellow workers, _____ to us, we will go out on strike and ask for even more benefits.

9. _____ for you when you get to the office, please just sit down and wait; you shouldn't have to wait for more than a few minutes.

10. _____ a warm day, our next class will be held in the park near school.

QUIZ 204   can, must, and *have to* in *if* clauses; *had better*

handbook p. 181

Fill in each blank with a verb phrase using can *or* can't *unless* must *or* have to *is given in parentheses.*

air	fight	keep away from	open	speak
bail out	find	leave	redone	squeeze in
come up with	gossip	play	renew	wash
do	hear	put up with	resign	work
do over	hush up			

Examples: a. If our enemy *can fight* dirty, so can we.

b. (have to) It'll be better if our teacher *doesn't have to squeeze in* more students.

c. I'll walk out of this debate if my voice *can't be heard* .

d. (must) If you *must gossip*, please don't gossip about me.

1. If you _____ the next dance well (it's a fast tango), I promise that I won't laugh at you if you promise not to step on my feet.

2. (have to) If I _____ of this plane, I won't be afraid.

3. (must) If you _____ from your company, please do it with dignity.

4. Mr. Long, if you _____ a good slogan for advertising our new product within a week, you shall be fired from this agency.

5. I'll be furious if I _____ my views (my opinions) at the next meeting; I want them to be heard.

6. (have to) If neither of us _____ tomorrow, we'll stay home and mow the lawn.

7. If Jack _____ , how long will he have to stay in jail?

8. If you _____ tobacco and alcohol, Mr. Perry, it'll be better for your health.

9. (have to) If this excellent composition _____ , I'll be very surprised.

10. (must) Sir, if you _____ to me, please don't shout.

11. If that teacher (one of the most experienced in the school) _____ _____ that student (the biggest troublemaker here), who can?

12. (have to) If this bowl _____ , I'll put it away right now.

13. Sir, if my passport _____ anywhere, what shall I do?

14. (have to) If this letter _____ , I'll have time to do something else.

15. Children, if you _____ , I'm going to give you all a spanking.

16. (must) Sandra, if you _____ the window, please put a sweater on.

17. Mrs. Brooks, if we _____ these new students (you say your class is too crowded), just where shall we put them?

18. (must) If you _____ your radio, you'd better turn it down a bit. You'll wake up all the neighbors.

19. Yes, they're going back to Mexico if their visas _____ .

20. (have to) If you _____ this company, who will take your place?

score _____ (20 points each)

QUIZ 205   *will* in *if* clauses

handbook p. 182

Place in the blanks appropriate verb phrases using will.

be	mind	seat
do	quiet down	wait

Examples: a. Your Majesty, if you *will be* so kind to sit down so that everyone else can, it will be most appreciated by the ladies and gentlemen assembled here.

b. (please) If you *will please wait* a few minutes, Madam, someone will be right here to serve you.

1. Gentlemen, if you _____ so good to listen to my suggestions, I think this problem we have with the government will eventually be solved.

2. Sir, if you _____ your own business, I will mind mine.

3. (please) Class, if you _____ , I will be able to continue with the story of Little Red Riding Hood.

4. If you _____ these exercises every day, Mr. Samuels, you should be feeling your old self within a few days.

5. (please) Ladies and Gentlemen, if you _____ , the meeting will begin.

QUIZ 206   unless, even if, and in case

handbook p. 182

Write in each blank an appropriate verb phrase (affirmative only) in the simple present tense.

betray	get down on	lose	swear
censor	go off	misplace	thicken up
cut off	invite	reach	torture
do over			

Examples: a. I'll never believe him even if he _swears_ on the Bible that he's telling the truth.

b. Laura Canfield will never be satisfied unless she _reaches_ the top of the business world.

c. You should keep an extra house key at your neighbor's in case you _lose_ yours.

1. The movie will still be good even if it _____ by the government.

2. Mr. Griffin, this letter shouldn't be sent out unless it _____ .

3. You should always keep candles in the house in case the power _____ _____ .

4. We will win this battle, Ladies and Gentlemen, unless we _____ .

5. She says she won't marry him unless he _____ his beard.

6. I should have your address in case I _____ your phone number.

7. I will never forgive her even if she _____ her hands and knees and begs me for forgiveness.

8. You should watch this while it's cooking in case it _____ too quickly.

9. The party won't be any fun unless interesting people _____ .

10. General, this prisoner will never confess to his political crimes even if he _____ .

QUIZ 207   questions with conditional clauses
handbook p. 183

Complete the following yes–no and information questions with appropriate verb phrases.
Provide subjects and objects when needed.

he	bail out	lay off	spoil	him
it	catch up with	put back together	take up with	it
we	check out	see off	tell off	them
you	get into	show up		

Examples: a. How <u>will you get into</u> your house if you're locked out by accident?

b. (have to) If it becomes serious, <u>will you have to take it up with</u> your lawyer?

1. (have to) If you get a job with the State Department, _____
   _____ by the FBI first for security clearance?

2. If business continues to be so slow, how many more workers _____
   _____ ?

3. (be able to) If your brother ends up in jail, _____ ?

4. Mr. Likes, in case a student falls behind because of illness, how _____
   _____ the rest of the students when he returns to school?

5. (be able to) Robbie, if you take this clock apart, _____
   _____ ?

6. (be able to) Sam, if this rowboat begins to leak, _____
   _____ ? Have we got a bucket?

7. (have to) If your parents leave this afternoon, _____
   _____ at the airport?

8. If this isn't kept in the refrigerator, _____ ?

9. (probably) Should it happen to rain, _____ at
   the meeting late?

10. (be able to) If your boss gives you a hard time, _____
    _____ ?

QUIZ 208 real conditions; *if* meaning *when*

handbook p. 183

Write in each blank an appropriate verb phrase in the simple present tense. Provide subjects and objects when needed.

you	attend to	catch on	help out	them
your boss	bawl out	come up with	mean	you
your mother	break down	do	take	
	bring out	go	turn in	

Examples: a. (usually) If your father goes to Europe on business, *does your mother usually go* with him?

b. (often) If we've been having lots of rain, our computer *often breaks down*.

1. (usually) If our company is introducing a new product, it _____ _____ in September so that we can take advantage of the coming Christmas sales.

2. (always) If no one in the office has a good idea, my boss _____ _____ one. She's the cleverest person I've ever met.

3. (ever) If you make a mistake at work, _____ _____ ?

4. (usually) If our baby is crying, it _____ _____ she's hungry.

5. (ever) If your parents are busy in their store, _____ _____ ?

6. (usually) If my father has had a particularly hard day, he _____ _____ shortly after dinner.

7. (rarely) If something goes wrong in this office building, it _____ _____ right away; the maintenance department is poorly organized.

8. (always) If I tell my grandfather a joke, he _____ _____ , and he usually has an even better joke to tell me.

9. (have to) If it's not raining, I _____ an umbrella to work.

10. (have to) If you can't go into your office, _____ _____ your work, or does your secretary do it?

QUIZ 209   present-unreal conditions

handbook p. 183

Fill in the blanks with appropriate verb phrases. Do not use the passive voice. Use only _would_ in result clauses.

Examples: a. The children are bored because they have nothing to do (it's raining out).
They _wouldn't be_ so bored if they _had_ something to do.

b. Because he always eats dinner late, he never sleeps well.
If he _didn't eat_ dinner so late every night, he _would sleep_ better.

1. I'm not a billionaire—nothing much unusual happens in my life.

My life _____ completely different if I _____ a billionaire.

2. He smokes two packs of cigarettes a day, and he has a bad cough.

If he _____ so much, he _____ such a bad cough.

3. I don't speak English as well as I'd like; that's why I'm here.

I _____ here in this class if I _____ English well.

4. They have only a little money in the bank, so they never travel much.

If they _____ a lot of money, they _____ a trip around the world.

5. Fortunately, my boss isn't out of the office today.

If he _____ here, I _____ too much work to do.

6. I realize I'm not you—we're not at all the same.

I _____ my life very differently if I _____ you.

7. Life costs a lot in London, so we don't live there; we can't afford it.

We _____ there if we _____ better off (more prosperous).

8. I'm not the president of this country. Look at what he's doing.

I _____ things differently if I _____ he, that's for sure.

9. I know how to pronounce her name, but I don't know how to spell it.

If I _____ how to spell it, I _____ able to look it up in the phone book.

10. She wears too much makeup on her face; she sometimes looks like a clown.

She _____ a more attractive woman if she _____ less makeup.

QUIZ 210   continuous forms in *if* clauses

handbook p. 185

Write an appropriate verb phrase in each blank.

act	feel	run	snow	treat
be	give	sleep	take	worry
do				

Examples: a. If I *weren't doing* this quiz right now, I'd probably be watching TV.

b. She would get out of bed and go to school today is she *weren't feeling* so tired.

1. He'd enjoy his job more if he _____ so many new responsibilities all the time; he's overloaded with work.

2. If my roommate _____ now, we'd be able to turn on the stereo.

3. I'd quit my job if I _____ by my boss as badly as yours has been treating you. How can you ever put up with it?

4. Yes, the trains would probably be running on time this morning if it _____ . Bad weather conditions usually cause delays of one kind or another.

5. No, she never worries. If she _____ about her problems at work, she wouldn't be laughing all the time, would she?

6. He's an honest businessman. If he _____ on the up and up (honest) in this deal, I wouldn't have anything to do with him.

7. We'd go for a drive up to the mountains if our car _____ better; the radiator boils over in high altitudes.

8. I wouldn't be so busy if I _____ so much homework by my grammar teacher all the time.

9. George, I wouldn't be annoyed with you if you _____ so silly. Why don't you grow up and stop being so childish? You're almost 30 years old.

10. If my roommate _____ a nap now, I wouldn't be making so much noise, nor would I be playing the radio so loudly.

QUIZ 211   unless and even if

handbook p. 185

Fill in the blanks with appropriate verb phrases.

| be | find | give | need | torture |
| bribe | force | go | starve | |

Examples: a. How tasteless this food is! I couldn't eat it even if I *were starving*.

           b. She wouldn't go out with anyone unless her parents *gave* their permission.

1. Listen, Mr. Macho, I wouldn't marry you even if you _____ the richest man in the world.

2. (have to) He wouldn't drop out of school unless he _____ to work to support his wife and child.

3. I would never help the mob out even if I _____ a million dollars. I'm an honest policeman.

4. General, I would never reveal this information even if I _____ .

5. (have to) I could never steal unless I _____ food for my family.

6. I wouldn't marry anyone at this time of my life even if I _____ madly in love with the person; I'm too busy with my career.

7. He's a very shy young man; he wouldn't ask a woman for a dance at a party unless he _____ to do so by one of his friends.

8. For religious reasons, he wouldn't take any kind of medicine even if he _____ it in order to live. He doesn't believe in doctors.

9. I wouldn't go to the FBI about this situation unless it _____ very serious, and it's not.

10. I wouldn't live in that house even if I _____ a millionaire; it's too big.

score _____

QUIZ 212   could in conditional clauses

handbook p. 186

Write in each blank an appropriate verb phrase using *could*.

afford	get away with	make	solve
bail out	go	marry	speak
find	have	see	take advantage of

Examples: a. I love to travel, but I'd never take a trip unless I *could afford* it.

           b. I wouldn't want to go on a trip around the world if you *couldn't go* with me.

1. Even if he _____ his father's high position in the government, he'd never do it. He wants to become a success on his own.

2. We wouldn't be having any problems with this project if the right person _____ for the job. We're willing to pay a lot.

3. If Tad and his wife _____ a child, they'd adopt one.

4. Even if she _____ the richest man in town, she wouldn't ever do it; she's too much in love with her boyfriend.

5. If this crime _____ by the FBI, no one could solve it.

6. She'd be doing better at work if she _____ English better.

7. He just loves his job, but his salary isn't much. If only he _____ more money, he'd be quite happy.

8. Even if she _____ her husband, she wouldn't do it; she wants him to remain in jail.

9. Anatole, your face is covered with paint. If only you _____ yourself in a mirror right now, you wouldn't be able to stop laughing.

10. Even if I _____ it (there was no chance of my being caught by anyone), I would never steal anything from anyone—I'm too honest.

score _____

QUIZ 213   questions with conditional clauses

handbook p. 186

Complete the following yes–no and information questions with appropriate verb phrases using would. *Provide subjects when needed.*

she	deal with	happen	pay
you	do	lend	take care of
	go	like	take over

Examples: a. What *would you do* if you were a billionaire?

b. (have to) *Would you have to go* to your parents if you ran out of money?

1. (be able to) If I asked you for a loan, how much _____ me?

2. (probably) If you were at the beach right now, what _____ ?

3. If you were I, Sir, how _____ this problem?

4. If you were she, Mike (now put yourself in my wife's shoes), what kind of house _____ to live in?

5. (have to) If you wanted to get an apartment in your hometown, about how much rent _____ ? I'm just talking about a regular apartment—nothing fancy.

6. If you were me, Sam, how _____ my greedy landlord?

7. If you needed a job, where _____ to find one?

8. If you left this company, Mr. Siddons, who _____ your position?

9. Miss Brown, what _____ if you walked down Main Street in the middle of the day wearing nothing but a bikini?

10. Jim, if your mother wanted to get in touch with you when you are in Sri Lanka, how _____ it?

score _____ (5 points each blank)

QUIZ 214   past-unreal conditions

handbook p. 187

Fill in the blanks with appropriate verb phrases. Use only <u>would</u> *in the result clauses.*

Examples: a. Our side didn't fight very hard, and the battle was lost.
If we <u>had fought</u> harder, the battle <u>wouldn't have been lost</u>.

b. Our car broke down on our way to the station, so we missed the train.
We <u>wouldn't have missed</u> the train if our car <u>hadn't broken down</u>.

1. His sister slipped on an icy sidewalk and fell down; she broke her wrist.
She _____ if the sidewalk _____ so slippery.

2. He was fired because he'd been careless on the job.
He _____ from the job if he _____ so careless.

3. He drank a lot of coffee, so he didn't sleep very well.
If he _____ less coffee, he _____ so poorly.

4. We got lost last night because we didn't have the right directions.
We _____ lost last night if we _____ the right directions.

5. I didn't give him an answer because I hadn't understood his question.

If I _____ his question, he _____ an answer.

6. I didn't have an appetite last night, so I skipped dinner.

I _____ dinner if I _____ an appetite.

7. They'd cooked the meat for five hours; it was very tough.

It _____ so tough if it _____ so long.

8. We didn't take this quiz at the beginning of the course; it was too difficult.

If we _____ it at that time, it _____ too difficult.

9. She hadn't told me the truth, so I didn't feel bad about breaking my promise to her.

I _____ my promise to her if she _____ to me.

10. My mother met my father at a school picnic many years ago.

If he _____ to that picnic, he _____ my mother, and I wouldn't have been born.

score _____ (10 points each blank)

QUIZ 215   continuous forms in *if* clauses

handbook p. 187

Write appropriate verb phrases in the blanks.

arrest	drive	play around	use
bite	get	speed	wear
catch	mind	spill	

Examples:
a. A: I'm sure someone was using notes during the last test. B: No, impossible! Our teacher has eyes in the back of her head, and if anyone *had been using* notes, he *would have been caught.* I'm sure of it.

b. The police stopped the thieves' car because they were driving with their headlights off. Just think—they *wouldn't have been caught* if they'*d been driving* with their lights on.

1. She was arrested because she was wearing a bathing suit on the street (it was a very conservative town). She _____ if she _____ more appropriate clothes.

2. You spilled your milk because you were acting like a baby at the table. The milk _____ on the floor if you _____ so childishly.

3. I didn't even get one bite when I went fishing yesterday. But I'll tell you, I _____ a lot of fish if they _____ .

4. The police stopped us and gave us a ticket. We _____ one if we _____ through town so fast.

5. He kept asking me all of these personal questions (he was a perfect stranger to me), and I got a little angry. I _____ angry at him if he _____ his own business.

score _____

QUIZ 216   unless and *even if*; *could have* in result clauses

handbook p. 188

Fill in each blank with an appropriate verb phrase in the past perfect tense.

be	bribe	give	help	offer
betray	find	have	marry	tutor

Example: a. According to the newspapers, he would never have been caught unless a member of his family *had betrayed* him.

1. No, I wouldn't have gone out yesterday even if it _____ a nice day; I was too busy with chores at home.

2. They must have had visas. They couldn't have traveled in the Soviet Union last summer unless they _____ them.

3. I'm afraid that student couldn't have passed the final examination even if he _____ beforehand by one of his teachers.

4. My grandfather is always saying he wouldn't have had a happy life unless he _____ my grandmother.

5. Even if she _____ guilty of killing her neighbor, I wouldn't have believed it. She could never have done such a thing.

6. She would never have consented to marrying that man even if she _____ _____ a palace to live in and diamonds and furs to wear.

7. The warden is certain that the prisoners couldn't have escaped from their cells unless the prison guards _____ .

8. Unless my teacher _____ me some kind of assistance, I don't think I could have done this quiz at the beginning of the course.

9. Even if I _____ a million dollars, I could never have betrayed my country as some spies did in the last war.

10. He couldn't have gone all the way through the university unless he _____ _____ financially by his wife and her parents.

QUIZ 217   *could have* and *might have* in result clauses

handbook p. 188

Fill in the blanks with appropriate verb phrases.

be	eat	get	make
become	enter	have	pass
die	fix	invite	take

Examples: a. (might) The meat at dinner last night looked a little spoiled, so I didn't touch it. I *might have gotten* sick if I *had eaten* it.

b. (could) I didn't have any money last August, but I *couldn't have taken* a vacation even if I *had had* the money because I was working the whole month.

1. (could) Unfortunately, the garage had closed by the time we got there. Our car _____ if we _____ there before closing time.

2. (might) A: The party was very crowded last night, wasn't it? B: Yes, don't you think it _____ more successful if fewer people _____ _____ ?

3. (could) He hadn't passed the physical examination, so he wasn't able to enter the army. Actually, he _____ the army even if he _____ the physical—he can't read and write.

4. (might) He had been very successful in political life when he died at the age of forty-two. If he _____ at such a young age, he _____ _____ the president of the country one day.

5. (could) We had wonderful products but weak management, so our company went out of business. We _____ a fortune if we _____ _____ able to get rid of all the poor managers.

QUIZ 218   *could have* in conditional clauses
handbook p. 188

Fill in the blanks with appropriate verb phrases.

accompany	be	fire	see
afford	find	go	send

Examples: a. When our children were younger, if we *could have afforded* it, they *would have been sent* to the best schools in the city.

b. I couldn't get to the airport when my friend left for Europe; I was too busy at work. I *would have been* so happy if I *could have seen* her off.

1. I'm sure if my company _____ someone to take over my position last month, I _____ at once—they want to get rid of me.

2. He _____ so lonely on his last business trip if his wife _____ him, but she wasn't able to; there had been a death in her family, and she had to go back to her hometown.

3. Because he couldn't afford the long trip to Australia, he wasn't able to be at his daughter's graduation. If he _____ her graduate from the university, he _____ very proud of her.

4. If we _____ at your reception for the First Lady, we _____ _____ very disappointed. Fortunately, we were able to be there.

5. When we went to Argentina (it was an eleven-hour flight), if we _____ it, we _____ first class, but there was a difference of almost a thousand dollars.

score _____

QUIZ 219   present result following past condition
handbook p. 189

Fill in the blanks with appropriate verb phrases in the past perfect tense.

check over	make	spend	tell
get	meet	study	wear
have	occur	take care of	

Examples: a. (never) The world would be a completely different place today if World War II *had never occurred*.

b. (never) If my father *had never met* my mother, I wouldn't be sitting here now.

1. Mr. Smith, if your house _____ more regularly when it was new, you wouldn't be having so many problems with it now.

2. Oh, no, look—our plane is taking off. If we _____ here just a few minutes earlier, we'd be on the plane right now.

3. Son, if you _____ the best education that money could buy when you were younger, you wouldn't be in such a good position now. Count your blessings. (old saying)

4. If we _____ hotel reservations, we wouldn't be sleeping in this car tonight.

5. Mrs. Bryant, if you _____ so much time in the sun when you were younger, you wouldn't be having so many problems with your skin now.

6. If my car _____ by the mechanic at the garage before I'd started out on this trip, it might be running better now.

7. If he _____ for the last exam, the teacher wouldn't be so annoyed with him now.

8. My feet wouldn't be so tired now if I _____ better shoes when I went shopping.

9. She wouldn't be so worried now if her children _____ her where they were going.

10. If I _____ English more when I was younger, I might be a full-time student at the university right now.

score _____ (20 points each)

QUIZ 220   *have to* and *be able to*; present versus past result

handbook p. 189

Fill in the blanks with appropriate verb phrases using *have to* and *be able to*.

do over	go	sit down	work
drop out of	see	take	

Examples: a. (have to) If I'd forgotten to buy laundry soap, I *would have had to go* back to the store to get some—I must do the laundry today.

b. (be able to) Yes, Sir, if you'd made a reservation earlier, you and your wife *would be able to sit down* immediately, but the restaurant is now full, as you can see by just looking around.

1. (be able to) You _____ the Pope if you had gone to the Vatican while you were in Rome.

2. (have to) If you'd had a government scholarship while you were a student at the university, you _____ at a part-time job in the evenings; you'd have had more time free for studying.

3. (have to) If you'd saved more money while you were working on your sum—
mer job, you _____ school now.

4. (be able to) If we hadn't put by a little money every month during last
winter, we _____ a vacation this summer, and we're
really looking forward to going to Miami.

5. (have to) If there had been only one mistake in that letter (I sent it yesterday),
it _____ .

score _____ (20 points each)

QUIZ 221   special conditional form
handbook p. 190

Complete the following sentences with appropriate verb phrases using the past perfect tense. Provide subjects.

I	we	be	inquire
it	you	bear	know
they		invest	take care of

Example: a. <u>Had I been</u> Christopher Columbus, I would have stayed home.

1. _____ more wisely, they wouldn't have lost so much
money in the last recession.

2. _____ in the early part of the eighteenth century, I
would like to have been born in France.

3. _____ twenty years ago what we know now, we
would have done things differently.

4. _____ by the director in the very beginning, this problem wouldn't be such a big one today.

5. _____ at the right office, you wouldn't have gotten
the wrong information.

score _____

QUIZ 222   questions
handbook p. 190

Complete the following yes–no and information questions with appropriate verb phrases using <u>would have</u>. Provide subjects when needed.

he	you	call	go	pay
they	your wife	do	happen	spend
		drive out	lend	

name _____

Examples: a. If you'd decided to take a trip to Europe, how *would you have gone*?

           b. If you'd been sick yesterday and had to stay home from work, who *would have done* your job?

1. (have to) If your father hadn't paid that tax, _____ a penalty?

2. (be able to) If you could have gone to the convention in San Francisco last March, _____ with you?

3. (have to) If you'd had to borrow $100,000 from the bank, how much in—terest _____ ?

4. (have to) If they'd bought that old house on the corner, how much money _____ in order to fix it up?

5. If you'd run out of money on your vacation, who _____ first?

6. If you'd gone to California last summer, _____ in your car?

7. Terry, what _____ last Saturday night if your parents had finally decided to let you go out?

8. (be able to) If you'd wanted to borrow money from your grandfather, how much _____ you?

9. (have to) If your apartment had needed painting, _____ it yourself?

10. If you'd walked into the party without any clothes on, what _____ ?

score _____ (5 points each)

REVIEW QUIZ V

Write in each blank the appropriate from of the base form given in parentheses.

Examples: a. (have to work) I *wouldn't-have to work* if I were a billionaire.

           b. (get along with) I'd quit my job right away if I *didn't get along with* my boss.

1. (have) If she _____ any money, she always goes to her mother for some.

2. (rain) We'd like to go for a hike now in the woods if it _____ .

3. (use) If room 312 _____ tomorrow, you may give your ex-am there.

4. (have to work) I'd have more time to study if I _____ every day.

5. (mind) I _____ going shopping if it hadn't been raining.

6. (okay) You can't take off tomorrow unless your boss _____ it.

7. (have to stop) If we _____ for gas, we would have made much better time.

8. (be) Of course I'd help you out if you _____ in some kind of financial trouble.

9. (eat) If she _____ candy (particularly chocolate), she always puts on weight right away.

10. (go) If we hadn't gone to Hong Kong, we _____ to Shanghai.

11. (go) She _____ to church unless her husband went with her.

12. (be able to get) If I _____ tickets, I'd have seen that show.

13. (invite) He wouldn't have gone to the conference even if he _____ .

14. (have to study) If you'd studied more last semester, you _____ so hard now; you should have been thinking more about the future.

15. (be able to get) If you don't have your identification card with you when you go to the dance tonight, you _____ in.

16. (be) I'd never borrow money unless I _____ in great need of it.

17. (want) I'm going to the movies tonight even if my wife _____ to go.

18. (have to go) Timmy, if you brushed your teeth regularly three times a day, you _____ to the dentist so often; you must get into the habit.

19. (be able to travel) If I didn't have a passport, I _____ .

20. (pass out) If he drinks too much beer, he always _____ .

QUIZ 223   past real conditions

handbook p. 190

Fill in the blanks with appropriate verb phrases using the simple past tense or its continuous form.

be	go	look
eat	go out	wear
get	have	work

Examples: a. I remember in the sixth grade, Tommy Tunnel would always be flying paper airplanes if the teacher *wasn't looking.*

b. (have to) Why do you have to borrow my car, Son? Why, when I was your age, if I *had to go* somewhere, I would always have to walk.

1. My grandfather used to always look at the sun to figure out the time if he _____ his pocket watch (he usually wore two).

2. I've got wonderful memories of my childhood on a dairy farm. I remember how my father would let me help him milk the cows if he_____ short of help.

3. What a great college roommate you were, Dick! I remember you would always lend me money if I _____ any, and you always made your bed.

4. I remember when my grandparents were still alive; if my grandmother _____ at the table, my grandfather would always say a prayer before dinner.

5. While I was sick with the flu, if I _____ something, I'd throw it up right away.

6. I remember in the seventh grade, when Mr. Leedy was my teacher, he would always make me stand in the corner if I _____ my homework assignments regularly.

7. I remember as a child if I _____ in some kind of trouble, one of my sisters was.

8. (have to) It's long ago, but I still remember how my father would take my mother and me to a movie on Friday night if he _____ the next day.

9. It's way back in my memory, but I can still remember how my mother would always put a lamp in the front window if my father _____ home late.

10. While we were in Buenos Aires, if we _____ in the evening, we would always go dancing.

REVIEW QUIZ W

Write in each blank an appropriate form of the base form given in parentheses.

Examples: a. (blow up) I was there; I saw the terrorists *blow up* the car, and then run away.

           b. (able to attend) If we'*d been able to attend* the conference, we would have.

1. (have to cook) If the power had gone off last night, we _____ _____ dinner on the kerosene stove.

2. (be) If I _____ tired when I get home from work, I usually take a little nap.

3. (give) Would the students object to _____ the final examination today?

4. (lay off) No one should _____ unless the company starts losing money.

5. (get on) He walked across the street in order _____ the shady side.

6. (have) _____ any breakfast, I began to get hungry around ten.

7. (invite) The party won't be a success unless interesting people _____ _____ .

8. (have to have) If Mr. Ellis _____ an operation, he would have gone to the best surgeon in New York City.

9. (be) Hank, I'd never think of dropping out of school if I _____ you.

10. (be) Oh, yes, Rickie, in those days during the war, if there _____ _____ a shortage of beef, many people would eat horse meat.

11. (be) You'll be able to see all your old friends if you _____ at the meeting tomorrow.

12. (enjoy) If we hadn't saved our money, we _____ ourselves on this vacation now.

13. (drive) Would you please stop _____ so fast; you're like a maniac behind the wheel.

14. (correct) During the last course, if the teacher _____ the quizzes, the students would do it.

15. (unwrap) When _____ your present, try not to rip any of the paper.

16. (have) So far, no one _____ a problem with this quiz. It's a fast class.

17. (be) If I _____ you, Mr. Snoopy, I'd mind my own business.

name _____

18. (have to go) If he'd been a good boy last night, he _____ to bed early.

19. (touch) I wouldn't risk _____ those live wires; you'd better watch out.

20. (take) _____ a break for three hours, the students were exhausted.

score _____ (5 points each)

REVIEW QUIZ X

Write in each blank one word. Write an "X" in the blank if a word is not required. Contractions like don't and didn't count as one word.

Examples: a. X though Tad Rogers is only fourteen, he's going out with girls.

   b. My brother lets me drive his car once *in* a while.

1. This office is being used for only the time _____.

2. Helga Eisner speaks English well, but she _____ makes mistakes sometimes.

3. _____ the very cold weather, the pond behind our house still hasn't frozen over.

4. What delicious cake this is! _____ you like some?

5. My father took my sister and _____ out to dinner last night; it was my birthday.

6. _____ to the Second World War, no war had ever been so widespread and destructive.

7. People must have _____ love in order to be truly happy.

8. I'm making a fool out of myself, _____ I?

9. I wouldn't mind _____ for a walk now. Would you?

10. I'm planning to give _____ my father a box of Cuban cigars for his birthday.

11. _____ not go to the movies tonight; I'd rather go shopping.

12. Officer, please let us _____ pass through the barricades—it's urgent.

13. If you go to _____ Netherlands, you'll see a lot of windmills.

14. _____ quitting his job at that company, he's been a much happier man.

15. French has been easy this semester, but mathematics _____.

16. Her boyfriend wants to go to the game on Saturday, but she doesn't want _____.

17. _____ to the rain, there has been heavy flooding in the northern part of the city.

18. You'd _____ stop gambling; you'll lose your pants as well as your money.

19. Wasn't it _____ October, not September, that your friend left for America?

20. They're staying at _____ Panorama Hotel when they go to Kathmandu; they'll have a good view of the city.

score _____ (5 points each)

REVIEW QUIZ Y

In each of the following sentences, there is one mistake. Cross out that mistake and put in a correct word if one is needed.

Examples:
a. Chemistry is difficult for me this semester, and so ~~are~~ *is* physics.

b. She's being given the instructions, ~~hasn't~~ *isn't* she?

1. What time will our limousine arrive to the front door of the White House?

2. The teacher let the class to go home early because of the serious storm.

3. His life has been completely different for entering the university.

4. I am very angry to make a rational decision at this time.

5. He doesn't want to go to home yet, and his wife doesn't either.

6. Instead to putting our money in the bank, we should invest it in real estate.

7. Never I could hurt a defenseless animal, and neither could you.

8. A lots of people have made a great deal of money in the oil business.

9. I need to go to the hardware store for to get a screwdriver.

10. News travel fast through the medium of radio.

11. Due of his extreme selfishness, few people care for him; he's difficult to like.

12. He's quite a nice boy in spite to his quick temper; he must learn how to watch it.

13. Yes, we can to go with you, but we'll have to bring our children with us.

14. She's such a honest woman that everyone trusts her.

15. Neither of them have the desire to speak and write English well.

16. Never he does any of the homework for the class; he's not interested.

17. If I would have had more money, I would have stayed in Tahiti longer.

18. They have a beautiful house at the Lake Tahoe; they've got a fantastic view.

19. His uncle has an European manner about him, doesn't he?

20. This quiz has been worth to do, hasn't it?

score _____

QUIZ 224   *like;* expressing similarity
handbook p. 191

Fill in the blanks with appropriate verb phrases.

act   feel   smell   taste
be   look   good

Examples: a. (always) She's *always acting* like the boss, but she really isn't.

b. This looks like coffee, but it *doesn't taste* like it. It's not; it's chicory.

1. Spanish _____ like German, but English does quite a bit.

2. This perfume _____ like gardenias; it's very seductive.

3. I _____ like a fool when I made that stupid mistake in front of everyone.

4. Luda Romanoff _____ like a princess, but she is.

5. For a young and romantic person, the end of the first romance _____ like the end of the world.

6. (ever) He _____ like a V.I.P. (very important person), but in actuality he is.

7. (always) He _____ like a big shot (V.I.P.), but he's just a low man on the totem pole (a person in the lowest position of responsibility).

8. Her job _____ just like mine, but she makes a heck of a lot more than I do.

9. John, when you get a little bit angry, your voice _____ just like your father's.

10. Darling, you _____ like a dream in your new dress last night; I could have sworn you were a movie star.

score _____

QUIZ 225 *like* versus *as*

handbook p. 191

Fill in each blank with <u>like</u> *or* <u>as</u>.

Examples: a. Even though it's late October, it almost feels *like* August; it's really hot to-day.

b. She writes just *as* she speaks, frankly and honestly.

1. Since his father died, he's been acting _____ the president of the family business.

2. Yes, he speaks _____ an educated man, but he didn't even finish elementary school. He's a self-made man.

3. He works _____ a slave, but he hardly makes enough money for his family to live on.

4. _____ most students, my roommate never has much money to spend on luxuries.

5. This cigar, Sir, tastes good _____ a fine and expensive cigar should.

6. Marilyn Monroe was best _____ a comedienne; her talent was not for dramatic stories.

7. Things such _____ refrigerators and washing machines are very expensive in many countries; they're very often highly taxed.

8. This food tastes _____ leftovers; it must have been in the refrigerator for a long time.

9. The world is not so large _____ it was; better transportation has brought people closer together.

10. Many nouns may be used _____ verbs.

QUIZ 226   *as if* and *as though*; unreal opinions
handbook p. 192

be	fry	lose	see
float	have	own	smoke

Fill in the blanks with appropriate verb phrases.

Examples: a. Tanya's face was as white as a sheet when she came into the room; she looked as if she *had seen* a ghost.

b. He's always acting as though he *didn't have* any money in the bank, but in actuality he's the richest man in town.

1. Signora Correlli acts as if she _____ the star in this opera company, but she's never sung a leading role.

2. Dickie, you look as though you _____ about to sneeze; here is a tissue.

3. (just) I saw Susan Law sitting in a coffee shop the other evening; she was alone and looked as if she _____ her best friend.

4. My girlfriend acts as though she _____ in love with me, but she's only pretending.

5. What a great mood I'm in this morning! I feel as if I _____ on a cloud.

6. I know it's August, but doesn't it feel as though it _____ September today?

7. When I walked into the room, it smelled as though someone _____ marijuana, but there was no one there.

8. Yes, the fish was not very good last night; it tasted as if it _____ in rancid oil.

9. A fellow in my office is always acting as if he _____ the president of the company, but he's punching a time clock every day just like me.

10. Every time the sergeant gives an order, he acts as if he _____ a general.

QUIZ 227   noun clauses derived from statements
handbook p. 193

Transform the following statements into that *noun clauses. Use a question mark when it is appropriate.* That *may be omitted.*

Examples: a. "Life is very short."
Most young people don't realize *that life is very short.*

b. "He stole the jewels."
Does the thief admit *he stole the jewels?*

1. "I'll eventually marry."
I suppose _____

2. "You must have a vacation now."
Do you feel _____

3. "I'll always remember you in my heart."
I promise _____

4. "There is life after death."
Do you believe _____

5. "I owe more taxes."
The government claims _____

score _____ (20 points each)

QUIZ 228   noun clauses derived from yes-no questions; *whether*
handbook p. 195

Transform the following yes–no questions into noun clauses introduced by whether *or* if. *Use a question mark when it is appropriate.*

Examples: a. "Does that store sell vegetables?"
Do you know *whether that store sells vegetables?*

b. "Will the news be announced soon?"
I'd like to know *if the news will be announced soon.*

1. "Did the boss come to work early today?"
My secretary doesn't know _____

2. "Is the elevator out of order?"
Excuse me, do you know _____

3. "Is it going to rain?"
No one can really predict _____

4. "Does she have a car?"

Does anyone know _____

5. "Will there be an election?"

It's hard to predict _____

QUIZ 229   whether or not

handbook p. 196

Transform the *following yes–no questions into noun clauses. Use* <u>whether or not</u> *five times, and use* <u>whether</u> . . . <u>or not</u> *five times. Use a question mark when it is appropriate.*

Examples: a. (<u>whether or not</u>) "Does he like me?"
I don't know <u>whether or not he likes me.</u>
b. (<u>whether . . . or not</u>) "Does he like me?"
Do you know <u>whether he likes me or not?</u>

1. "Am I in love?"

I keep asking myself, I really don't know _____

2. "Is that student married?"

By the way, would you happen to know _____

3. "Did I do the right thing?"

I'm still trying to decide _____

4. "Does he want to quit his job?"

Can't he make up his mind _____

5. "Did I put a stamp on that letter?"

I just can't recall _____

6. "Have I made a terrible mistake?"

I'm worried—I keep asking myself _____

7. "Is this answer correct?"

Don't you know _____

8. "Do you want to be my husband?"

Please tell me right now _____

9. "Will you be here tomorrow?"

Do you know now _____

10. "Does this word mean anything?"

The teacher doesn't know _____

name _____   score _____

QUIZ 230   noun clauses derived from information questions
handbook p. 196

Transform the following information questions into noun clauses so that you may complete the sentences. Use a question mark when it is appropriate.

Examples: a. "What time is it?"
Could you please tell me *what time it is?*

b. "How did he do that?"
I don't know *how he did that.*

1. "Where are the elevators?"
Why don't you ask the hall porter _____

2. "Where does the teacher usually correct our homework?"
Do you know _____

3. "How did they split up the money?"
I'd really like to know _____

4. "What did I eat for dinner last night?"
I can't remember _____

5. "What kind of tea is this?"
Doesn't the label on the package say _____

6. "How much money does he make?"
He won't ever tell the government _____

7. "Why did I go to your father?"
I'm afraid to tell you _____

8. "What are his telephone number and address?"
Would you happen to know _____

9. "Exactly how many students are there in your class?"
Can you tell me _____

10. "What is the correct formula for water?"
Does anyone in the class know _____

score _____   (20 points each)

QUIZ 231   the rule of sequence of tenses
handbook p. 197

Transform the following direct statements and questions into noun clauses so that you may complete the sentences. Follow the rule of sequence of tenses. Use a question mark when it is appropriate.

Examples: a. "Did they do well or poorly on the exam?"

Only a few students knew *whether or not they'd done well or poorly on the exam.*

b. "He's acting so strangely because he's fallen in love."

None of his friends knew *that he was acting so strangely because he had fallen in love.*

1. "He landed in America."

When Christopher Columbus stepped onto the shores of the New World, he didn't know _____

2. "She's laughing because she's just heard a funny story about you."

When you ran into her out in the hall, did you know _____

_____

3. "Did I get an invitation to that affair?"

I have a rather poor memory, and I wasn't able to remember _____

_____

4. "The radio isn't working right because it wasn't fixed properly."

My father said _____

_____

5. "What time is it?"

I was late because I didn't know _____

score _____

QUIZ 232 the rule of sequence of tenses; modals
handbook p. 198

Transform the following direct statements and questions into noun clauses so that you may complete the sentences. Follow the rule of sequence of tenses. Use a question mark when it is appropriate.

Example: a. "He must return some books to the library."
He forgot *that he had to return some books to the library.*

1. "Where did I put my shopping money?"

I couldn't remember _____

2. "She should go to the doctor at once."

Sarah knew _____

3. "They may go on a vacation if they save enough money."

They said _____

4. "The teacher is angry because someone in the class was cheating on the exam."

Did you know _____

5. "Did she give me a bad grade?"

I didn't want to ask the teacher _____

6. "Why can't he return the radio he bought?"

I wanted to know _____

7. "What happened to me after the accident?"

I couldn't remember _____

8. "I can't get a promotion in the company because I don't have enough friends at the top."

While I was working there, I knew _____

9. "I met Napoleon's Ghost."

I dreamed the other night _____

10. "Did I lock the front door?"

When I got to work the other morning, I couldn't remember _____
_____ , so I had to go back home to make sure.

score _____ (20 points each)

QUIZ 233 indirect speech

handbook p. 198

Transform the following direct statements into noun clauses so that you may complete the sentences. Follow the rule of sequence of tenses. Use a question mark when it is appropriate.

Examples: a. "I don't ever eat anything fattening because I don't want to put on weight."
He told his doctor *that he didn't ever eat anything fattening because he didn't want to put on weight.*

b. "We're going to take a vacation by ourselves without our children."
Did they tell you *that they were going to take a vacation by themselves without their children?*

1. "We want to introduce our daughter to your son."

Mr. and Mrs. Downes told my wife and me _____

_____

2. "I want to talk to you about the present I'm going to give you on your birthday."
Did he tell his wife _____

3. "My car still isn't working right even though it's just been fixed."

   When I saw him in the garage, he told me _____

   _____

4. "You can take your vacation after I've taken mine."

   When I spoke to my boss about it, she told me _____

   _____

5. "I'm not worried about hurting myself on my job because I'm always very careful with any of the machinery I use."

   The mechanic told me _____

score _____

QUIZ 234   indirect speech

handbook p. 198

Read the directions and look at the examples in Quiz 233.

1. "We're not happy with the political situation in our town."

   During our conversation, they told me _____

2. "My car cost less than yours but more than my wife's."

   Did he tell you when you spoke to him _____

3. "You must stop smoking before you kill yourself."

   My doctor told me in no uncertain words _____

   _____

4. "I don't want you to do the job, because I'm going to do it myself."

   She sounded a little angry when she told me _____

   _____

5. "We'll have to take our car to the garage before we leave on our trip."

   Did they tell you _____

6. "We ourselves are going to build our house, and nobody is going to help us."

   They were really bragging when they told me _____

   _____

7. "We're angry at you because you're always thinking of only yourselves."

   I was surprised when my neighbors told my husband and me _____

   _____

8. "I can't make myself do something that I don't want to do."

   She sounded very serious when she told me _____

   _____

name _____

9. "I want you to go with me to the store because I don't want to go by myself."
   She told her husband _____

10. "You'll be able to make more money when you've had more experience on the job."
    My boss told me the other day when I asked for a raise _____
    _____

score _____ (20 points each)

QUIZ 235   indirect speech
handbook p. 198

Transform the following yes–no questions and answers into noun clauses so that you may complete the sentences. Look at the examples carefully, and follow the rule of sequence of tenses.

Examples: a. "Do you live in Istanbul?" "Yes, I do."
I asked him *whether or not he lived in Istanbul, and he said that he did.*

b. "Can you help me fix my car?" "No, I can't."
I asked a friend of mine, who is a mechanic, *if he could help me to fix my car, and he said that he couldn't.*

1. "Do you have to speak English much at your office?" "No, I don't."
   I asked him _____

2. "Will you help me with my project?" "Yes, I will."
   I asked Maria Cuevas _____
   _____

3. "Are you going to take your car with you when you go to Puerto Rico?" "No, we don't think so."
   I asked Taka and Sumi Yamaguchi _____
   _____

4. "Did I do well on the final exam?" "Yes, you did."
   I asked Madame Costeau, my French teacher, _____
   _____

5. "Will you help me with my homework?" "No, I won't."
   I asked Fernando, my roommate, _____
   _____

QUIZ 236 indirect speech

handbook p. 198

Transform the following information questions into noun clauses so that you may complete the sentences. Follow the rule of the sequence of tenses. Use a question mark when it is appropriate.

Examples: a. "How much money do you make with your company?"
I thought it was none of his business when he asked me *how much money I made with my company.*

b. "Whom do you want me to marry?"
Shouldn't you have asked your parents *whom they wanted you to marry?*

1. "Why can't you tell me what you are doing out in the garden?"
She asked her little boy _____

2. "Where did you hide the keys to your apartment?"
Did you ask your roommate _____

3. "Why didn't you go to your teacher about the problem?"
Shouldn't you have asked them _____

4. "How many pieces of furniture were delivered to your apartment?"
Someone at the store called up and asked me _____
_____

5. "How much did you pay for your car?"
I really didn't think it was any of her business when she asked me
_____

score _____

QUIZ 237 indirect speech

handbook p. 198

Read the directions and look at the examples in Quiz 236.

1. "Why won't you help me with my homework?"
Did you ask Carlos _____

2. "What kind of car do you drive to work every day?"
For some reason, she didn't want to answer me when I asked her _____
_____

3. "Why didn't we stop at the last gas station?"
When they ran out of gas out in the middle of the desert, they asked
themselves _____

4. "Where can we find a good nursery school for our twins?"

Did your new neighbors ask you _____

5. "Why did you steal my money?"

I was really shocked when Juan Santana asked me _____

_____

6. "Why did I do such a foolish thing?"

Did you take time to ask yourself _____

7. "How old are you?"

Suma Saud only looked at me and said nothing when I asked her _____

_____

8. "How long does it take you to shave in the morning?"

During the job interview yesterday afternoon, I thought it a strange question when I was asked _____

9. "Where are the examinations that you corrected?"

When the teacher came into the room, the students asked her _____

_____

10. "How may I make up the work I've missed?"

I asked the teacher _____

score _____ (20 points each)

QUIZ 238 indirect speech; the distant past

handbook p. 201

Transform the following direct statements into noun clauses so that you may complete the sentences. Observe the rule of sequence of tenses, and change the underlined word or words accordingly.

Examples: a. "I'm not working tonight."

When I spoke to her on the phone last Friday, she told me *that she wasn't working that night*.

b. "Can you help me with my project tomorrow morning?"

I didn't want to say yes when my boss asked me *whether I could help him with his project the following morning*.

1. "I have a lot of things to do tonight because I'm leaving on a long trip early tomorrow morning."

I wanted her to go out to dinner with me, but she said _____

_____

2. "I'm very sleepy this morning because I didn't sleep well last night."

When I saw him in the school cafeteria, he said _____

_____

3. "I feel much better today than I did yesterday."
When her son came into the room, she told him _____

_____

4. "Why didn't you do your homework last night?"
Unfortunately, I didn't have an excuse ready when my grammar teacher

asked me _____

5. "I still remember Japan well even though I was there many years ago.
While my grandfather was talking to me about his years in Asia, he told me

_____

score _____

QUIZ 239   indirect speech; the distant past
handbook p. 201

Read the directions and look at the examples in Quiz 238.

1. "I don't think it'll be as cold tonight as it was last night."

The night watchman told me _____

2. "I don't want to go shopping by myself today because I'm worried that I won't be able to carry my packages home."

She told me _____

3. "Why don't you tell me about your adventures now before I tell you about mine?"
He asked me _____

4. "I'm laughing because I've just heard a funny story a few minutes ago about you and your wife and what happened on your vacation."

I didn't know what she was talking about when she told me _____

_____

5. "I'll fight for my country even if it means I may lose my life to-morrow."
He was serious when he said _____

6. "I must tell you about the wonderful man I met last night."

Right away she told me _____

7. "Are you going to speak to your lawyer _this_ morning about the problem you were telling me about _yesterday?_"

   My boss asked me _____

8. "Why can't you charge me the same price you charged my wife _yesterday?_"

   He asked the salesman (he sounded a little angry) _____

   _____

9. "I'm very happy because I finally found a good job two days _ago_."

   When I ran into him on the street, he told me _____

   _____

10. "I want to be by myself _now_ and think about things."

    She told me _____

score _____

QUIZ 240 commands in indirect speech

handbook p. 202

Transform the following direct commands into appropriate infinitive phrases.

Example: a. "Please copy this material out of your textbooks."
The teacher told us _to copy that material out of our textbooks._

1. "Please stop pointing your finger at me."
   Mr. Owens sounded angry when he told me _____

   _____

2. "Don't laugh at me."
   He was being serious when he told his girlfriend _____

   _____

3. "Please tell me what you did with my wallet."

   She asked her husband _____

4. "Give me all the money you have on you."
   After the thief (a tall and mean-looking man) had stuck his gun in my ribs,

   he told me _____

5. "Don't make the same mistakes in your life that I made in mine."

   My father told me shortly before he died _____

   _____

6. "Please put yourself in my shoes."
   I understood her situation much better after she'd asked me _____

   _____

7. "Don't make a fool out of yourself at the party."
   Before he left the house, his mother told him _____

   _____

8. "Stop talking about yourself so much."
   I didn't want to tell her _____

9. "Don't be so bossy."
   I got angry and told my boss _____

10. "Don't tell anyone that I gave you a present."
    She whispered into my ear _____

score _____ (5 points each)

REVIEW QUIZ Z   review; *say* versus *tell*

Write in each blank an appropriate form of say *or* tell .

Examples: a. I was just *saying* to Mr. Browning he'd better reconsider our company's offer.

b. I *wouldn't have told* the story to the children unless they'd asked me to.

1. How dare you _____ me what to do—I'm not your slave.

2. _____ anything about this to my neighbors; I don't want them to know.

3. Would you mind _____ me what's bothering you? Don't be so petulant.

4. Little Jackie _____ her prayers every evening before she gets into bed.

5. Cindy, don't be a tattletale (a person who gossips); you promised you _____ anyone this secret.

6. _____ stories about women you go out with, Harold, is not very gentlemanly.

7. The prisoner has already _____ us everything that he's going to say.

8. A: Daddy, what is black and white and read all over? B: Why, Danny, a newspaper, of course. Now let me _____ you a riddle. See if you can guess it.

9. No, she's speaking truthfully. If she _____ a lie, I would know.

10. If you say you want to help me, I'll believe you, but _____ the truth.

11. _____ a word to anyone about this; we want to keep it a secret.

12. She's always _____ she's going to get a divorce, but she's only kidding.

13. I wouldn't risk _____ that story to the boss; he might fire you.

14. If she _____ she loved me, I wouldn't have believed her.

15. _____ your prayers before you go to bed, children.

16. Even if he'd begged me on his hands and knees, I _____ anything to him about my future plans.

17. Please _____ anyone what I've just told you; I don't want anyone to know.

18. _____ you'll do this work tomorrow; don't put it off any longer.

19. Miss Tattletale insisted on _____ every detail of the scandal.

20. _____ you're sorry, just don't do it again.

score _____

QUIZ 241 noun clauses derived from exclamations

handbook p. 203

Fill in each blank with an appropriate verb phrase.

come	have	pay	save
do	make	put up with	say
eat	make up	run	tell

Examples: a. I was really astonished at how fast Ted *was running*; I'd never seen him in such good physical shape before.

b. I'm disappointed at how little money I *saved* last winter.

1. Did you see how fast I _____ the last quiz?

2. I remember what wonderful apple pies your grandmother _____ when I would visit your family on my school holidays.

3. Did you notice what a beautiful figure that woman sitting under the umbrella _____?

4. Cindy, I'm amazed at how fast you _____ your lunch. Are you trying to catch a train?

5. He's always boasting about how much money he _____ by his company.

6. (have to) I'm disgusted at how much corruption the people of this town _____ every day.

7. The teacher is surprised at how few students _____ to school today; only half the class is here so far.

8. I'm shocked at what you _____ now; I just can't believe it, nor will I ever be able to.

9. Everyone is talking about how many mistakes I _____ since my marriage.

10. I was amazed at how easily he _____ all those stories during our meeting yesterday afternoon. He almost seemed to believe them himself.

score _____

QUIZ 242   infinitives following information words

handbook p. 204

Write appropriate infinitives in the blanks.

chop off	pick	skin	take apart
deal with	sand	start	take up
get rid of	shoe	store	thicken

Examples: a. Would you please show me how *to take apart* this radio; I want to see how it was made.

b. A burglar I used to know (he was fairly honest at the time I knew him) taught me how *to pick* a lock.

1. A friend of mine who lives on a farm taught me how_____a rabbit.

2. The directions in the recipe don't say how _____ the soup.

3. Do you know how _____ pests like Joe and Jay?

4. Our son doesn't know what _____ at the university; he can't make up his mind about the future.

5. I'm afraid I don't know how _____ businesspeople in this town; they're too sharp for me.

6. Would you please show me how _____ wood so that I won't get any bumps.

7. When I was a child on the farm, my grandfather taught me one day how _____ a chicken's head on a block of wood; it made a terrible impression on me.

8. I'm just riding through this town, and I'm looking for a person who knows how _____ a horse; mine just threw (lost) one of hers.

9. We can't decide where _____ these antiques—in the basement, or in the attic.

10. When I was in the Boy Scouts, I learned how _____ a fire without matches.

score _____

QUIZ 243 *that* noun clauses after verbs of urgency

handbook p. 204

Supply an appropriate verb phrase in each blank.

cut off	give	quit	serve
eat	hang	reorganize	tell
get out of	play	return	throw out

Examples: a. The King suddenly rose from his throne and demanded that the prisoner's head *be cut off.*

b. My boss has firmly but politely suggested I *quit* my job.

1. It is forbidden in the Koran that a Moslem _____ the flesh of the pig.

2. It is politely requested by the hotel management that radios _____ after eleven o'clock at night. We will appreciate your cooperation.

3. Ladies and Gentlemen, I propose that all the papers we're now working on _____ , and that we start all over again.

4. We demand that the enemy _____ to us the land that is rightfully ours.

5. Listen, I'm not suggesting (I'm demanding) that you _____ this room at once and never come back.

6. The people of the village demand that the captured guerrillas _____ at dawn.

7. Sir, I'm not begging, I'm only asking that I _____ my fair share of the money we made on the project.

8. She knelt down on her knees and begged that I _____ her husband about the scandal in her family; he'd leave her if he ever found out.

9. The president of the company recommends that the firm _____ from top to bottom. He wants to increase productivity by 30 percent.

10. He's a very difficult customer and always insists that he _____ before anyone else is.

QUIZ 244   *that* noun clauses after adjectives of urgency

handbook p. 205

Put an appropriate verb phrase in each blank.

allow	call	hush up	make
be	deal with	keep	rush
boil	enter	leak out	say

Examples: a. It's imperative that fresh troops *be rushed* to the front, or else the battle will be lost.

  b. It's absolutely essential that you *deal with* these matters as soon as possible.

1. It is vital to the security of this country that the guerrillas _____ to roam the countryside and murder innocent people.

2. Rather than being at the meeting by yourself, isn't it better that your boss _____ there with you?

3. Ladies and Gentlemen, it is essential that this information _____ to the press—we don't want the government to be wrongly accused.

4. It is mandatory that all requests for promotion in this company _____ _____ in person at the president's office.

5. Operator, I must have a line—it's urgent that the fire station _____ ____ at once.

6. Excuse me, is it necessary this water _____ before it's drunk.

7. Listen, it's best you _____ nothing to anyone about this situation; the family wants no one to know about this scandal, and they want it to be hushed up.

8. It's best that this information _____ a secret between you and me and nobody else.

9. Is it advisable that this student _____ the university now, Professor? Is she properly prepared?

10. Sh! It's best that we _____ . Some people might be listening in on our conversation, and we don't want them to find out what we're talking about.

REVIEW QUIZ AA

Write in each blank an appropriate form of the base form given in the parentheses.

Example: a. (stand) It's essential that the people of the nation <u>stand</u> united in this crisis.

1. (eat) I'm a little surprised at my roommate; how dare he _____ food all the time and never buy any.

2. (do) I'm not used to _____ such hard work as this; it's breaking my back.

3. (have) If I'd had time, I _____ dinner, but I had a meeting.

4. (give away) I don't think these old chairs are even worth _____ .

5. (do) I was mad at her because she'd made me _____ something that I didn't want to do.

6. (be) If I _____ you, young woman, I wouldn't waste my money on foolish fashions of the day; always stick to the traditional.

7. (run) The police yelled to the thief to stop, but he kept on _____ .

8. (work on) Have you finished _____ that project yet?

9. (make) I was watching a potter _____ a pot on a potter's wheel.

10. (feel) I can't help _____ sorry for that poor old man; he's so alone in the world.

11. (die away) Many Indian tribes don't want to let old customs _____ .

12. (hush up) Children, would you mind _____ ? Your daddy and I are talking.

13. (have) _____ an injection of morphine, the patient felt little pain.

14. (be) Betsy, your grandmother would never allow that if she _____ alive today.

15. (fire) If I _____ from my job, I would have gotten angry at my boss.

16. (put) My teacher suggested _____ the last paragraph at the beginning of the composition, so I'm doing the whole thing over.

17. (have) We _____ no problems in the company this year so far.

18. (finish up) Are you looking forward to _____ the semester?

19. (live) My sister _____ at the YWCA for the time being.

20. (have to go) If I'd had a toothache, I _____ to the dentist.

REVIEW QUIZ BB

Circle the correct answer. Circle both answers if either choice is correct.

Example: a. (A, **An**) ounce of prevention is worth a pound of cure. (old saying)

            b. (**For,** X) how many years have we known each other?

1. Just how many people (*do,* X) live in Tokyo, Sir?

2. My grandmother's eyes have become (*so, very*) weak; she can no longer sew.

3. They've got apple trees growing in (*the,* X) back of their house.

4. Annie, look at your face (*in, on*) the mirror; it's smeared with chocolate.

5. What (*in, on*) the world are you talking about?

6. Slim Downes is from Galveston, Texas—it's a port city on (*the,* X) Gulf of Mexico.

7. There's a large sign (*at, on*) the north side of my grandfather's silo.

8. No one in my class has a car, nor (*does,* X) anyone in yours have one.

9. It was (*so, such a*) beautiful day that we took a hike through the meadows.

10. (*The,* X) Netherlands is a small but very prosperous country.

11. During last spring, if the weather (*was, were*) nice, I'd always go swimming.

12. I was (*too, very*) hungry to wait any longer; I just had to eat then.

13. What time will your train arrive (*in, at*) Grand Central Terminal?

14. I think I lost my watch while I was sitting (*in, on*) the second row.

15. She was so excited, (*that,* X) she couldn't think straight.

16. Yes, he usually goes to (*the,* X) church on Sundays, but his wife rarely does.

17. Your father is (*laying, lying*) down, so please quiet down.

18. How many (*crisis, crises*) have we had to face together in this war?

19. (*Does, Do*) everyone want to go back to the beginning of the book and start over?

20. Please don't forget to put your name (*at, on*) the top of the page.

QUIZ 245 *wish* in the present

handbook p. 205

be	have	run	tell
burn	know	sit	work
go	live	speak	

Write an appropriate verb phrase in each blank.

Examples: a. I wish that I <u>spoke</u> English as well as my teacher does.

   b. (have to) I wish I <u>didn't have to go</u> to the chiropractor today, but I do.

1. I wish that life _____ so short.

2. (have to) We wish we _____ you this terrible news.

3. I wish I _____ that man's number; I'd like to call him up.

4. We wish Granddaddy _____ here with us now; we all miss him so much.

5. (have to) I wish I _____ at the office so early every morning.

6. The airconditioner is broken; I wish it _____ now. This apartment is like an oven.

7. I wish I _____ how to cook; I can't even fry an egg.

8. We wish our old car _____ so much gas; it's a real gas guzzler.

9. He wishes his girlfriend _____ with him, but her parents would never allow it.

10. (have to) She's very rich and bored and has nothing to do. She sometimes wishes she _____ so that she would have a reason for getting up in the mornings. The poor woman doesn't know what to do with herself.

QUIZ 246 *wish* in the past

handbook p. 206

Fill in the blanks *with appropriate verb phrases.*

bear	do	know	study
break down	get	promote	take care of
buy	have		

Examples: a. Is there anything you've done in your past life that you now wish you
        hadn't done?

   b. I wish I *had studied* English more when I was younger; I would have been
        able to learn faster than I do now.

1. She wishes that she _____ more opportunity to study
   when she was younger, but she was always too busy trying to make a living.

2. I wish I _____ that situation before it became so serious.

3. We wish our car _____ yesterday; we missed an important appointment.

4. Now that he has so many responsibilities, he wishes that he
   _____ to a higher position; he misses his old job where
   he had more free time.

5. I wish that I _____ ten years ago what I know now; I
   would have made millions.

6. He wishes he _____ a better deal when he bought his car.

7. Oh, I wish I _____ that stupid thing. Now, my dear, don't
   cry over spilled milk. (old saying)

8. When she got home from the store with the new dress, she wished that she
   _____ it; it was the wrong color.

9. (have to) Being a union boss isn't so easy; I wish I _____
   the meeting with the workers yesterday. I had to tell quite a few of them
   that they were to be laid off.

10. She's so unhappy, she wishes she _____ . She's a
    teenager, and it's her first broken heart.

QUIZ 247 *wish* with *could*; past and present
handbook p. 207

Fill in the blanks with appropriate verb phrases using <u>could</u> or <u>could have.</u>

be	have	paint	stop
cook	keep	see	work
do	make	sleep	

Examples: a. I wish that I <u>could make</u> any kind of wish and that it would come true.

   b. I wish I <u>could have slept</u> longer this morning, but I had to get up and come to class.

1. I wish something _____ about this situation right now.

2. I wish that I _____ dinner earlier last night so that I might have been able to go to the movies with my friends.

3. I wish I _____ as well as my mother can, but I'll never be able to.

4. We wish our apartment _____ before we moved in, but our landlord said that he couldn't afford to have it done, and we didn't want to do it ourselves, so it still needs painting.

5. He wishes he _____ smoking, but he has no will power.

6. What a silly wish, Ronnie! Why wish that you _____ invisible? What on earth would you do if you were able to disappear?

7. I wish my roommate _____ our secret, but he wanted to tell it to his sister, and she told everyone else in town.

8. I wish that my teacher _____ miracles, but she can't; if she could, I'd be able to speak English as well as she does.

9. He's become very rich and famous (and also egotistical); he wishes that all of his old school friends _____ him now. He loves to show off.

10. Yes, it must have been exciting. I wish I _____ at your graduation to see you receive the award. I would have felt so proud.

score _____

QUIZ 248 *wish* with *would*; future
handbook p. 207

Fill in the blanks with appropriate verb phrases using <u>would.</u>

be	get out of	let	stop
come	give	marry	talk
drive	learn	put	turn down

Examples: a. I wish my neighbor's dog _would stop_ barking; it's driving me crazy.

b. (please) Children, I wish you _would please get out of_ the house for a while and leave me in peace.

1. Darling, I wish you _____ me. Remember that two can live more cheaply than one.

2. She's getting tired of it; she wishes her friends _____ about her behind her back.

3. (please) Driver, I wish you _____ more slowly. I want to get to the station, but I want to get there alive.

4. Jamie, I wish you _____ your elbows on the table while you're eating.

5. I certainly feel lonely tonight. I wish somebody _____ me a call.

6. The children wish their mother _____ them stay up late tonight (they want to watch their favorite program on TV), but she won't; she's very strict about bedtime.

7. He wishes his wife _____ how to cook; he's tired of always having to be in the kitchen.

8. (please) Susan, I wish you _____ your stereo; you should be more considerate of the neighbors and me.

9. I wish that all my wishes _____ true.

10. Tom, I wish you _____ so egotistical. Stop talking about yourself all the time.

score _____

QUIZ 249 hope

handbook p. 208

Fill in the blanks with appropriate forms of the verbs below.

beat   conquer   get   marry
become   do   have   rain
complete enter   make

Examples: a. We hope that it _won't be raining_ tomorrow; we want our picnic to be a success.

b. Aren't you hoping _to have_ a lot of fun this coming summer?

1. Young man, what are you hoping _____ when you get out of school?

2. I certainly hope that I _____ a fool out of myself at tomorrow morning's meeting; I want to make a good impression.

  3. Columbus hoped that he _____ to the East, but he ended up in the West.

  4. He's hoping physics _____ too hard for him later on in the course; he wants to get a good grade.

  5. The teacher is hoping the students _____ well on the final exams; she's very proud of them.

  6. Napoleon hoped that he _____ Europe, but he failed.

  7. Doesn't your boyfriend hope _____ you, eventually?

  8. I hoped that I _____ Brown University last September, but I wasn't accepted (they didn't even tell me why).

  9. We hoped that the project _____ more quickly than it was; the contractors were very late in getting started.

10. Everyone is hoping that our team _____ in the next game, but it looks bad (a lot of our players are out with injuries).

score _____ (5 points each)

QUIZ 250   abridgement of noun clause after *wish*

handbook p. 209

Fill in the blanks with appropriate words.

Examples: a. You can't lend me any money, can you? I wish you *could.*

         b. My parents never listen to me—I wish they *would.*

  1. I'm not a billionaire—I wish I _____ .

  2. The teacher will probably give us an exam tomorrow—I wish he _____ .

  3. I didn't have any breakfast this morning—I wish that I _____ .

  4. I can't work miracles—I wish I _____ .

  5. I wasn't at the last meeting—I wish I _____ .

  6. My grammar isn't so good as I'd like it to be—I wish it _____ .

  7. We were at that party—we now wish that we _____ (it was raided by the police).

  8. My roommate doesn't ever help out in the kitchen—I wish he _____ .

  9. James has to get up early every morning—he wishes he _____ .

10. No one was at the station to meet me—I wish someone _____ .

11. You can't be at the seminar tomorrow, can you, Professor? I wish you

_____ .

236

12. I went to bed very late last night—I now wish that I _____ (I can't keep my eyes open).

13. No one in my family can be at my graduation—I wish everyone _____.

14. We weren't invited to the reception for the President's brother—we wish we _____.

15. It'll probably rain today—I wish it _____.

16. I was told beforehand about my surprise birthday party—I wish I _____ _____.

17. None of my friends are rich—all of them wish that they _____.

18. I'm sorry, I'm not able to help you at this time—I wish I _____.

19. I couldn't go out last night—I wish I _____.

20. I wasn't able to see my friends off at the airport—I wish I _____.

score _____ (5 points each)

REVIEW QUIZ CC

Write in each blank an appropriate form of the base form given in the parentheses.

Example: a. (build) To solve the problem, my neighbor has suggested a fence *be built* between his house and mine; he says he'll pay for having it done.

1. (do) I've asked Timmy to stop whistling in the house, but he keeps on _____ it.

2. (leave) He wishes he _____ the office early today, but he can't.

3. (listen) Ladies and Gentlemen, I want you _____ to what I have to say.

4. (steal) Listen, Eddie, you wouldn't be in such trouble now, if you _____ _____ the judge's car.

5. (be) It was only early August, but it felt as though it _____ late September. There was a chill in the air.

6. (sue) Yes, you're right, my company doesn't look forward to _____ by the government.

7. (make) He now wishes he _____ such a fool out of himself at the last meeting.

8. (stop) I wish the children _____ making so much noise, but they won't.

237

9. (cook) I wish I _____ the steak so long; it was as tough as rubber.

10. (win) She hoped that she _____ first prize in the contest, but she didn't.

11. (have to work) If I _____ yesterday, I wouldn't have been able to see you.

12. (bet) I wouldn't risk _____ on that horse if I were you.

13. (have to go) You _____ to the bank for a loan if you had taken better care of your finances.

14. (complete) You don't think this project is worth _____ , do you?

15. (be) I don't care for that clerk; she acts as if she _____ the president of the store.

16. (take up) Have you ever considered _____ stamp collecting as a hobby?

17. (never / bear) She's so unhappy that she wishes she _____.

18. (sign) Sir, please don't try to make me _____ something that I don't want to sign.

19. (feel) I can't help _____ sorry for the poor—they need more opportunity.

20. (move) I suggest _____ all the furniture in this room into the garage.

score _____ (5 points each)

REVIEW QUIZ DD

In each of the following sentences, there is one mistake. Cross out that mistake and put in the correct word (or words) if needed.

Examples: a. These spoons are ~~more~~ cheaper than those, much less in fact.

               helping
        b. I must thank you for ~~to help~~ me on the last project.

1. We wish the weather on our vacation would have been better than it was.

2. I'm not used to eat with my fingers, and neither are you.

3. Would you mind to stop at the store for a jar of pickles?

4. You'd rather be a lender than a borrower, hadn't you?

5. Only once I have eaten caviar, and once was enough—I didn't like it.

6. How delicious this ice cream is; do you like some?

7. Unless our car had fixed, we wouldn't have been able to go for our drive.

8. If you would have gone to the movie, you would have enjoyed it a great deal.

9. The people of the world demand that the hostages are released at once.

10. Despite of the bad weather, there were no serious traffic delays.

11. Only deer is protected by the government in this forest.

12. The telephone was invented for Alexander Graham Bell.

13. My doctor made me stopped smoking; he did it by hypnotizing me.

14. Never in her life she's been deeply in love; she's waiting for the day.

15. The color of her eyes are blue (as blue as the sky, in fact).

16. How essential is it that I am at the next conference?

17. The King has demanded that the revolutionary is beheaded.

18. I wouldn't get involved with this matter if I was you.

19. Before you leaving the room, please turn off the lights and close the windows.

20. How close are we at the end of this book?

score _____

QUIZ 251   *who* and *that* as subjects of essential adjective clauses

handbook p. 210

Fill in the blanks with appropriate verb phrases. Do not use any modal auxiliaries.

arrest	do	know	receive
bark	go	lie	rock
deliver	have	live	use

Examples: a. (never) I used to have a teacher at the university who *had never received* a university degree himself, but he was an internationally known artist.

b. (always) We have a dog that *is always barking,* but none of the neighbors ever complain.

1. A person who _____ how to read or write can still vote in the national elections, can't he?

2. The equipment that _____ tomorrow has cost this company millions of dollars.

3. People who _____ in glass houses shouldn't throw stones. (old saying)

4. All of the office equipment that _____ at the conference today has been rented from a nearby office supply company.

5. The hand that _____ the cradle rules the world. (old saying)

6. Does this gold pen that _____ here on my desk belong to any of you in this class?

7. (never) She used to go out with a man who _____ to school, but he was a famous writer of mystery stories. He'd taught himself how to read and write.

8. (ever) I have a friend who _____ any homework, but she always gets high marks.

9. A person who _____ a university education has a better chance of getting a good job.

10. The man in the office who _____ by the police yesterday had been stealing money from the company.

score _____

QUIZ 252 *whose* introducing essential adjective clauses

handbook p. 211

Complete the following essential adjective clauses with appropriate verb phrases. Do not use modal auxiliaries.

be	fly	live	sound	work
chase	have	own	take	yowl

Examples: a. Do you think a person whose family *has* connections in the government has a better chance of getting a job at the State Department?

b. Those are the people whose house I *lived* in while I was studying at Berkeley.

1. (have to) I have a friend whose parents _____ ; they just spend all their time traveling.

2. I know someone whose family _____ a skyscraper in New York City.

3. (have to) We have a neighbor whose husband _____ insulin every day; he has diabetes.

4. I met a woman at the reception whose husband _____ across the Atlantic Ocean in a balloon.

name _____

5. (always) We have a neighbor whose dog _____ the mailman.

6. I'd like you to meet the man whose wife _____ the next president.

7. I have a nephew whose voice _____ just like mine.

8. He has a girlfriend whose father _____ a V.I.P. in the government.

9. (always) I have a neighbor whose cat _____ ; I think he's lonely.

10. I want you to meet someone whose father _____ important connections in this company. He'll get you a good job.

score _____

QUIZ 253 nonessential adjective clauses; *which*

handbook p. 211

Write in the blanks appropriate verb phrases. Do not use modal auxiliaries.

be	have	tear down
cost	make	test out
die	swim	yowl

Example: a. Class, when Christopher Columbus, who didn't know where he _was_, landed in America, he thought he had arrived in India.

1. (never) Dora Moore, who _____ a singing lesson in her life, sounds as though she's been professionally trained.

2. (always) Their cat, who _____ , keeps my wife and me up at night.

3. Ladies and Gentlemen, this automobile, which _____ in Detroit, is powered by a small steam engine; it's a revolutionary design.

4. (already) The Browns, who _____ seven children, would like one more.

5. When I first met Priscilla Davenport, a woman who _____ across the English Channel three times, she was teaching swimming to children in New Zealand.

6. That house, which _____ today, was condemned by the city.

7. The patient, who _____ because he hadn't received good care, was trying to get out of the hospital so that he could die at home in his own bed.

241

8. Yes, Ladies and Gentlemen, this product, which _____ by my company now, is going to revolutionize the dry-cleaning industry.

9. Jonathan Grimes, who _____ a philanthropist all his life, died peacefully in his sleep last night at the age of 103.

10. Madam, this perfume, which _____ a hundred dollars an ounce, will go perfectly with your personality. You'll enjoy wearing it, and your husband will love it.

score _____

REVIEW QUIZ EE *contrasting essential and nonessential clauses*

Set off with circled commas the adjective clauses where they are nonessential.

Examples: a. The Statue of Liberty⊙which was a gift from the people of France⊙has been standing at the entrance to New York Harbor since 1886.

b. He has a girlfriend whose roommate is my oldest sister.

1. The electric light bulb which was invented by Thomas Alva Edison was one of the most important inventions of the nineteenth century.

2. People who are blind cannot live by themselves.

3. The Second World War which started in 1939 and ended in 1945 changed the world more than it had ever been changed before.

4. People who are married cannot live in that dormitory. It's for singles only.

5. Ma'am, this watch which was a birthday gift from my father on my twenty-first birthday is solid gold. How much can I pawn it for?

6. Children who never want to play are not normal.

7. Sir, this proposal which should have been typewritten is not acceptable to our committee. It must be redone properly.

8. Ladies and Gentlemen, these strange-looking objects which were found in some caves near this city were used as tools almost 50,000 years ago.

9. The Bible which was the first book to be printed has been the most widely read book of all time.

10. Wild ducks that have clipped wings cannot fly.

QUIZ 254   relative pronouns as objects of verbs and prepositions
handbook p. 213

Fill in the blanks with appropriate verb phrases:

call	go	put	vote
consult	introduce	speak	work
fall	live	swear	write

Examples: a. The man to whom I *was introduced* at the meeting had once been an astronaut.

b. The woman who he *had sworn* at turned out to be a police officer.

1. The woman for whom the people _____ in the election turned out to be the wrong choice.

2. The person who she _____ with since the beginning of the year has turned out to be a good roommate.

3. The government official to whom I _____ replied within a few days.

4. The person who I _____ to a few minutes ago when you came into the office is my boss.

5. The doctor whom they _____ never came and the patient died.

6. The lawyer who I _____ with turned out not to know what he was talking about (I lost the case).

7. The person for whom he _____ is not an easy person to get along with.

8. The table on which he _____ the newspaper is in the hall.

9. The woman with whom he _____ in love on a beach in Italy was eventually to become his wife.

10. The person who I _____ with to school every day has a car.

QUIZ 255 unmarked essential adjective clauses

handbook p. 214

Fill in the blanks with appropriate verb phrases.

dream about	give	make	talk about
eat	inherit	pack	turn on
fall	lose	publish	

Examples: a. (always) The man she's *always talking about* is the man she's going to marry.

b. The purse she*'d lost* was eventually turned in to the Lost and Found Department and returned to her.

1. The medicine the patient _____ twice a day is to keep him relaxed and out of pain.

2. The food we _____ at dinner usually appears on the table at lunch the following day.

3. The friends I _____ since my arrival in this town are all being very nice to me.

4. The program I _____ became a little boring, so I switched over to channel 13.

5. The books our company _____ are better than any of the other publishers'.

6. (recently) The antiques he _____ are worth thousands of dollars.

7. On my trip to Europe, the clothes I _____ were not right for the climate. I almost froze to death.

8. The man she _____ in love with on her vacation the previous summer eventually became her husband that spring.

9. The examination the students _____ today is the final.

10. (always) The person I _____ exists only in my imagination.

QUIZ 256 *where* introducing essential adjective clauses
handbook p. 214

Write in the blanks appropriate verb phrases.

break down	do	shine	think
come	give	sleep	work
cost	rain	take advantage of	

Examples: a. While we were in New England, we stayed in a hotel where George Washington *had slept*.

b. (always) They're looking for a place to retire where the sun *is always shining.*

1. I'm looking for a butcher's where good beef _____ much.

2. (always) At that time, we were living in an apartment where the plumb-ing _____, and there was often no heat, but the place was cheap.

3. I certainly don't enjoy being in a situation where I _____. Do you?

4. He's really lazy; he's looking for an institute where no homework _____ _____.

5. Have you ever lived in a house where nothing _____ right? Well, that's my house.

6. (ever) I'd like to live in a place where the winter _____; I don't like cold weather.

7. Would you happen to know a restaurant (nothing fancy) where a good, wholesome dinner _____ much?

8. (ever) While we were in Australia, we lived in an area where it _____. The sky was always a bright blue.

9. (have to) He's looking for a job where he _____ much; he's an artist, and he wants to use all his creative energies for his painting projects.

10. I used to work in a factory where the management _____ much for the workers; they were interested only in profits.

QUIZ 257   the present perfect and past perfect tenses in essential adjective clauses

handbook p. 215

Fill in the blanks with appropriate verb phrases in the present perfect or the past perfect tense. Use ever *in each verb phrase.*

be	fly	produce	take
build	have	ride	tell
do	hear	see	try on

Examples: a. When I first saw Madam Tebaldi perform, she had the most beautiful voice that I'*d ever heard*.

b. (have to) Without a doubt, it was the most difficult examination that I'*d ever had to take.*

1. The ambassador's limousine was the most luxurious car I _____ _____ in.

2. Isn't this the most beautiful fur coat that you _____ in this store?

3. (have to) Probably, this is the most difficult thing I _____ _____ in my whole life.

4. Ladies and Gentlemen, this will be the most spectacular musical comedy that _____ on Broadway. We'll all make millions.

5. Without a doubt, Nepal was the most beautiful country I _____ _____ in.

6. (have to) This is the most terrible news that I _____ anyone.

7. This dam is the largest that our construction company _____ _____.

8. (have to) This meeting is probably the most serious meeting that I _____ with the president since I started working at this company.

9. Grandpa's trip to Los Angeles was the first time he _____ on a plane.

10. My roommate has the most beautiful eyes that I _____.

name _____   score _____

QUIZ 258 causatives with *have* + actor + base form + object
handbook p. 215

Fill in each blank with an appropriate verb phrase containing <u>have</u> + actor + base form.

a butler	a jéweler	the mechanic	check	dye	reset
a carpenter	the dentist	my barber	come	fix	retype
a cleaning person	the doctor	my secretary	cover	pull out	serve
an exterminator	a maid	your hairdresser	cut	put	

Examples: a. Tomorrow, I'<u>m going to have my secretary retype</u> this letter; it's full of typos.

b. (have to) I'<u>ve had to have the mechanic put</u> a new battery in my car twice this year.

1. Because she and her husband were leaving for a two-month winter vacation, she _____ all the furniture in the house.

2. Yesterday, we _____ the porch; it's safe to walk on now.

3. (have to) I _____ this diamond; it may fall out if I don't have it done.

4. _____ your hair, Madam; it wouldn't look natural.

5. (have to) My neighbors _____ to their house at least three times. Termites are literally eating their house down.

6. My wife doesn't like my hair long; I _____ it short. Summer is coming, and I'm going to be doing a lot of swimming.

7. If I could have afforded it, I _____ the guests at my dinner party the other evening.

8. Their house looked wonderful for the dance the other night because they _____ in and clean it up. It usually looks messy.

9. (have to / ever) I've been lucky; I _____ a tooth, and I'm almost ninety years old.

10. (have to) Mr. Browning _____ his blood count every two months.

QUIZ 259 causatives with *have* + object + past participle

handbook p. 216

Fill in each blank with an appropriate phrase containing <u>have</u> *+ object + past participle.*

a tooth	her hair	the problem	develop	paint	renovate
all her dresses	his hair	these trousers	do	press	shorten
color film	it	your house	fix	pull out	take care of
her clothes	my car	your phone	make	put	

Examples: a. It costs a lot *to have color film developed* these days.

b. (have to) I *have to have these trousers pressed* before I can wear them again.

1. (have to) Stella Sands _____ three times a week; she's an actress and appears on TV a lot. What a beauty she is!

2. Darn it! I wish that I _____ last week. I'm without wheels.

3. (have to) Mr. Pickens, if you had taken better care of your house (Why did you let it run down?), you _____ last year.

4. _____ red, please. It will make it look like a barn.

5. If you _____ by your lawyer last year, you wouldn't be having so much trouble with the government now.

6. (have to / never) I _____ since the time that I was losing my baby teeth.

7. Because of the sudden change in fashion, she _____ _____ (that's why she doesn't have anything to wear now).

8. _____ by the bed; it's a convenient place to have one.

9. Mrs. Richhouse spends a lot of money on _____, and she always looks like a million dollars (which she happens to have).

10. Remember, class, a man _____—he has it cut.

QUIZ 260 causatives with *get* + object + past participle
handbook p. 216

Fill in each blank with an appropriate phrase containing *get* + object + past participle.

his hair	the bedroom	your car	change	lengthen
my apartment	the floors	your face	cut	lift
our TV	the pump	your hair	dye	paint
that leak	this skirt	your schedule	fix	sand

Examples: a. (have to) I *had to get my apartment painted* before I moved in; it really
            needed it.

b. *Don't get your schedule changed*; stay with us in this class.

1. I _____ white last winter if I could have
   afforded it.

2. (have to) We _____ today; it's flooding the
   kitchen floor.

3. I _____ last week, but it's still too short,
   isn't it?

4. We _____ last month; they really look nice
   now.

5. We _____; it'll be cheaper than buying a
   new one.

6. He _____ yesterday; he couldn't get an appointment.

7. _____ yellow; you don't want it to look
   like a taxi.

8. Mr. Jenkins, _____; it'll make you look ten
   years younger.

9. (have to) We _____; we can do it ourselves.

10. _____ short; you look better when it's
    long.

QUIZ 261   persuasion with *get* + object + infinitive
handbook p. 217

Fill in each blank with an appropriate object (+ *not*) + infinitive.

a stubborn mule	you	your dog	bark	keep off	say
my dog	your cat	your monkey	bite	make	scratch
my son	your child	your parrot	eat	move	smoke
the policeman	your children		give	play	watch

Examples: a. I'm looking for a way to get *my dog to keep off* the bed.

b. How do you get *your child not to watch* too much TV?

1. How did your doctor get _____?

2. How did you get _____ so many words?
He sounds like a person.

3. How do you get _____ at strangers when
they come into the house?

4. Doctor, what is a good way to get _____
his nails?

5. How did you get _____ such wonderful
tricks?

6. Well, Mr. Speedy, now how are you going to get _____

_____ you a speeding ticket?

7. How did you get _____ the furniture with
her paws?

8. What is a good way to get _____? Mine
won't budge an inch.

9. How on earth do you get _____ spinach?
Mine won't touch it.

10. How do you get _____ their beds?

score _____ (5 points each)

REVIEW QUIZ FF

In each of the following sentences, there is one mistake. Cross out that mistake and put in
the correct word if one is needed.

Examples: a. She told ~~to~~ everyone that she was getting married soon.

b. I wish I ~~spoke~~ had spoken to my boss about the project yesterday.

1. When I asked to her the question, she told me nothing.

2. You couldn't teach grammar unless your English was good.

3. We're both lazy—neither of us do the daily homework.

4. Would you enjoy to go for a swim now?

5. Can you tell me how many oranges are there in the crate?

6. When I was a child, if I were sick, I would stay in bed.

7. Do you know what does this word means?

8. That selfish child insists in getting everything she wants.

9. I went to the post office for to get some stamps.

10. If I slept more last night, I wouldn't be so tired now.

11. Bryan has to work very hard; he wishes he doesn't.

12. The company gave a raise to both my brother and I.

13. You'd rather stay home tonight, hadn't you?

14. He hardly knows nothing about his wife's friends.

15. I wish I didn't make that mistake yesterday.

16. Since their argument, they've stopped to speak to each other.

17. We believe it's best that the president resigns from his office.

18. You won't get better unless you don't take your medicine.

19. I was writing very fast, and I couldn't avoid to make a few mistakes.

20. I wish you enjoy your courses next semester.

score _____ (5 points each)

REVIEW QUIZ GG

Fill in each blank with an appropriate form of the base form given in the parentheses.

Examples: a. (come) Unless snow *comes* tomorrow, we won't be able to go skiing.

b. (come) I'll do that work if my boss *doesn't come* in tomorrow.

1. (cry over) There's no use _____ spilled milk. (old saying)

2. (be) Even if everyone in the club _____ here now, there wouldn't be a great many people.

3. (watch) We let the children _____ TV until very late last night.

4. (renovate) We don't think this house is worth _____. Do you?

5. (eat) She's an American and not used to _____ a lot of rich and spicy food.

6. (be) How necessary is it that I _____ at their baby's baptism?

7. (see) I wish I _____ *Romeo and Juliet* on TV the other night—I love that play.

8. (be) If I _____ tired now, I'd lie down and rest for a while.

9. (eat) We _____ outside yesterday if it hadn't been raining.

10. (know) We _____ each other for more than thirty years now.

11. (do) Please don't postpone _____ this work any longer; it must be done at once.

12. (give) The class has suggested to the teacher that he _____ no final exam.

13. (leak out) Someone in the government let the information _____ _____.

14. (run out of) We _____ gas if we'd stopped at the last station.

15. (fix) Because it _____, I'm not wearing my favorite watch now.

16. (pay) I'd never have done that job unless I _____ a lot.

17. (clean) I wouldn't have minded _____ the kitchen if you'd asked me to do it.

18. (be) He wishes he _____ so busy all the time; he's overloaded with work.

19. (serve) Mrs. Robinson insists on _____ at once.

20. (be able to do) You _____ very well if you had taken this quiz at the beginning of the course.

REVIEW QUIZ HH

Fill in each blank with one word. Contractions like <u>don't</u> or <u>doesn't</u> count as one word.

Examples: a. I've had little free time this semester, and I'll have even <u>less</u> next term.

b. <u>What</u> a beautiful day for the last day of class!

1. _____ we'd had a very dry spring, our garden looked lovely that summer.

2. I was _____ tired last night that I couldn't sleep—I kept tossing and turning.

3. _____ eleven years, my mother and father have had their candy store.

4. They've got _____ of money, but they don't know how to spend it.

5. You'd _____ watch out—there are many pickpockets around here.

6. I didn't benefit from yesterday's meeting, and no one else _____ _____ either.

7. Why won't you obey me, son? _____ I your father?

8. Our daughter really doesn't know _____ she wants to get married or not.

9. _____ to the pilot strike, no planes will be able to take off; we'll have to take the train.

10. My roommate and I haven't been studying; _____ of us is ready to take the final exam.

11. What time did you _____ down for your nap yesterday afternoon?

12. _____ now, we've had a lot of luck in our business; we don't know what's happened.

13. It was _____ the fifth row that I sat down in a broken desk and broke my arm.

14. _____ to the meeting, I found out that I was going to be elected president.

15. These are _____ big apples that I can't believe it—are they real?

16. _____ the hot weather and terrible crowds, we enjoyed the parade.

17. I'm glad that the semester is over; _____, I'm going to miss my class.

18. Would you like to give me your address _____ that I may write to you?

19. In the beginning, the teacher told us it was imperative that everyone _____ the homework. He was right.

20. Let's take our last break together, _____ we?

Commonly Used Multiple-Word Verbs and Certain Expressions

Note: Appearing in the following list are some of the more common multiple-word verbs, most of which occur in the quizzes. Those marked (S) are transitive and separable; those not marked are intransitive or inseparable. When a preposition is given in parentheses in the entry, that preposition is used when there is an addition to the phrase (usually a prepositional phrase); for example:

brush up (on), "review." You'd better *brush up* (on your grammar); the exam is tomorrow.

act out, "illustrate by acting" (S). The children *acted* the story *out* beautifully.

argue over (or **about**). Let's not *argue over* (*about*) this silly matter any longer.

ask out (S). He wants to go out with her on a date, but he's afraid to *ask* her *out*.

attend to, "take care of." My lawyer *attended to* the matter, and my problem with the government just disappeared.

bail out: a. "release (someone) from jail on payment of money" (S). Her neighbor's son got into trouble last weekend and ended up in jail—she had to *bail* him *out*.
b. "extricate from a difficult situation" (S). Our company hasn't been doing well lately, but the banks are going to *bail* it *out*.
c. "empty a boat of water" (S). Our boat was filling up with water (we'd sprung a leak), and we were trying to *bail* it *out* as fast as we could.
d. "parachute from an airplane." The pilot *bailed out* of the burning plane at four thousand feet.

bank on, "have confidence in." You can *bank on* my friends; they're all dependable.

bawl out, "rebuke severely" (S). I got to work late, and my boss *bawled* me *out*.

beat up, "give a thorough beating to" (S). Some big boys down the street *beat* our little boy *up* yesterday; we're going to talk to their parents.

bite off (S). Here, Dickie, would you like a piece of this candy bar? *Bite* some *off*.

block out, "obstruct from view or exposure" (S). That large tree *blocks* the sun *out*; let's cut it down.

blow away (S). There was a lot of smoke from the fire, but the wind *blew* it *away*.

blow down (S). We had a banana tree in the garden, but the strong wind in the last hurricane *blew* it *down*.

blow out: a. "extinguish" (S). Don't spill any wax on the table when you *blow* the candles *out*.
b. "explode (in reference to tires)." On our trip last month, two of our tires *blew out*.

blow up: a. "explode; destroy by explosion" (S). The terrorists *blew* the wrong car *up*.

b. "become very angry." When I asked my father to lend me some more money, he suddenly *blew up*.

c. "make larger (as in photography)" (S). She liked the photograph of herself, and she had it *blown up* five times.

break down: a. "stop working properly." Our car *had broken down*, and we had to have it towed to the nearest garage.

b. "lose one's composure or health." If you don't take it easy, you're going to *break down*.

c. "analyze" (S). We *broke* the hospital bill *down* and found that it was wrong.

break in: a. "tame" (S). We're *breaking* this horse *in;* he's almost ready to ride.

b. "train" (S). This is my new secretary; I'm *breaking* her *in*.

c. "make an illegal entry." Someone *broke in* last night (through the window) and stole all of my wife's jewelry.

d. "make something new more comfortable; begin the initial operation of a machine" (S). I can't wear these new shoes to go shopping or sightseeing; I'm just *breaking* them *in*. I'm not driving very fast; this is a brand new car, and I'm *breaking* it *in*.

break out: a. "appear (as with rashes, pimples, and other skin ailments)." When he eats chocolate, his face always *breaks out* in pimples.

b. "occur suddenly." Just as they arrived in the country, a revolution *broke out*.

c. "escape." Several convicts *broke out* of prison last night.

break up, "separate into smaller parts" (S). The students were rioting, but the police *broke* them *up*.

break up (with), "put an end to a romantic relationship." She and her husband are *breaking up* (with each other); they no longer get along.

bring about, "cause" (S). What *brought* the Russian Revolution *about*?

bring out: a. "introduce to society or the marketplace" (S). Our company is *bringing* a new mouse trap *out*, and we're going to make a million.

b. "publish" (S). The publishers *brought* this book *out* in the spring.

bring up: a. "raise or rear" (S). Dick's parents *brought* him *up* on a farm.

b. "bring into a conversation" (S). Let's have a light conversation; please don't *bring* anything serious or controversial *up*.

brush off: a. "remove dirt and dust by brushing" (S). *Brush* that jacket *off* before you put it on.

b. "reject; dismiss abruptly" (S). He's always trying to be friendly with her, but she always *brushes* him *off*.

brush up (on), "review." You'd better *brush up* (on the irregular verbs) before you take the final exam.

burn down, "burn completely (for buildings)" (S). The building *burned down*, but no lives were lost. Who *burned* it *down*?

burn out, "stop working (usually in reference to electrical equipment)." The motor in the fan has finally *burned out*. The light bulb in the closet has *burned out*.

burn up: a. "burn completely (for combustible material)" (S). She threw the old love letters into the fire and *burned* them *up*.

b. "make angry" (S). Your talking about me behind my back just *burns* me *up*.

butt in (on), "interrupt." Please don't *butt in* (on our conversation); it's rude.

call back, "return a phone call" (S). Please *call* me *back;* I'll be in all day.

call down, "reprimand" (S). He *called* his son *down* for being so lazy.

call for, "come or go to meet and get." Please *call for* me at nine; I'll be waiting for you.

call off, "cancel" (S). They've *called* their wedding *off;* they've decided they don't really love each other.

call on: a. "pay a formal visit." The Ambassador *called on* the King today.
    b. "be asked to speak." The teacher always *calls on* me first; I'm her favorite.

call out, "announce" (S). I'm waiting for someone to *call* my name *out.*

call up: a. "telephone" (S). No one could *call* me *up* yesterday; my phone was out of order.
    b. "draft into military service" (S). The government has *called* thousands of men and women *up;* many people say war is coming.

calm down, "relax" (S). I was nervous, but the soft music *calmed* me *down.*

carry out, "obey orders" (S). Yes, Sir, I'll *carry* these orders *out* right away.

catch on (to), "understand (usually in reference to jokes)." Everyone was laughing at his wife's joke, but his face was blank; he hadn't *caught on* (to the joke).

catch up (with), "overtake." You're behind in your class, but if you study hard, you'll be able to *catch up* (with the rest of the students).

check in (with), "inquire." My boss asked me to *check in* (with him) before I leave work today.

check off (S). The teacher *checked* the names *off* as she was reading the list.

check out, "test or evaluate" (S). You'll enjoy that restaurant; you should *check* it *out.*

cheer up, "encourage cheer and happiness" (S). I was feeling depressed and unhappy, but a friend of mine came over and *cheered* me *up* with some funny stories.

chew up, "chew completely" (S). Children, *chew* your food *up* before you swallow it.

chicken out, "lose one's bravery." I was going to dive off the high board (almost thirty feet), but I *chickened out* at the last moment.

chop off (S). He *chopped* his thumb *off* in an accident with a hatchet.

chop out, "remove by chopping" (S). On that head of lettuce, *chop* the spoiled part *out.*

chop up, "chop completely" (S). *Chop* the vegetables *up* before you put them in the soup.

clam up, "stop talking." Whenever I ask her a personal question, she always *clams up.*

clean off, "clean completely (usually in reference to tables)" (S). Please *clean* this table *off.*

clean out, "remove articles from in order to clean (usually in reference to closets, drawers, and large containers)" (S). We're also going to *clean* the closets *out;* they're in a mess.

clean up, "clean completely" (S). We're going to *clean* the house *up* today.

clear away, "remove articles from (usually from a table or desk top)" (S). Waiter, would you please *clear* these dishes *away;* we've finished.

clear out (of), "leave." When the police arrived, everyone *cleared out* (of the room).

clear up: a. "become fair weather." The rain has stopped, and it's finally *clearing up.*
    b. "explain" (S). This is a serious matter; you'd better *clear* it *up* with the boss yourself before someone else talks to him.

come off, "succeed or take place." I worked hard on planning that meeting, but it never *came off.*

come up with, "imagine or think up." I'm trying to *come up with* a good title for my next composition.

cool off, "make cooler" (S). Why don't we turn on the airconditioner and *cool* the bedroom *off* before we go to bed.

count on, "depend on." You can always *count on* me; I'm very dependable.

cross out, "remove a written mistake by making a cross mark" (S). Please *cross* all the mistakes *out* and put in the appropriate corrections.

cross up, "betray or cheat" (S). I'm furious that my business partner has *crossed* me *up.*

cry over, "worry about." Don't *cry over* your past mistakes; they weren't all your fault.

cut down: a. "cut to the ground" (S). The lumberjack *cut* the tree *down* with the biggest axe I'd ever seen.
    b. "decrease the consumption (of)." He's *cut down* on smoking and feels better.

cut in (on), "interrupt." I hate to *cut in* (on your conversation), but I must speak to both of you at once.

cut off: a. "abruptly stop someone from speaking" (S). The telephone operator *cut* my wife and me *off*.

b. "remove by cutting, or amputate" (S). The patient's leg couldn't be saved, and the surgeon had to *cut* it *off*.

c. "disinherit" (S). He never liked his children, so he *cut* them *off* in his will.

cut out, "stop" (S). Children, you're making a lot of noise; please *cut* it *out*.

cut out (of), "remove by cutting" (S). What a beautiful picture this is! I'm going to *cut* it *out* (of the magazine).

cut up, "cut into small pieces" (S). *Cut* the meat *up* before you fry it.

deal out, "distribute" (S). The dealer *dealt* the cards *out*, and I got four aces.

deal with, "negotiate with; take care of." My lawyer is *dealing with* the problem now.

decide on (or *upon*), "choose." Which color have you *decided on* to paint your house?

die down, "decrease in intensity." The storm finally *died down* after ten hours.

die out (away) "end." Many old customs in our country have *died out* (away).

dine out, "dine in a restaurant." It costs a lot to *dine out* in a fine restaurant.

dish out, "serve" (S). My grandmother always *dishes* the food *out* at dinner.

do over, "do again with corrections" (S). Please *do* this composition *over*.

do without, "manage without." We have to *do without* a vacation this year; we're broke.

drag on, "proceed slowly." The meeting was *dragging on*, so I finally left.

dream about (sometimes *of*), He's always *dreaming about* castles in the air.

dress up, "dress in a formal or elegant style" (S). For the occasion, she *dressed* herself *up* in her best finery. Shall we *dress up* for dinner?

drive away: a. "repel" (S). The spray *drove* the mosquitoes *away*.

b. "leave by driving." She stepped on the gas and *drove away*.

drop in (on), "unexpectedly visit." I don't like to *drop in* (on my friends) without calling first.

drop off: a. "deliver" (S). I have to *drop* these packages *off* at the post office.

b. "decrease." The company's sales have been *dropping off* recently.

drop out (of), "leave; stop attending (usually in reference to schools)." Some students become discouraged and decide to *drop out* (of school). Note: Frequently used with the expression *drop out of sight*: As I watched the ship sailing toward the horizon, it gradually *dropped out of sight* (disappeared).

eat in, "eat at home." Let's not *eat in*; let's go out and have Chinese food.

eat out, "eat at a restaurant." Let's not *eat out*; let's stay home and save money.

eat up, "eat completely" (S). He cooked a whole chicken for himself and *ate* it all *up*.

end up, "arrive at a place, usually unexpectedly." Columbus wanted to go to India, but he *ended up* in America instead.

fall behind, "not keep up; lose ground." He wasn't doing any homework, so he *fell behind* the rest of the class.

fall down. A horse *fell down* in the race and broke its leg; it had to be destroyed.

fall in, "collapse (used in reference to buildings)." The roof of the old building *fell in*. Note: Commonly used with the expression *fall in love*: Romeo *fell in love* with Juliet at first sight (immediately).

fall off, "decrease." Sales for our company always *fall off* in the summertime.

fall out of. They were breaking up because they'd *fallen out of* love.

fall out (with) . . . (*about* or *over*), "quarrel; have an argument." He and his brother *fell out with* each other. They *fell out over* a woman.

fall through, "fail." We were supposed to go to Sweden, but our plans *fell through*.

figure on: a. "expect." We're *figuring on* ten people being at the meeting.
b. "intend." I'm *figuring on* doing my homework this evening after dinner.

figure out, "solve; understand" (S). Would you please help me *figure* this puzzle *out*.

fill in: a. "complete a form, quiz, etc. by writing in the blanks" (S). Please *fill* the blanks *in* with appropriate words.
b. "substitute." Mrs. Clark is *filling in* for her husband at the office while he's away on a business trip.

fill out, "complete by writing" (S). Have you *filled* your application form *out* yet?

fill up, "fill completely" (S). How much gas today, Sir? My tank is almost empty; *fill* her (it) *up*, please.

find out, "discover" (S). He was stealing money from the government, and the FBI *found him out*.

finish up, "finish completely" (S). I'm going to *finish* my homework *up* and go to bed.

fix up: a. "decorate; renovate" (S). We're *fixing* the house *up*; it's costing a lot.
b. "make something okay" (S). There's no problem now; I've *fixed* it *up* with the police.

flip over, "turn over" (S). Don't you think it's time to *flip* the pancakes *over*?

focus in (on), "draw a sharp focus on individual things or people" Class, today we're going to *focus in on* the problems of each student.

focus on, "concentrate on." Most of the quizzes in this book *focus on* a particular subject.

fool around, "behave in an active but relaxed manner." I like to take it easy on Sundays; I just *fool around* with my family and friends.

foul up, "create disorder" (S). We were expecting to do good business last weekend, but the bad weather *fouled* our plans *up*.

freeze over, "freeze completely as in lakes, rivers, and bays." Hudson Bay *freezes over* every winter; however, the Hudson River *freezes over* only once in a great while.

freeze up, "become cold and reserved." When I asked her how old she was, she suddenly *froze up*.

get along: a. "manage." With inflation and high prices, it's difficult to *get along* these days.
b. "have a good relationship." My cat and dog *get along*, which is unusual.
c. "be on one's way." I have to be *getting along*; I've got a lot of errands to run.

get away with, "commit a bad act without being punished." He's *gotten away with* many crimes. A lot of people *get away with* murder these days.

get by: a. "manage." Despite the high cost of living, we're *getting by*.
b. "pass." Please let me *get by*; I'm in a big hurry.

get even with, "have revenge." I'll *get even with* you for getting me into trouble.

get into, "enter." How do you *get into* the Boy Scouts?

get in the way, "obstruct." Children, please don't *get in the way*; you're always under my feet.

get in touch with, "contact; call." *Get in touch with* me when you're in town next.

get off, "leave a conveyance, dismount a horse, etc." We *got off* the train at Victoria Station. Do you *get off* a horse on the left or right side?

get on: a. "enter a conveyance, mount a horse, etc." Have you ever tried to *get on* a camel?
    b. "progress." Everyone is *getting on* very well at school.
    c. "have a good relationship; get along." How are you and your roommate *getting on* these days?

get on one's nerves, "make one nervous." That loud music is *getting on my nerves.*

get out (of), "leave." What time are you going to *get out* (of work) today? *Get out* (of my life) and never speak to me again.

get over, "recover from; recuperate." He's *getting over* his bad cold now.

get over with, "finish" (S). Do the job now; *get it over with.* Don't put it off.

get rid of, "eliminate or exterminate." What's the best way to *get rid of* mice? It's difficult to *get rid of* a foreign accent.

get through, "finish." What time are you going to *get through* at work today?

get together (with), "gather; unite." I'd like to *get together* (with you) soon.

get up: a. "stand up." Everyone *got up* when the general entered the room.
    b. "arise; cause to arise" (S). My roommate *gets me up* at six o'clock every morning. What time do you usually *get up?*

give away, "give without charging money" (S). The old furniture up in the attic wasn't worth much, so I *gave it all away.*

give back, "return" (S). That's my money—would you please *give it back*.

give in (to), "yield." If you wait for him to accept your offer, he'll eventually *give in* (to you). Children, don't *give in* (to temptation) and eat too much candy.

give out, "distribute; assign" (S). Has the teacher *given* the homework assignment *out* yet?

give up: a. "abandon; reject" (S). The ship was sinking fast, so they *gave it up.* He knew cigarettes weren't good for him, so he *gave them up.*
    b. "surrender" (S). After more than a hundred days of heavy fighting, the rebels finally *gave themselves up.*

go on (with), "continue." *Go on* (with your story); I'm fascinated.

go out: a. "temporarily leave." Why did the teacher *go out* during the examination?
    b. "stop burning." The lights *went out* as soon as the earthquake occurred.

go out of business, "stop doing business forever." His company was losing money, so it *went out of business.*

go out (with), "go on a date." They *went out* (with each other) for a long time before they finally decided to get married.

go over, "review; look over." Please *go over* your homework before turning it in.

go with, a. "harmonize." How beautifully your sweater *goes with* your skirt!
    b. "be romantically involved." Mary *goes with* John; they're both very much in love.

goof off, "fool around; waste time." We usually just *goof off* during our lunch time.

goof up, "disrupt; foul up" (S). I was going to make a good deal, but I *goofed it up.*

gossip about. What on earth are you two *gossiping about?*

grind up, "grind completely" (S). I'm going to *grind* all this meat *up* for a meat loaf.

grow into, "become large enough for." We buy our son's clothes too large for him, and he gradually *grows into* them.

grow out of, "become too large for." Our daughter has become very tall; she's *grown out of* all her clothes.

grow up, "become an adult." Our children are quickly *growing up.*

hand back, "return by hand" (S). The waiter gave me the bill, and I *handed* it *back* without looking at it.

hand down, "bequeath" (S). My grandfather gave this watch to my father, and my father *handed* it *down* to me.

hand in, "submit" (S). When you *hand* your homework *in*, don't forget to put your name on it.

hand out, "distribute; give out" (S). Professor Kline is *handing* the final grades *out* in tomorrow morning's class.

hang around, "congregate; fool around." "Don't ever *hang around* pool halls," my father always told me.

hang out: a. "hang around." College students *hang out* at the coffee shop on the corner.
b. "hang (articles of clothing) outside" (S). I *hung* the wet clothes *out* to dry.

hang up: a. "place (article of clothing) on a hook or a hanger" (S). *Hang* your jacket *up* in the closet, please.
b. "replace a telephone receiver; end a telephone call" (S). Did you *hang* the receiver *up* when you finished your call?

hang up on, "end a telephone conversation abruptly." While I was talking to him on the phone, he got angry and *hung up on* me.

have on, "be wearing" (S). What a fabulous gown the Countess *has on*! And She has a bracelet on her wrist that must have cost a fortune.

help out, "assist" (S). Would you please *help* me *out* on the project.

hold on: a. "wait." Would you please *hold on*; Mr. Smith is talking to a customer on the other line.
b. "grasp." *Hold on* to my hand, Susie, while we're crossing the street.

hold up: a. "rob with a gun" (S). Someone *held* me *up* last night—she got all my money.
b. "delay" (S). Bad weather *held* our plane's departure *up*.
c. "last; endure." Do American cars *hold up* as well as Japanese cars?

hold your horses, "slow down." Children, you're walking too fast; *hold your horses*.

horse around, "fool around; joke around." The two boys were just *horsing around* when they suddenly started fighting; the teacher had to break them up.

hush up, "be quiet" (S). The little girl started crying when the teacher told her to *hush up*. The children were making a lot of noise, but their father went upstairs and *hushed* them *up*. (See *shut up*.)

iron out, "solve (usually in reference to a problem)" (S). Don't worry about a thing: we'll be able to *iron* this problem *out* in no time at all.

joke around, "fool around; goof off, horse around." Some boys were *joking around* outside in the hall during class, and our teacher got annoyed.

keep away (from), "stay away from." *Keep away* (from the stove), children.

keep off, "keep away from" (S). Please *keep* your hands *off* the merchandise.

keep on: a. "continue wearing" (S). I'm going to *keep* my jacket *on*; it's cold in here.
b. "continue." I told her to stop, but she *kept on* laughing at me.

keep out (of), "stay out of." She angrily told him to *keep out* (of her life).

keep up, "maintain" (S). He *keeps* his house *up* beautifully, but he's a terrible cook.

keep up (with), "maintain the same speed or level." Try to *keep up* (with the class); if you fall behind, try to catch up.

kick out (of), "eject; suspend" (S). Fortunately, they *kicked* that troublemaker *out* (of school). After the revolution, a lot of rich people were *kicked out* (of the country).

kid around, "joke around; fool around." Some children were *kidding around* with our new kitten, and one of them got scratched.

kneel down, "go into a kneeling position." Upon entering the chapel, she *knelt down* to pray.

knock down (S). The little boy *knocked* the big boy *down,* and a fight started.

knock off: a. "cause something to fall" (S). I *knocked* that Chinese sculpture *off* the shelf by accident.
b. "quit work." What time do you usually *knock off?*

knock out, "render unconscious (usually in reference to boxing)" (S). The Mexican fighter *knocked* the Costa Rican *out* in the third round.

lay off, "fire" (S). Due to the recession, the auto companies have *laid* thousands of workers *off.* They're taking no one on.

lay over, "delayed (usually in reference to planes)" (S). Our plane was *laid over* in Dublin for a couple of hours.

leak out: a. "release by leaking." Don't let any water *leak out* of the bucket.
b. "secretly reveal" (S). The government *leaked* the sensational news *out* for political reasons.

leave out, "omit" (S). Don't *leave* any answers *out* on your examination.

let down, "disappoint" (S). I'm depending on you for your help; don't *let* me *down.*

let out, "release" (S). Judge, please *let* me *out* of jail.

let up, "decrease." It's been raining all day, but it's beginning to *let up.*

lie down, "recline." He'd like to *lie down* for a little nap.

lie low, "hide." The rebels *lay low* in caves up in the mountains while the army was looking for them.

listen in (on), "eavesdrop, secretly listen." I never *listen in* (on my boss's phone calls); they're none of my business.

load up, "load completely" (S). We *loaded* the car *up* the night before so that we could take off early the next morning.

lock out (of) (S). She *locked* herself *out* (of her house) last night.

lock up, "lock completely" (S). Don't forget to *lock* the house *up* when you go out.

look after, "protect; tend to, take care of." *Look after* your own interests first.

look at. Oh, *look at* the sunset! Isn't it beautiful?

look for, "search for." May I ask what you're *looking for* in life?

look forward to, "anticipate with pleasure." She *looks forward to* graduating from the university and going out into the world on her own. Her grandmother isn't *looking forward to* the day that she retires.

look into, "investigate." Mr. Sherlock Holmes himself *looked into* the matter and found nothing of a suspicious nature.

look out (for), "be careful; be on guard." *Look out* (for pickpockets) when you're in the public market.

look over, "examine" (S). You might enjoy reading this book. Why don't you *look it over?*

look through, "search." I forgot which book I'd hidden my money in, so I had to *look through* every book on the shelf.

look up: a. "Search for (usually in reference to dictionaries, encyclopedias, etc.)" (S). When you don't know a word, *look* it *up* in your dictionary.
b. "contact; get in touch with" (S). I tried to *look* her *up* when I was in Miami, but I was told she'd moved out of town.
c. "improve." Business has been bad, but things are starting to *look up.*

make out: a. "succeed; get along." How are you *making out* on your new job?
b. "complete a form or document" (S). Has your grandfather *made* a will *out* yet?
c. "understand" (S). It was so foggy last night that I couldn't *make* the street signs *out.*
d. "pretend." He's always *making out* that he's a millionaire.
e. "construct." This ancient Egyptian necklace is *made out* of gold and lapis lazuli.

make up: a. "invent" (S). Children like to *make* stories *up,* and so do adults.
b. "compensate for" (S). I have to *make* some assignments *up* for my writing class; I didn't have time last week.
c. "apply cosmetics" (S). She never *makes* herself *up,* and she always looks beautiful.
d. "become reconciled after a quarrel or argument." My neighbors are no longer fighting; they've finally *made up.*

make up one's mind, "make a decision" (S). Hamlet couldn't *make* his mind *up.*

mess around, "fool around, goof off." What are you doing today? Nothing, really, just *messing around.*

mess up, "mess completely" (S). Our son can cook very well, but he always *messes* the kitchen *up* when he does.

mix up: a. "blend" (S). *Mix* all the ingredients *up* before you add the milk.
b. "confuse" (S). His complicated directions *mixed* me *up* even further.

mop up, "mop completely" (S). The floor was filthy (very dirty), so I *mopped* it *up.*

move away. They haven't lived in this town for a long time; they *moved away* ten years ago.

move over. Would you please *move over* and make some room for me.

nibble on, "eat sparingly." Let's *nibble on* a little something with our coffee; dinnertime is a long time away.

object to. Why do you *object to* calling off the meeting? I don't *object to* it at all.

pass around, "hand around" (S). John, why don't you *pass* your photographs *around* and show them to everyone.

pass away (or on), "die [old-fashioned]." His grandmother *passed away* recently.

pass out: a. "distribute; give out" (S). The teacher has already *passed* the new material *out.*
b. "faint." He drank so much alcohol that he eventually *passed out.* During the conference, the heat and humidity in the room became so intense that several people *passed out.*

pass over: a. "skip" (S). When they called out names from the list, they *passed* mine *over.*
b. "hand over" (S). Please *pass* the salt *over.*

pass up, "not take advantage of an opportunity" (S). It was a wonderful opportunity, but we decided to *pass* it *up* (we were too busy with other things).

pick on, "tease; ridicule." Please don't *pick on* me so much; I'm getting sick of it.

pick out: a. "select" (S). He *picked* the right answer *out.*

b. "remove by picking" (S). She *picked* a cinder *out* of her eye.

pick up: a. "lift up" (S). She dropped her handkerchief, and a gentleman standing next to her *picked* it *up* for her.

b. "call for; arrange to meet or get" (S). I'll *pick* you *up* at five o'clock; will you be waiting for me? I've got to *pick* some medicine *up* at the drugstore.

play around, "fool around; mess around, joke around." He was *playing around* with a gun and shot himself in the leg accidentally.

point at. Don't *point at* people, Billy; it's not polite.

point out, "indicate" (S). Yes, the teacher *pointed* several mistakes *out,* but she didn't ask me to do the composition over.

pry into, "investigate; snoop." How dare the FBI *pry into* my private affairs.

pull off: a. "remove by pulling" (S). He *pulled* his coat *off* in a hurry and sat down to work.

b. "succeed with" (S). She didn't think the project would be a success, but she managed to *pull* it *off.*

pull out: a. "remove by pulling" (S). The dentist had to *pull* all of the patient's teeth *out.*

b. "break an agreement." The bank was going to lend us money to start a new business, but it *pulled out* at the last moment, so we had to borrow from our parents.

punch out, "remove by punching; knock out" (S). He works on a machine that *punches* holes *out.* The Rumanian *punched* the Albanian *out* in the fifth round.

put away, "return something to its original and proper place" (S). Children, please *put* your school materials *away* when you get home from school.

put back together, "assemble" (S). He took his alarm clock apart, and now he can't *put* it *back together.*

put by, "save" (S). Are you *putting* some money *by* for your old age?

put down: a. "suppress" (S). Because of their superior weapons, the government soldiers were able to *put* the revolutionary forces *down.*

b. "criticize" (S). She's always *putting* her husband *down,* and he doesn't deserve it. Please don't *put* me *down* so much; I try to do my best.

c. "lower; place" (S). Please *put* that package *down* on the floor.

put off, "postpone" (S). This is an important assignment; don't *put* it *off* any longer.

put on: a. "don" (S). She *put* her coat *on* and left in a big hurry.

b. "be ostentatious or snobbish." He's always *putting on* airs of superiority.

c. "tease; attempt to deceive" (S). You're not being serious, are you? You're just *putting* me *on,* aren't you?

put one's foot in one's mouth, "say something indiscreet." Only after I'd made that stupid remark did I realize I'd *put my foot in my mouth.*

put out: a. "extinguish" (S). Before *putting* the lights *out,* be sure to lock the house up.

b. "annoy; irritate" (S). It certainly *put* me *out* when she told me to shut up.

c. "expel; suspend" (S). He was making so much trouble at school that they *put* him *out.*

d. "inconvenience" (S). No, your visiting me at this time isn't *putting* me *out;* I've got nothing else to do with my time.

put up: a. "raise" (S). When the police cornered the bank robber in an alley, they said, "*Put* your hands *up* and don't make a move."

b. "provide (usually in reference to money)" (S). The bank is going to *put* all the money *up,* but we're going to do all the work.

c. "preserve; can" (S). My mother *puts* strawberries *up* every June.

d. "accommodate" (S). They've got a lot of room in their house; they can *put* at least twenty people *up* comfortably.

e. "erect" (S). His father's construction company is *putting* new houses *up* all over town.

put up with, "endure; tolerate." On the very first day the teacher said, "I won't *put up with* cheating in this class." I can no longer *put up with* my boss's terrible manners; I'm quitting right now.

quibble over, "pay attention to unimportant details." Let's not *quibble over* a few dollars here or there.

quiet down: a. "become quiet." The lights lowered, the audience *quieted down*, the curtain rose, and the play began.

b. "make quiet" (S). She started to read a story to the children in order to *quiet* them *down* before they went to bed.

rain out, "postpone or cancel because of rain (usually in reference to baseball)." More games were *rained out* last season than in any other season in the history of baseball.

ring back, "call back" (S). I'll *ring* you *back* in a few minutes, so don't go out.

ring up, "call up (chiefly British)" (S). Any time you feel like a little chat, just *ring* me *up*.

rip off: a. "remove by ripping" (S). The doctor and the nurse *ripped* the burn victim's clothes *off*.

b. "cheat; steal" (S). He was angry because some clever businessmen from the city had *ripped* him *off*.

rough up, "treat roughly" (S). The mobsters *roughed* one of the witnesses *up*, so he was afraid to testify at the trial.

run across, "find unexpectedly; meet by chance." While I was looking for some old photographs, I *ran across* this old love letter.

run around (with), "associate with." He *runs around* (with some troublemakers) a lot, and his parents are worried about him.

run away (from* or *with), "escape." Look! The dog is *running* away (from us).
She *ran away* (with the delivery boy from the grocery store) and got married.

run down: a. "make unkind remarks about oneself or others; disparage" (S). Don't *run* yourself *down* so much all the time; you're a clever and talented person. She says she's my friend, but she's always *running* me *down* to others.

b. "(put) in bad health" (S). He's so *run down*, he's staying home and resting for a few days. Don't *run* yourself *down*; good health is your most precious possession.

c. "stop (usually in reference to a spring machine." My new watch is automatic, so it never *runs down*.

d. "hit while moving" (S). Don't drive so fast; you might *run* a pedestrian *down*.

run errands. Would you rather do the chores today or *run the errands*?

run into: a. "collide with." The ship *ran into* an iceberg and sank within a few hours.

b. "meet by chance." While I was traveling in a remote part of China, I *ran into* an old school friend of mine from California; it's a small world, isn't it?

run out (of), "exhaust the supply of." When we were in the desert, we had little water; we eventually *ran out* (of water). Look at the time! We must hurry up; we're *running out* (of time).

run up, "increase (usually in reference to a bill)" (S). You're going to *run* a big phone bill *up* if you keep making so many long-distance calls.

rush off: a. "leave in a rush." Don't *rush off*; can't you stay a little longer?
b. "take quickly" (S). *Rush* this material *off* to the printer's right away—it's urgent.

scratch out, "remove by scratching" (S). She *scratched* the old tenant's name *out* on the mailbox and put on her own.

see about: a. "consider." I don't know whether I want to buy this radio or not; I'll just wait and *see about* it.

b. "attend to." I have to *see about* a lot of things at work tomorrow.

see off, "say good-bye to" (usually in reference to travel) (S). I went to the airport to *see* my friends *off*.

sell out, "sell completely" (S). By the time I got there, the store had already *sold* everything on sale *out*.

send out (S). They'd already *sent* several hundred invitations *out* when their daughter suddenly decided to call her wedding off.

set off, "leave (usually in reference to a trip or journey)." When are you *setting off* on your next trip around the world?

set up, "arrange" (S). I want to *set* everything *up* before my guests arrive.

settle down: a. "stay in one place and make a home." He's almost thirty-five now, and he realizes he has to *settle down* instead of living out of a suitcase.

b. "relax" (S). Yes, Doctor, the medication has *settled* the patient *down*.

shape up, "improve" (S). The coach is really *shaping* our team *up* this year.

sharpen up: a. "sharpen completely" (S). I *sharpened* all the kitchen knives *up*.

b. "improve; make better" (S). The director is trying to *sharpen* the musical *up* with some more dance numbers.

ship out, "be sent overseas (usually in reference to the navy)" (S). She wanted to have a post on land, but the navy *shipped* her *out*.

show off, "brag; display" (S). He thinks he's got the best of everything; he's always *showing off*. Now he's got a new car, and he's driving it around town *showing* it *off*.

show up: a. "appear." He waited for his cousin for three hours, but she never *showed up*.

b. "be better than others" (S). He studied hard, got good grades, and *showed* everyone else in the class *up*.

shut off, "cause to stop working or running" (S). Be sure to *shut* the water *off* before leaving the kitchen.

shut up: a. "close" (S). Many people in Alaska (those who can afford it) *shut* their houses *up* in the winter and go to California or Hawaii.

b. "stop talking" (S). "*Shut up*," she screamed at him in a fit of anger. (See *hush up*.) Note: Almost always, *shut up* used in this sense is an extremely impolite expression. Students sometimes use it not realizing that it is inappropriate. Perhaps, when it is necessary to make someone be quiet and stop talking (very often children), the expression *hush up* or *quiet down* will draw less offense.

sit down, "be seated." Why don't you take your coat off and *sit down*, Ma'am?

sit up, "sit straight." Teddy, please *sit up* in your chair; don't slouch.

size up, "analyze" (S). I *sized* the situation *up* and realized I'd better get out of the town fast.

slow down (or **up**), "decrease speed" (S). *Slow* that machine *down*—it's going too fast to be safe. Please *slow up*—you're speaking too fast for me.

smarten up, "improve; become wiser" (S). She *smartened* herself *up* with some new clothes. She finally *smartened up* and split up with her boyfriend.

snoop into, "look into the private affairs of others." He's always *snooping into* other people's business; everyone calls him Snoopy.

sort out, "classify" (S). Someone in the mailroom *sorts* my mail *out* before it comes to my office.

speak of, "mention." Janice never *speaks of* her former husband.

speak out, "say aloud." Everyone at the meeting wanted to say something against the proposal, but no one *spoke out*.

speak up, "speak more loudly." Why are you whispering? Please *speak up*; I can't hear you.

speed up, "go faster" (S). As soon as we get out of town, we can *speed up*. The teacher is trying to *speed* his class *up*; it's going too slowly.

split up: a. "divide" (S). The thieves *split* the money *up* among themselves.
b. "separate (usually in reference to a romantic or marital relationship)." They're *splitting up*; they're no longer in love with each other.

spread around, "distribute" (S). Someone is *spreading* terrible rumors about me *around* town. Money in our society must be more evenly *spread around*.

spring up, "appear suddenly." A lot of new shops have *sprung up* in my neighborhood recently.

squeeze in, "enter (or allow to enter) by squeezing" (S). The bus was crowded, but ten or so more passengers *squeezed in*. Yes, we'll *squeeze* you *in*; the more, the merrier.

squeeze out (of), "remove by squeezing" (S). How much juice can you *squeeze out of* an orange? It's easy to *squeeze* money *out of* my father when he's in a good mood.

stand around, "wait around without any purpose." It was a boring party; we just *stood around* for three hours doing nothing; no one even danced.

stand away (from), "keep away from." *Stand away* (from this hot stove).

stand by, "wait for." I'm *standing by* for a seat on the next plane to Kuala Lumpur.

stand for: a. "represent." The fifty stars in the flag of the United States *stand for* the fifty states of the Union.
b. "tolerate." The professor said she wouldn't *stand for* any sleeping in the class.

stand out, "be conspicuous." He's very tall and has bright red hair, so he always *stands out* in a crowd.

stand up: a. "get up." Everyone *stood up* when I entered the room; it made me feel great.
b. "intentionally not show up for an appointment with" (S). She had a date with her boyfriend, but he *stood* her *up*; she's very hurt.

stand up for, "defend; support." If you ever have to go to court, or if you ever have any trouble, I'll always *stand up for* you; you're one of my oldest and best friends. We must *stand up for* our rights.

stand up to, "face with determination." You must *stand up to* your roommate (don't be afraid of him) and tell him what's wrong. You must *stand up to* your boss; don't let her treat you like a slave.

start out, "begin" (S). The teacher always *starts* the class *out* with a joke.

stay up, "not go to bed." She's *staying up* and waiting for the children to come home from the dance. Don't *stay up*—I'll be home late.

stick with, "stay with; adhere to." *Stick with* me, everyone; I've got the right directions, and we won't get lost.

switch off, "turn off" (S). Please *switch* the lights *off* and go to sleep.

switch on, "turn on" (S). *Switch* the lights *on*, please; it's getting dark in here.

take advantage of, "utilize an opportunity; use people." You should *take advantage of* the free time you have today and do some homework. You shouldn't *take advantage of* your friends.

take after: a. "resemble a parent." In looks, he *takes after* his father, but he *takes after* his mother in personality.
b. "follow the example of." John wants to *take after* his father and be a teacher.

take apart, "disassemble" (S). He *took* his calculator *apart*, and now he doesn't know how to put it back together.

take back, "return" (S). I'm *taking* this shirt *back* to the store; it doesn't fit right.

take care of, "protect; watch, deal with." I'm *taking care of* my neighbor's house while she's out of town on business. Would you mind *taking care of* my children today?

take charge of, "assume responsibility for." Who's going to *take charge of* the office while your boss is on vacation?

take down, "write down; take dictation" (S). Yes, I *took* her phone number *down,* but I forgot where I put it.

take for, "mistake for" (S). I *took* Helga *for* her sister; they look alike.

take for granted, "assume to be true; accept without question" (S). You can't *take* everything you read *for granted*; many people don't know what they're writing about. Stop *taking* your friends *for granted.*

take in: a. "include." Their three-week tour of Europe *took in* seven countries.
b. "deceive" (S). His clever conversation almost *took* me *in,* but I eventually realized he was telling me a pack of lies.
c. "make smaller (usually in reference to clothes)" (S). I've lost some weight recently; I've got to find someone to *take* all my clothes *in.*

take off: a. "remove" (S). My shoes were hurting my feet, so I *took* them *off.* He's lost weight; he's *taken* at least ten pounds *off.*
b. "ascend; leave in a hurry." The plane couldn't *take off* because of the heavy fog on the runway. While I was speaking to him, he suddenly *took off.*
c. "not work" (S). He *took* three days *off* and went up to the mountains to do some fishing.

take on: a. "hire" (S). The company is *taking* a hundred new workers *on.*
b. "assume." She *takes on* the air of a rich woman when she gets dressed up.

take out: a. "remove; delete, leave out" (S). Don't leave the wine in the refrigerator; *take* it *out* and let it get to room temperature. Your paragraph will be better if you *take* all the commas *out.*
b. "have a date with" (S). She knows a movie star who often *takes* her *out.*

take over, "take control of" (S). When he and his wife and their twelve children stay in a hotel, they *take* it *over.*

take place, "occur." Many new and exciting things *have taken place* in my life recently.

take up: a. "consider" (S). The committee will be *taking* the matter *up* tomorrow.
b. "begin (often in reference to habits and careers)" (S). Their son is going to *take* medicine *up* at the university. When did you *take* smoking *up*?
c. "shorten" (S). Those curtains are a little long; *take* about three inches *up.*
d. "occupy" (S). We have a St. Bernard dog; she *takes* a lot of room *up* in our apartment.

take up with, "begin an association with." Their son is *taking up with* some tough young men who hang around down at the pool hall.

talk over, "discuss" (S). He *talked* his problem *over* with his father.

talk to someone about. He *talked to* his priest *about* his family problems.

taste of. Everything at dinner last night *tasted of* garlic.

tear down, "demolish" (S). It was a beautiful old building, but they *tore* it *down.*

tear off (S). I showed my ticket to the usher, but he didn't *tear* the stub *off.*

tear out (of), "remove by tearing" (S). She *tore* the whole page of "Joneses" *out* (of the phone directory).

tear up, "tear or rip into pieces; rip up" (S). She *tore* the photograph of her old boyfriend *up* and threw it away.

tell off, "rebuke severely; bawl out" (S). She got angry at her boss and *told* him *off.*

test out, "try" (S). Before you buy a pen, always *test* it *out* first.

thaw out, "thaw completely" (S). If we're going to have strawberries for dessert, we'd better take some out of the freezer and *thaw* them *out*.

thicken up, "make thicker" (S). She usually *thickens* the gravy *up* with flour.

think about: a. "consider." He is *thinking about* buying a scooter.
b. "have an opinion (in clauses beginning with *what*)." What do you *think about* the President? I often wonder what people *think about* me.

think of: a. "consider." What on earth are you *thinking of*? He's *thinking of* quitting his job and looking for a new one.
b. "have an opinion (in clauses beginning with *what*)." What do you *think of* me? No one in town knows what to *think of* the scandal in the Mayor's office.
c. "remember." Yes, I'll give you my passport number as soon as I can *think of* it.

think up, "imagine or invent" (S). He's a clever person; he's always *thinking* something *up* that will make a lot of money.

throw away, "discard" (S). She *threw* all those old shoes *away*.

throw out: a. "discard; throw away" (S). She *threw* all her old letters *out*.
b. "eject; kick out" (S). Peter was making so much noise in the theater, that the management kicked *him out*.

throw up, "vomit" (S). Baby ate some potatoes, but she *threw* them *up*.

tire out, "tire completely" (S). Our long trip certainly *tired* the two of us *out*.

tow away, "remove by towing" (S). I parked in front of a fire hydrant by mistake, and the police *towed* my car *away*.

try on, "test (for articles of clothing)" (S). Why don't you *try* this beautiful dress *on*?

try out, "test (for machinery and mechanical devices)" (S). Would you like to *try* this typewriter *out*, Sir? It's our latest model.

tune in. On our short wave, it's easy to *tune in* to the BBC Home Service.

tune up, "put in tune" (S). The orchestra is already *tuning up*; the concert will begin any minute now. I have to *tune* my guitar *up* before I play anything.

turn away, "not permit to enter; reject" (S). The rioting students tried to enter the building, but the police *turned* them *away*.

turn down: a. "decrease the volume or brilliance of" (S). Please *turn* the radio *down*; it'll wake up all the neighbors. *Turn* that light *down* a bit, please; it's hurting my eyes.
b. "reject" (S). They offered him a million dollars as a bribe, but he *turned* them *down*. She gets proposals of marriage all the time, but she always *turns* them *down*.
c. "prepare (a bed) for sleeping" (S). She likes to *turn* the children's beds *down* while they're still taking their baths.

turn in: a. "go to bed." He gets up when the sun rises and *turns in* when it sets.
b. "submit" (S). I still have this application; I mustn't forget to *turn* it *in*.
c. "betray (usually in reference to the police)" (S). We knew our neighbor was a thief, so we *turned* him *in* to the police; he's in jail now.

turn off: a. "stop the operation of" (S). Did you *turn* the lights *off* when you left the classroom? How on earth do you *turn* this thing *off*?
b. "cause displeasure or dislike" (S). The speaker's loud and vulgar manner *turned* everyone in the audience *off*.

turn on: a. "start the operation of" (S). Let's *turn* the radiator *on*; it's getting cold in here.
b. "become unfriendly toward." She'd always been a good friend of his when she suddenly *turned on* him and became one of his worst enemies.
c. "cause excitement in oneself or others (often in the sexual sense)" (S). I'm sorry, but that kind of music just doesn't *turn* me *on*.

turn out: a. "extinguish (an electric light)" (S). *Turn* the lights *out* and go to sleep, everyone.
b. "produce" (S). Hollywood produces some fine films, but it also *turns* a lot of junk *out*.

      c. "result." Tell me how the election in your town *turns out,* will you?

      d. "expel" (S). Because of cheating, the two students *were turned out* of the university.

turn up: a. "appear." I'd been waiting for her for almost an hour when she finally *turned up.* I'd been missing that wallet for a couple of months when it suddenly *turned up* under the cushion of a chair.

      b. "find" (S). Mr. Holmes has *turned* several important clues *up;* he thinks he's solved the case.

      c. "increase the volume or brilliance of" (S). Please *turn* the radio *up;* I'm a little hard of hearing (my hearing is poor). Please *turn* the lights *up;* this place is like a dungeon.

wait for. How long have you been *waiting for* me? They're just *waiting for* the day that they have their own house.

wait on, "serve." During the Christmas season, it's difficult to find people in the stores to *wait on* you.

wake up: a. "awake." I'd just *woken up* when the rooster started crowing.

      b. "awaken" (S). I'd just gone to sleep when the phone *woke* me *up*—there was nobody on the line.

walk out on, "leave someone abruptly." He was shocked when his companion at the party suddenly *walked out on* him with another man.

warm up, "make warm again" (S). Look at these lovely leftovers in the refrigerator; let's *warm* them *up* for supper.

watch out, "be careful." *Watch out,* everyone; we're going to hit a big bump.

wear down, "deteriorate" (S). His job is extremely hard; it's *wearing* him *down.*

wear off, "decrease gradually." Doctor, the effect of the morphine is *wearing off;* the patient is beginning to feel pain.

wear out: a. "use until old" (S). She's *worn* all her clothes *out,* but she can't afford to buy anything new.

      b. "exhaust" (S). Getting around this town by public transportation is *wearing us out.*

well off, "rich." Yes, they're very *well off;* they're *better off* than anyone else in town.

wind up, "end; end up" (S). How on earth did we ever *wind up* in this place? They *wound* the meeting *up* with coffee and cake.

wipe out: a. "destroy" (S). The hurricane *wiped* several towns along the coast *out.*

      b. "exhaust greatly" (S). All his difficult courses and loads of homework this semester have almost *wiped* him *out*—he's exhausted.

wipe up, "wipe clean" (S). Children, you spilled the milk on the floor; you should *wipe* it *up.*

work on. My boss and I are *working on* a very exciting project now.

work out: a. "solve" (S). This problem baffles me; I just can't *work* it *out.*

      b. "be proved successful or satisfactory." Do you think their marriage will *work out?*

      c. "exercise." He goes to a gym twice a week and *works out.*

worry about. There's no need to be nervous; what on earth are you *worrying about?*

wrap up: a. "wrap completely" (S). Yes, this is a beautiful shirt; *wrap* it *up*—I'll take it.

      b. "complete" (S). They *wrapped* the project *up* three weeks before their deadline.

wring out, "wring completely" (S). He took the clothes out of the laundry basket and *wrung* them *out.*

write down (S). Yes, I was given the directions, but I didn't *write* them *down.*

zero in (on), "focus in on." What exactly is the problem? We must *zero in* (on it).

Commonly Used Phrases
with *Do* and *Make*

1. The verb *do* is used in the following phrases:

do an assignment. Please *do* all your assignments as neatly as possible.

do one's best. If you always try to *do* your best, you'll always do well.

do business with. No one likes to have to *do* business with dishonest people.

do a calculation. Would you like to *do* these calculations with my calculator?

do a chore. On Saturdays, he tries to *do* all his chores in the morning and run his errands in the afternoon.

do the cleaning (or *the cooking, the washing,* etc.). When do you usually *do* the cleaning?

do a dance. The children are now going to *do* a dance. Let's watch.

do the dishes. I'm not going to *do* the dishes; I'm just going to put them in the sink and let them soak.

do an exercise. How long does it usually take to *do* an exercise?

do a favor. Please *do* me a favor and don't tell this secret to anyone.

do one's hair (usually in reference to women). Does your mother *do* her hair herself, or does she go to a beauty salon?

do one's homework. *Do* your homework every day, and you'll always do well in class.

do the hunting. A female lion *does* all the hunting; the male never does.

do a job. When he *does* a job, he almost always does it well.

do the laundry. A lot of people like to *do* the laundry on Mondays.

do a problem. I'm trying to *do* these problems for my algebra class, and they're not easy. *Note: To do a problem* means *to solve a problem; to make a problem* means *to create a problem:* Please don't *make* so many problems for yourself.

do a puzzle. If you can *do* this puzzle, I'll give you a hundred dollars.

do a quiz. How long does it usually take you to *do* a quiz?

do research. How much pure research does your company *do*?

do something for someone. Her rich brother doesn't ever *do* anything for her.

do studying. I've got a lot of studying to *do* today—I can't waste a minute.

do taxes. He's looking for a good accountant to *do* his taxes. *Note: To make taxes* means *to create taxes.*

do one's work. Mr. Tracy, would you please *do* your work and stop complaining?

2. The verb *make* is used in the following phrases:

make an appointment. What's the best time for you to *make* an appointment?

make an arrangement. Who's responsible for *making* the final arrangements?

make a bed. My roommate knows how to *make* her bed, but she never does.

make believe, "pretend." Children like to *make* believe they are adults.

make a bet. Would you like to *make* a bet with me? I'll give you the odds.

make a cake. I'm having guests for dinner, so I'm *making* a cake.

make a call. How often do you *make* a long-distance call?

make a change. We'd like to *make* a few changes around here.

make change (for money). Our little boy doesn't know how to *make* change yet.

make a commitment. He refuses to *make* a commitment; he's not sure of himself.

make a comparison. Professor Smith often *makes* incorrect comparisons.

make a date (an appointment). How would you like to *make* a date with a movie star?

make a deal. Let's *make* a deal; if you wash the dishes, I'll dry.

make a decision. My boss and I have to *make* critical decisions every day.

make a difference. Would you like to go out or stay home tonight? It doesn't really *make* a difference.

make a discovery. Young children, who are explorers, *make* new discoveries every day.

make do, "manage with little available." We don't have much money; we'll just have to *make* do. *Make* do with what you've got and be happy.

make an error. Does your roommate *make* many errors when he speaks?

make an excuse. I hope my boss isn't there when I get to the office late; I don't want to have to *make* any excuses.

make a face, "change the appearance of one's face." Jimmy, why did you *make* such an ugly face when I asked you that question?

make a fool of. Don't let anybody *make* a fool of you.

make friends. It's often difficult to *make* friends in a large, strange city.

make friendships. On a trip we often *make* friendships that don't last very long.

make fun of. Children, don't *make* fun of people less fortunate than you.

make good. Jane Sills is a woman who's always *made* good her promises.

make an impression. If you want to *make* a good impression at a job interview, don't chew gum or smoke.

make an improvement. Many improvements have been *made* in our company recently.

make a list. Barbara always *makes* a shopping list, but she always loses it.

make a living. With inflation and high taxes, it isn't so easy to *make* a living these days.

make love (have sexual relations). The signs the anti-war marchers were carrying said, "*Make* love, not war."

make a mistake. He's *made* a great many mistakes, but he's always learned from them.

make money. A lot of people are looking for a way to *make* money without working.

make a movie. It can cost millions of dollars to *make* a movie.

make a noise. Children, please don't *make* any noise; your father is resting.

make peace. Let's *make* peace; it's stupid to fight.

make a plan. Let's *make* plans for our vacation now; summer is coming soon.

271

make a plane (*train, bus*), "catch a plane." I'm in a big hurry to the airport; I've got to *make* a plane to Chicago.

make a problem. Please don't *make* any problems for me; I've already got enough.

make progress. The class has been in session for only a few days, and the students have already *made* a lot of progress.

make a promise (or *resolution* or *vow*). They're always *making* promises, but they never keep them.

make a speech. No one *made* any speeches last night after dinner, fortunately.

make a statement. Has the President *made* any statements concerning the recent scandal in the government.

make a toast, "drink to." Ladies and Gentlemen, let's *make* a toast to our leader. Note: Do not confuse *make a toast* with *make toast*: Do you always *make toast* at breakfast?

make trouble. Those boys are always *making* trouble; they're real troublemakers.

make a try. Don't give up yet; you'll hit the target. *Make* another try.

make a turn. When you get to the intersection, don't *make* a right turn, make a left.

make war. Those two countries are always *making* war with each other.

Commonly Used Irregular Verbs

base form	past form	past participle
arise	arose	arisen
awake	awoke, awaked	awaked, awoken
be	was	been
bear	bore	borne (*meaning* to carry)
		born (*meaning* to bear a child)
beat	beat	beaten
become	became	become
begin	began	begun
bend	bent	bent
bet	bet	bet
bite	bit	bitten, bit
bleed	bled	bled
blow	blew	blown
break	broke	broken
bring	brought	brought
broadcast	broadcast, broadcasted	broadcast, broadcasted
build	built	built
burst	burst	burst
buy	bought	bought
cast	cast	cast
catch	caught	caught
choose	chose	chosen
come	came	come
cost	cost	cost
creep	crept	crept
cut	cut	cut
deal	dealt	dealt
dig	dug	dug
dive	dived, dove	dived, dove
do	did	done

base form	past form	past participle
draw	drew	drawn
dream	dreamed, dreamt	dreamed, dreamt
drink	drank	drunk
drive	drove	driven
eat	ate	eaten
fall	fell	fallen
feed	fed	fed
feel	felt	felt
fight	fought	fought
find	found	found
flee	fled	fled
fly	flew	flown
forbid	forbade	forbidden
forget	forgot	forgotten (*British* forgot)
freeze	froze	frozen
get	got	gotten (*British* got)
give	gave	given
go	went	gone
grind	ground	ground
grow	grew	grown
hang	hung	hung
	hanged (*meaning* being hanged by the neck until dead)	hanged
have	had	had
hear	heard	heard
hide	hid	hidden
hit	hit	hit
hold	held	held
hurt	hurt	hurt
keep	kept	kept
kneel	knelt, kneeled	knelt, kneeled
knit	knit, knitted	knit, knitted
know	knew	known
lay	laid	laid
lead	led	led
leap	leaped, leapt	leaped, leapt
learn	learned (*British* learnt)	learned (*British* learnt)
leave	left	left
lend	lent	lent

appendix 3

base form	past form	past participle
let	let	let
lie (to recline)	lay	lain
lie (not to tell the truth)	lied	lied
light	lit, lighted	lit, lighted
lose	lost	lost
make	made	made
mean	meant	meant
meet	met	met
mistake	mistook	mistaken
overcome	overcame	overcome
pay	paid	paid
prove	proved	proved (*sometimes* proven)
put	put	put
quit	quit	quit
read	read (*pronounced* "red")	read (*pronounced* "red")
ride	rode	ridden
ring	rang	rung
rise	rose	risen
run	ran	run
say	said	said
see	saw	seen
seek	sought	sought
sell	sold	sold
send	sent	sent
set	set	set
shake	shook	shaken
shine (intransitive)	shone	shone
(transitive)	shined	shined
shoot	shot	shot
show	showed	shown, showed
shrink	shrank, shrunk	shrunk
shut	shut	shut
sing	sang	sung
sink	sank, sunk	sunk
sit	sat	sat
slay	slew	slain
sleep	slept	slept
slide	slid	slid
speak	spoke	spoken

base form	past form	past participle
speed	sped, speeded	sped, speeded
spend	spent	spent
spin	spun	spun
spit	spit, spat	spit, spat
split	split	split
spread	spread	spread
spring	sprang, sprung	sprung
stand	stood	stood
steal	stole	stolen
stick	stuck	stuck
sting	stung	stung
stink	stank	stunk
strike	struck	struck
strive	strove	striven
swear	swore	sworn
sweat	sweated, sweat	sweated, sweat
sweep	swept	swept
swim	swam	swum
swing	swung	swung
take	took	taken
teach	taught	taught
tear	tore	torn
tell	told	told
think	thought	thought
throw	threw	thrown
undergo	underwent	undergone
understand	understood	understood
wake	woke, waked	woken, waked
wear	wore	worn
weave	wove	woven
weep	wept	wept
win	won	won
wind	wound	wound
withdraw	withdrew	withdrawn
withhold	withheld	withheld
wring	wrung	wrung
write	wrote	written